# Nongovernmental Organizations and the World Bank

*Cooperation for Development*

EDITED BY

SAMUEL PAUL

AND

ARTURO ISRAEL

The World Bank
*Washington, D.C.*

Manufactured in the United States of America
First printing November 1991

The World Bank Regional and Sectoral Studies series provides an outlet for work that is relatively limited in its subject matter or geographical coverage but that contributes to the intellectual foundations of development operations and policy formulation. These studies have not necessarily been edited with the same rigor as Bank publications that carry the imprint of a university press.

The findings, interpretations, and conclusions expressed in this publication are those of the authors and should not be attributed in any manner to the World Bank, to its affiliated organizations, or to the members of its Board of Executive Directors or the countries they represent.



The complete backlist of publications from the World Bank is shown in the annual *Index of Publications,* which contains an alphabetical title list and indexes of subjects, authors, and countries and regions. The latest edition is available free of charge from Publications Sales Unit, The World Bank, 1818 H Street, N.W., Washington, D.C. 20433, U.S.A., or from Publications, The World Bank, 66, avenue d'Iéna, 75116 Paris, France.

At the time of writing, Samuel Paul was an adviser on public sector management in the World Bank's Country Economics Department, and Arturo Israel was the head of that department's Public Sector Management and Private Sector Development Division.

*Cover design by Sam Ferro.*



***Library of Congress Cataloging-in-Publication Data***

Nongovernmental organizations and the World Bank : cooperation for development / edited by Samuel Paul and Arturo Israel.
p. cm. — (World Bank regional and sectoral studies)
Includes bibliographical references.
ISBN 0-8213-1924-8
1. Non-governmental organizations—Developing countries. 2. World Bank—Developing countries. I. Paul, Samuel, 1930– II. Israel, Arturo. III. Series.
HC60.N55 1991
338.9'009172'4—dc20 91-31438
CIP

# The Biology of *Trypanosoma* and *Leishmania*, Parasites of Man and Domestic Animals

# Nongovernmental Organizations and the World Bank

*Cooperation for Development*

**WORLD BANK**

**REGIONAL AND**

**SECTORAL STUDIES**

90 0540368 9

# Contents

Figures

# Preface

Recent years have witnessed the emergence of nongovernmental organizations (NGOs) as an increasingly visible and forceful presence on the international development scene. They have not only championed and financed the causes of environmental protection, poverty alleviation, and other social concerns in many developing countries, but have also been active advocates of policies in these and other areas. The NGO movement that has a long history in the more industrialized countries has in recent decades established links with similar movements in developing countries. NGOs from both industrial and developing countries participate jointly in a variety of development initiatives. There are, of course, several developing countries, notably in Asia and Latin America, that have had a tradition of indigenous NGO work long before the cooperative NGO programs began.

A significant new development is the pattern of interaction emerging between NGOs and other actors on the development scene. In a number of developing countries, NGOs have begun to work with governments, shedding the traditionally adversarial mode of operation between the two. On the international scene, bilateral and multilateral donors are increasingly cooperating with NGOs: donors are listening to the views and advice of NGOs on developmental issues, and donors and NGOs are working together on specific projects funded by the donors. These new relationships and transactions can potentially be beneficial to the development process. But whether they will in fact turn out to be so will depend on how the parties involved plan their joint activities, understand each other's goals, strengths, and weaknesses, learn from their experiences, and adapt as they go along. Given the relative newness of these cooperative endeavors, there is much that we still do not know about the nature of these interactions, the processes involved, and their outcomes.

The World Bank, whose official cooperation with NGOs began in 1981, has maintained a serious and long-term interest in this subject. As a major international development agency, the Bank has all along explored ways to work with NGOs and to facilitate cooperative efforts between developing country governments and NGOs. At the present time, the Bank is engaged in a major effort to promote the involvement of NGOs in its projects in different countries. Of the 228 projects approved by the Bank in 1990, 50 have involved NGOs—in contrast to an annual average of 16 projects during the preceding 17 years.

This book is the culmination of an attempt to take stock of the World Bank's cooperation with NGOs in recent years against the backdrop of the evolving role of NGOs in development. The intended audience of the book is policymakers and public officials in developing countries, the NGO community, and development professionals in general, including World Bank staff. It is hoped that this volume will help improve the understanding among those involved of the potential role and contributions of NGOs in the development process.

The idea of a book on NGOs and the World Bank was initiated in 1988 by Arturo Israel, who at the time was chief of the Public Sector Management and Private Sector Development Division of the Bank. It was felt that the basic objective of the book can best be achieved by pooling the reflections of both Bank staff members and outside experts on the subject. Four of the contributors are or were Bank staff members when they wrote their chapters. Samuel Paul wrote the overview chapter and was primarily responsible for editing the volume. Lawrence Salmen, Paige Eaves, and David Beckmann reviewed the World Bank experience in working with NGOs (Chapters 4 and 5). The other two contributors, David Korten and David Brown, are scholars who work with NGOs and have written extensively on them. Their chapters (2 and 3) focus on the nature, scope, and evolution of NGOs, and offer valuable guidance on understanding their potential and limits.

The Country Economics Department and the External Affairs Department of the World Bank provided the support and resources required to complete the preparation of this volume. We are grateful to Mary Shirley for her comments on the overview chapter and to Ernestina Madrona for her excellent secretarial assistance.

# 1

# Nongovernmental Organizations and the World Bank: An Overview

*Samuel Paul*

The emergence of nongovernmental organizations (NGOs) as a "third sector" in the economy has been an important phenomenon of the 1980s.[1] NGOs have been heralded as new agents with the capacity and commitment to make up for the shortcomings of the state and the market in reducing poverty. This trend has been reinforced by cumulative evidence from the developing world on the positive contributions of NGO interventions and other grass-roots initiatives to poverty reduction. International donors, developing country leaders and governments, and scholars have thus begun to pay greater attention to the role, potential, and limits of NGOs in the development process.

Increased reliance on the state to intervene directly to reduce poverty began in the 1960s, after the market and the "trickle-down" approach failed to affect significantly the depth of poverty in many developing countries. Observers were struck by the worsening of income distribution that often accompanied economic growth. Some argued that the slow progress of poverty reduction was due not only to "bureaucratic failure" but also to the market catering primarily to elites and export enclaves and ignoring the basic needs of the poor (Kothari 1984; Rose-Ackerman 1980; and Drabek 1987). An alternative development model supported by NGOs advocated "bottom-up" projects that involved the poor directly in income-generating and social activities. The purpose was to enhance their income-earning capacity and to "empower" them to develop on their own.

Poverty reduction requires resources, the capacity to adapt programs to diverse and uncertain conditions, and a strong performance orientation supported by the demand pull of the poor themselves. Neither developing country governments nor NGOs possess all these attributes. The limits to action by government lie in its difficulties in responding and adapting its services to the needs of the poor, in weak public accountability for results, and in the aversion of bureaucrats and politicians to the mobilization of public demand. Even under democratic regimes, the poor's access to public services and programs tends to be limited by the reliance of government on standardized services that are not calibrated to particular needs and by the poor's inability—due to weak political and organizational power—to demand change and hold the bureaucracy accountable for performance. When essential goods are in short supply, the chances are that elites will have disproportionate access to them. Under such conditions, bureaucrats will be less inclined to inform and educate the poor, or to improve the delivery of services to them (Paul 1988; and James 1982).

Major swings in development paradigms often ride the crest of optimism cushioned by assumptions difficult to test at the time. The fact that the market and the state have not succeeded enough in reducing poverty does not mean that NGOs will do better. There is, however, a strong case for a careful and dispassionate assessment of NGOs' distinctive competence and role in the development process. As they work closely with the poor, for example, NGOs may enhance the access of the poor to public services and augment their political power through organization. NGOs' command over financial resources may be limited, however, and their capacity to access technology, research, and other infrastructure tends to be modest. NGOs are typically founded by leaders committed to a cause but not necessarily interested in replicating their endeavors nationally or internationally. But as the following chapters argue, NGOs tend to be active as catalysts for change and responsive to the needs and problems of beneficiaries. Given their greater local knowledge and commitment, they are more likely than governments to have the interest and skills to adapt development projects and programs to local conditions. Their small size and proximity to beneficiaries can make them more accountable for results. The state, the market, NGOs, and other grass-roots initiatives, in short, have different but complementary strengths. In the context of poverty alleviation, there is a clear case for a division of labor that exploits such comparative advantages. As a recent World Bank report (1990) has noted:

> *Donors and recipients have given too little attention to sociocultural and political factors and have not been sufficiently aware of the important role that the poor themselves can play in initiatives designed to assist them. Evidence supports the view that involving the poor in the design, implementation, and evaluation of projects in a range of sectors would make aid more effective. Involvement of women has contributed to the attainment of objectives in many agricultural development projects in Sub-Saharan Africa; participation of local community organizations has improved performance in many urban poverty projects; organizations of beneficiaries in aid-supported irrigation schemes have made important contributions to the maintenance and operation of project works; and involvement of organized groups of low-income borrowers has facilitated repayment of loans in small-scale credit programs.* (133)

## Rationale and scope of the book

This book is a collection of papers on the role, potential, and limits of NGOs in development. It combines a global review of what NGOs are and what they can do in the development process with an analysis of the experience of one international development agency, the World Bank, in working with NGOs in its operations.

Any organization that is not a part of government qualifies as an NGO, but the term typically denotes organizations that are both nongovernmental and not-for-profit.[2] This broad definition covers a wide range of organizations. Our primary concern in this book is with a segment of this large set—NGOs that focus on the development activities and issues of the developing world. The scope of their work may be local, national, or international, and their areas of interest may span one or more sectors of the economy.

NGOs have been a subject of intellectual inquiry in many countries in recent years.[3] The emergence, growth, and survival of NGOs as an institutional form alongside profit-making enterprises and the government is the phenomenon that invited this inquiry. A brief review of the theoretical perspectives on NGOs is attempted below as a backdrop to the detailed discussion of the role and potential of NGOs in development in the following chapters.

The literature on NGOs is multifaceted, covering the economic, political, and managerial dimensions of the nonprofit sector. There is a sizable literature on the economics of the nonprofit sector that consists of theories of the role of NGOs and of their behavior (Hansmann 1987; and Rose-Ackerman 1980). The dominant approach is to explain the phenomenon of NGOs in terms of the failure of the market and of the state. Several theories have been advanced, largely by western social scientists, to explain the emergence of NGOs.[4] The *subsidy theory* asserts that this institutional form is a response to the many implicit and explicit subsidies made available to NGOs by the state (Weisbrod 1988). Donations to NGOs in support of activities such as education, health, poverty alleviation, and welfare are encouraged through a variety of subsidies to both charitable organizations and their financial contributors. The deductibility of donations on the donor's tax returns stimulates giving because it reduces the after-tax cost to the donor. Similarly, the tax subsidies to the NGO increase the amount of output (different services that society values) available to society beyond what might have been produced without the subsidies. A different view of the rationale of NGOs is provided by the *public goods theory*, which states that NGOs exist to satisfy the residual unsatisfied demand for public goods in society. It argues that the state tends to provide public goods only at the level that satisfies the median voter; where demand exceeds this level or where heterogeneous demands exist, NGOs step in to fill the gap. Public television and medical research illustrate the point. NGOs supplement the funds provided by governments for public television in some countries so that a wider range of programs can be offered to the public. This theory does not explain, however, why NGOs also provide services without characteristics of public goods (for example, health care, higher education, and so on).

The *contract failure theory* suggests that NGOs arise where ordinary contractual mechanisms do not provide the public with adequate means to police producers (Hansmann 1987). Under these conditions, for-profit firms have an incentive and opportunity to exploit customers by offering less service than was promised and paid for. The contract failure theory is more general than the public goods theory and views NGOs as a response to possible opportunistic behavior by both private and public service providers. The argument here is that when contracts are difficult to define, people are likely to "trust" NGOs more than commercial firms. When the public is unable to monitor or evaluate certain outputs and services (for example, disaster relief and care of the elderly), they are likely to turn to organizations with no profit motive for producing and delivering the outputs and services. This public behavior can be explained in terms of the values and goals that people perceive in NGOs, a theme that is discussed in some detail in the following chapters.

Finally, the *consumer control theory* explains the existence of a category of NGOs in terms of the superiority of direct consumer or patron control when the market and government are unable to ensure the desired performance (Ben-Ner 1986). It is argued that consumer control may help eliminate information asymmetry and the adverse consequences of monopoly for members. Examples are professional associations and member-controlled clubs. The reasons that NGOs have survived in some sectors and not in others, the ways in which their behavior differs from that of profit-oriented entities, and comparisons of their efficiency with that of other institutional forms have also been explored in the literature. These theoretical perspectives provide alternative explanations of why NGOs emerge and survive in society and point to the conditions under which this institutional form is likely to perform better than the market and the state.

Studies of the politics of the nonprofit sector have focused on the reasons that NGOs perform public functions that normally fall within the purview of the government (Douglas 1987). Voluntary action is viewed here as an adaptive response to the constraints of the majority rule and equitable distribution criteria of the state. A modest body of knowledge exists also on the dynamics of managing NGOs. This branch is concerned with planning, financing, budgeting, controlling, and evaluating NGO activities (Ramanathan 1982). The focus here is on the internal management problems of NGOs, an applied area of direct relevance to the training and development of NGO staff. Finally, there are numerous micro-level studies of NGOs and of their performance and problems.

Similar theoretical and empirical work on NGOs in developing countries is only beginning to emerge. While there is no lack of case studies of individual NGOs and of the many development experiments and projects undertaken by them, there are few studies of the NGO sector, nationally or regionally, and few careful assessments of NGO collaborations with international donors. An exception is the special issue of the journal *World Development* (Supplement, Autumn 1987), which pulled together an impressive set of both country- and issue-oriented papers on NGOs. A scanning of these papers highlights the paucity of reliable data and of analytical work. Of the papers in this special issue and the nearly 420 references cited in the bibliography, hardly any provided a systematic analysis of the growth or other trends and patterns of NGO development. In general, the literature on developing country NGOs seems to have a strong inward-looking orientation, an understandable preoccupation with their problems, and an advocacy bias driven by their focus on action and change.

The theoretical perspectives on NGOs in the developed world might apply equally well to developing country NGOs, but the theories' validity and relevance for these NGOs have not yet been explored. Developing country NGOs differ from their counterparts in more developed countries in important respects. The former are typically much smaller and depend on less skilled staff and technological resources. External linkages (for example, links with international donors and governments) are more important for NGOs in developing countries than for those in developed countries. What is the effect of small size and limited resources on performance? What are the implications of external linkages for NGO behavior in developing countries? Much research remains to be done on these and other related issues.

The World Bank's official cooperation with NGOs began in 1981, when the NGO-World Bank Committee was established. The Bank's increasing involvement in poverty-focused activities had set the stage. The Bank was engaging NGOs in a scattering of Bank-financed projects in several sectors, and initial discussions between the Bank and NGOs examined this emerging experience in collaboration. A group of industrial country NGOs with operational programs in the developing countries pioneered systematic dialogue with the Bank. They hoped that the Bank might be a new source of funding for them, and the Bank hoped that these NGOs might lend political support to funding for the International Development Association, the Bank's concessional affiliate. These discussions were formalized in the NGO-World Bank Committee and were also pursued through a series of country-level "trilateral" (government-NGO-World Bank) meetings. Developing country NGOs played a growing role in these discussions.

In the mid-1980s, the practical importance of developing country NGOs in some sectors was increasingly recognized within the Bank. At the same time, advocacy NGOs concerned with poverty and the environment became vocally critical of the Bank, and many urged increased efforts by the Bank to engage developing country NGOs in its operational work. At the start of 1988, the Bank began an institution-wide effort to expand its work with NGOs. While Bank-NGO cooperation has clearly expanded, there is as yet relatively little assessment of this cooperation and its effect on development.

No single book can hope to fill these gaps or to provide a global assessment of the contributions of NGOs and their collaborative programs with donors or governments. A beginning can be made, however, by focusing on some of the broader concerns about NGOs, their role, and their potential. This volume represents a modest endeavor to improve our understanding of the NGOs working on developing country problems by analyzing their evolution and their strengths and weaknesses. The book attempts first to examine the nature, potential, and limits of NGOs and their international patterns of evolution from a broad, developmental perspective. Against this backdrop, it then attempts a critical assessment of the experience of the World Bank in working with NGOs and in facilitating government-NGO cooperation in Bank projects.

This book consists of five chapters. This chapter provides an introduction to the general theme of the book, an overview of the findings of the subsequent chapters, and a forward-looking view of their implications. Chapters 2 and 3 analyze the concept, the evolution, and the strengths and weaknesses of NGOs, bearing in mind regional variations and the international forces at work. Chapters 4 and 5 are devoted to a discussion of the World Bank's policies toward NGOs and its experiences in working with NGOs through its projects in the developing world. Since many donors and governments collaborate with NGOs on different fronts, the World Bank's experience is no more than a case study and is not presented here as a representative example. On the other hand, the Bank is the largest international development agency in the world, and its policies, approaches, and experience in this area may be of interest not only to NGOs, but to many international donors and governments and to the development community in general.

## Themes and findings: A summary assessment

Chapter 2, by David C. Korten, focuses on the historical evolution of NGOs, an empirical analysis of NGO-government and NGO-donor relations, and concerns germane to the future role of NGOs. NGOs have had a long record of participation in international assistance. That the funds channeled through NGOs to the developing world are currently equivalent to nearly 9 percent of official development assistance testifies to the scope and significance of the growing role of NGOs. Korten shows how NGOs have played diverse roles in international assistance, including the delivery of relief and welfare services, human resources development, political activism and empowerment, and policy advocacy. Over the past three decades, official funding of NGOs for international assistance has expanded steadily, reaching a peak in the 1980s.

Using the limited data available on the NGO sector, Korten shows that there has been a substantial growth in the number, size, and sophistication of modern NGOs in the post-colonial developing world. Regional variations are significant, however. Latin American NGOs have been more politically active than others. Asian NGOs have, despite their political activism, collaborated more often with governments than their counterparts in other regions. In general, African NGOs have been engaged in lower-profile and more conventional service-delivery efforts.

In most developing countries, NGO-government relations are characterized by natural tensions, with governments trying to minimize political competition and NGOs jealously guarding their autonomy. An interesting recent phenomenon is the emergence of NGOs in some of the East European socialist countries and the roles they are playing in the reform process. Whether tensions are managed constructively depends greatly on the ideological orientation of NGOs and the type of political regime in power.

According to Korten, perceptions of legitimate development roles for NGOs are influenced by two contrasting views of the nature of development. Those who view development in terms of allocating investment resources to maximize economic growth tend to emphasize NGOs' potential as low-cost service providers. Those who focus more on the human and political empowerment dimensions of development see NGOs as a political and social force for strengthening pluralism, protecting the rights of marginalized groups, and curbing the power of the state vis-à-vis the people.

The likely directions of future movement relevant to NGOs and their relations with governments and donors are summarized by Korten as follows:

- There will be greater pressure on NGOs in future to support sustained and large-scale service delivery. This is in contrast to the temporary and shifting nature of the relief services to which many NGOs are accustomed. This trend has an important implication for public assistance agencies, which need to rethink their policies concerning NGO funding if their goal is to ensure sustained service delivery on a large scale.
- NGOs' roles in advocacy and development education are likely to receive much greater attention than in the past, given the growing awareness among NGOs—of both developed and developing countries—about the structural determinants of poverty and the environmental destruction that conventional development practice has been slow to address. Donor agencies will come under increasing pressure to come to terms with groups concerned with human rights, the environment, women's issues, and peace.
- The pace and intensity of NGO interactions with governments are bound to grow under these conditions. Interactions arising from service-delivery roles tend to be relatively passive, but the activist, advocacy, and protest roles of NGOs can be expected to be stormier and more acrimonious.
- NGOs from both developed and developing countries may increasingly play a catalytic role in people-to-people cooperation. Many problems can be handled through voluntary citizen action, where sharing experience and jointly solving problems provide the key. NGOs, with their international links, access to knowledge, and cost-effective exchange modes, may well emerge as the dominant medium for such people-to-people cooperation.

In Chapter 3, L. David Brown and David C. Korten analyze the rationale of NGOs from a number of perspectives. They argue that the comparative advantage of NGOs lies in their ability to innovate, to adapt to local conditions, and to reach and to work with the poor. These positive features are a function of their basic values, special skills, small size, limited resources, flexibility, and freedom from political constraints. Their weaknesses stem from some of the same characteristics—particularly their value commitments, small size, independence, and administrative flexibility. The authors then examine the pros and cons of markets, hierarchies, and clans in the context of development and point out that NGOs approximate value-driven, clan-type organizations. The chapter warns that, in relating to NGOs, donors should avoid equating small with simple. Though small, NGOs are simple neither in organizational form nor in development roles.

Brown and Korten distinguish different categories of NGOs—service-delivery agencies, development-catalyst organizations, sector-support and networking organizations, public service contractors, and people's organizations. Because NGOs vary in their missions and distinctive strengths, it is important that their activities be compatible with their concerns and capabilities. In general, NGOs will be most effective in operating environments that value both voluntarism and pluralism.

What are the ways in which large donors can work effectively with NGOs? Based on a review of international experience, Brown and Korten identify five promising areas for support.

• Direct financial support to NGOs is an important role that donors can perform provided funding takes the form of broadly defined grants tied to mutually agreed program missions. Donors should avoid financing mechanisms and practices that undermine the distinctive nature of NGOs.

• Strengthening sector-support institutions that assist NGOs (for example, those that provide technical help, training, and so on) can sometimes be even more beneficial than direct and short-term project support to NGOs. Donor financing and technical assistance in this area will have a multiplier and long-term effect on NGOs.

• Donors can help enlarge the political space for NGOs in their country environments. Freedom of association, public policies that encourage private philanthropy, and opportunities for interested NGOs to participate in the policy process are areas in which donor support, dialogue, and persuasion may nudge governments to provide a more hospitable policy and operating space to NGOs.

• The creation of feedback links from NGOs to donors is a strategically important step from which donors stand to benefit. This calls for greater mutual willingness to share information and to use both informal and formal mechanisms, such as advisory councils, to receive feedback on donor projects and policies.

• By involving NGOs in development tasks in which they have skills or experience, donors are likely to enhance the potential impact of NGOs in their local settings. This implies active involvement of NGOs in the donor projects with which they are associated, in planning, solving problems, and taking action—a far cry from NGOs' traditional role as mere implementors of projects designed and funded by others.

The central message of Chapter 3 is that no responsible donor should undertake to "assist" or "use" NGOs as part of its development programming unless it is prepared to make a substantial investment in understanding their nature, limits, and distinctive roles. In this spirit, Brown and Korten propose issues for further research. They point out that careful studies of the NGO sector on a country and regional basis are essential to improve our knowledge of the patterns that exist at the field level. Research is needed also on the question of how to create and manage the learning process by which a functioning set of small local initiatives by NGOs or others is transformed into a large-scale local development action. The role of funding mechanisms in assisting this transformation is also an important subject. Case studies could be undertaken to analyze and compare NGO experiences as sources of feedback in the design, implementation, and evaluation of donor or government projects.

In Chapter 4, Lawrence F. Salmen and A. Paige Eaves present the findings of a review of NGO roles and contributions in a sample of recent World Bank projects. This review is the first of its kind for the Bank. Though this analysis focuses on the admittedly limited experience of one among many international development agencies and donors, its conclusions and insights are relevant to other donors, development agencies, and governments. Salmen and Eaves identified 217 World Bank projects approved during 1973-88 that involved NGOs. These projects accounted for less than 6 percent of all Bank projects of the period. From this universe, they selected a representative sample of 24 projects for detailed study. They divided NGOs into five functional categories: community associations, policy-advocacy groups, service-provider/intermediary agencies, contractors, and cooperatives.

An important finding of their review is that the Bank involved NGOs far more during implementation (58 percent of the universe) than during design (12 percent). Service-provider NGOs (41 percent) and contractor NGOs (31 percent) were involved in Bank projects more often than the other types. Based on qualitative assessments, Salmen and Eaves found that NGOs have in general contributed positively to the success of Bank projects—by facilitating the participation of beneficiaries, highlighting environmental issues, and assisting in the delivery of services to low-income groups. Systematic studies of costs and benefits have not, however, been attempted. The benefits of NGO participation in Bank projects were:

- NGOs' demonstrated skills and experience in identifying community needs and promoting community participation
- Their articulate and forceful contributions to policy reform, especially in environmental issues
- Their cost-effective delivery of services to relatively vulnerable and inaccessible beneficiary groups; their facilitation of cost recovery
- Their long-term commitment to development efforts and their strong advocacy role on behalf of disadvantaged groups.

The review also highlighted some of the limitations of NGOs and the pitfalls in working with them in projects:

- The advocacy role of NGOs often injects antagonism into their relations with governments; this may spill over into donor-government relations.
- The primary concern of NGOs with local problems tends to make them less sensitive to larger macroeconomic issues and to the need for an enabling policy environment.

• Inter-NGO collaboration essential in many projects could be marred by the tendency of some NGOs to be hostile toward each other.
• The limited financial and managerial resources of NGOs may adversely affect their participation in projects unless donors anticipate such problems and take advance action to minimize them.

These findings by and large reaffirm the assessment by Brown and Korten of NGO strengths and weaknesses. For the World Bank, the question is how to involve NGOs in its projects so as to utilize their strengths while minimizing their limitations. Salmen and Eaves propose steps to this end. They argue, first, for action by the Bank to improve its understanding of NGOs, their mission, and comparative advantage. Second, NGOs should be encouraged, where appropriate, to contribute more to project design while continuing to take part in implementation. Third, Bank collaboration with borrower governments should help create an enabling environment in which NGOs can attain their full potential.

In Chapter 5, David Beckmann continues the assessment of the World Bank's experience with NGOs in its projects and in its dialogue on development issues. His update of the review of project-level NGO involvement beyond 1988 shows that the number of NGOs participating in Bank projects has increased significantly. Upstream NGO involvement (from implementation to design) has also grown somewhat (though it is difficult to assess intensity and quality). Both trends are positive.

Beckmann dwells on the evolution of the World Bank's policy dialogue with NGOs and on the role played by the NGO-World Bank Committee. He notes that environmental NGOs have influenced the Bank's policies and that the Bank's operational outreach toward NGOs was influenced by advice from the NGO-World Bank Committee. There is also some evidence of increasing efforts by Bank staff to seek out NGO perspectives on projects and, in some instances, on policy-related issues.

The emerging lessons from the Bank's collaboration with NGOs in projects and policy-related issues are several:

• Bank-NGO interactions of the past decade have been a learning experience for both sides. Within the Bank, operational staff have gained understanding of the potential and limits of NGOs. But there is a clear need to focus more on the quality of NGO involvement than on the numbers of NGOs or the funds disbursed through them. The growing upstream involvement of NGOs reflects a promising qualitative change.

• The Bank has made a modest beginning in strengthening the relations between governments and NGOs. But much more remains to be done if the potential of NGOs is to be effectively tapped by borrower countries. Studies of the NGO sector through the Bank's economic and sector work can be a useful aid in this process.[5]

• Given the tensions between NGOs and governments in many countries, the Bank has to be realistic in its expectations about the pace at which NGO involvement in its projects can be made to grow. Progress may be further constrained by the budgetary and time limitations under which Bank staff operate.

• NGOs have in recent years faced several problems in working with World Bank projects. NGOs are used to working with grants, whereas the Bank lends money to governments that in turn are responsible for the use of the loans. Multiple actors with divergent goals are more difficult to work with, especially for small agencies such as NGOs. Bank projects that deal with macroeconomic policy reforms offer little scope for NGOs that have limited interest or competence in policy matters. This is not to deny that a growing number of NGOs are getting involved in public policy issues in many countries.

In conclusion, Beckmann predicts that NGO-World Bank interaction will expand. Both NGOs and their links with governments will strengthen. The swing toward democracy in many parts of the world may well lead to increased public participation at the local level, often with the involvement of NGOs. Beckmann also expects growing interaction between the World Bank and NGOs in the shaping of public understanding of global development issues.

## Emerging issues and policy implications

The contributors to this volume have examined NGOs and their activities from different perspectives. Brown and Korten have given us a sweeping global review. Salmen, Eaves, and Beckmann offer a micro-level view of NGO experiences, having assessed them through the lens of a single development agency. Nevertheless, there is a surprising measure of agreement among them on the nature, potential, and limits of NGOs and on some of the emerging issues in dealing with them. The findings also point to certain directions for change and action that merit special attention.

• In general, there is considerable optimism about the potential role NGOs can play in development projects in collaboration with governments and donors. This is based on the greater openness toward NGOs shown by several donors and governments and on the positive demonstration effect of projects in which NGOs and donors have joined. The expectation that the NGOs' role in development will increase reflects a growing consensus on their strengths and competencies. There is, however, little hard evidence on their impact, costs, and other measures of performance.

• It is agreed that the NGO role should not be limited to project implementation, though that seems to be the mode most often used by governments and donors. NGOs' ability to contribute to project design, to provide feedback on implementation, and to interact on public policy issues is also recognized as valuable.

• The creation of an enabling environment for NGOs in developing countries is perceived to be a priority need. An important ingredient is the design of public policies that create incentives for NGOs to contribute effectively to the development process.

• Those who wish to tap the potential of NGOs should have a good understanding of their strengths and weaknesses. This applies equally well to governments and international donors and development agencies. For the World Bank, the importance of orienting its operational staff and management to this need cannot be overemphasized.

What are the major implications of these conclusions? What are the gaps in our knowledge of NGOs and the problem areas that merit special attention? Based on the data and findings of the different chapters, we present below six important themes for consideration by donors, governments, and the NGO community.

## Need for systematic studies of NGOs

As noted, a review of the NGO literature reveals our extremely limited knowledge of this sector. NGOs are not a homogeneous lot; there is no consensus on the definition of NGOs. Severe problems exist in gathering and analyzing available information. Being small, most NGOs lack systematic records, even on their own operations, growth, and financial transactions. We know little about total capital invested, sources of financing, manpower employed, and the quantitative and qualitative dimensions of NGO activities, even on a country basis. Nevertheless, it is not uncommon for supporters to claim capabilities and strengths for NGOs on a blanket, sector-wide basis.

It could be argued that quantitative assessments are partial and of limited value. There is no question that qualitative and micro-level studies of individual NGOs and their projects are important. One is not a substitute for the other. Systematic sector knowledge is a useful basis for diagnosing problems, discovering key patterns, and anticipating future needs. The assessment of individual NGOs by donors and governments, usually a prerequisite for involving them in projects, will be more meaningful when undertaken in the context of sector studies. This does not imply that the information loads and reporting requirements of NGOs should be increased. Sample surveys and special studies can be undertaken to develop the needed data base. NGO associations, donors, and governments can play a useful role by initiating studies on a country or regional basis and by getting qualified institutions and scholars to address the research issues raised by Brown and Korten.

## Dilution of the mission of NGOs: What can be done?

The growing demand for NGO participation in development projects has created a new dilemma for those committed to the NGO cause. On the one hand, it is encouraging that public agencies and donors recognize the contributions NGOs can make. New opportunities will most likely facilitate sustainable development and promote people's participation and empowerment over time. But pressure to take on increased loads can cause NGOs to dilute their commitment and stray from their basic mission. Easy availability of funds can be a source of distraction to NGOs used to struggling with limited resources. There is already some evidence that the demand for NGO services has led to the establishment of some nominal or opportunistic NGOs whose primary interest is in contract work for donors or other agencies.

While NGOs should guard against the dilution of their mission, donors and governments can also play a useful role in resolving this dilemma. First, donors and governments can take care to match NGOs with work that best uses their skills and commitment. As one example, an advocacy NGO should not normally be drawn into conventional service delivery. Second, donor and government staff should be sensitized to the overload and dilution problem, since they are the agents pressing NGOs to get jobs done. Such staff should become more discriminating in matching activities with NGO competence and more sensitive to the use of funds as a means to attract NGO participation. Third, as Brown and Korten argue, the capabilities of NGOs can be strengthened by allocating more funds for their development—even if this means less for contract work. This investment in NGOs will pay off in the long run.

**Alternatives to scaling up**

There is still another issue for NGOs and their collaborators to face. Both governments and donors have a strong interest in NGOs expanding their coverage to larger populations. This is particularly true of service delivery first targeted to a small geographical area—perhaps a few villages or a pilot project. Pressures soon emerge to replicate the services nationally or regionally through the existing NGOs. But should they expand at the cost of their values and strengths? There are several risks for NGOs in "scaling up." Large-scale operations undercut NGOs' ability to make local adaptations and speedy responses. Closeness to the people and capacity to get them to participate are difficult to sustain. The motivation and commitment of NGO workers can be adversely affected, because expansion causes an organization to become increasingly bureaucratic. What scaling up puts at risk are precisely the features and strengths for which NGOs are valued.

These costs must be weighed against the benefits that donors and governments see in scaling up. There is clearly a need to reach as large a population as possible so that development benefits are widely shared. A wholesale approach, whether in disbursing funds or delivering services, is administratively more manageable for a government or donor agency. Large-scale operations are generally believed to bring down the unit cost of service. But while efficiency criteria might support scaling up, the process tends to dilute or adversely affect the quality, relevance, and sustainability of services or benefits provided to people through the NGO.

What is the way out of this dilemma? It is in the interest of all concerned that NGOs scale up only to the point where their quality and other valued attributes are still not adversely affected. This limit may be high for international NGOs that are large and have a long track record. But for developing country NGOs, many of which have limited experience and resources—both human and technical—conventional scaling up may be a mistake. Other options that help augment the supply of services indirectly while preserving NGO strengths should be explored. Some examples follow:

• Rather than asking an NGO to expand and to shoulder increased responsibilities, donors and governments should enlist more NGOs to participate in the given task. This approach taps multiple sources of voluntary energy and promotes greater pluralism in society. It also calls for increased efforts by donors and governments to strengthen the core capabilities of NGOs and to finance the technical and professional support services that small NGOs require. Although some donors are reluctant to finance the overhead costs of NGOs, this kind of support is needed to increase the capacity of NGOs to take on projects, as the NGOs themselves are not building up the basic capabilities to utilize a larger volume of funds.

• Governments and donors can often get the benefits of scaling up by encouraging networks of NGOs to create linkages and collaborative arrangements. Coordination and internal conflict resolution are left to the networks, which can also facilitate learning and common services among members. The successful emergence of such NGO networks and their collaborative experiences with government agencies in Latin America seem to underscore the promise of this approach (Annis 1987).

• Under certain conditions, NGOs may play the role of "nursery," generating innovative development ideas that other agencies with greater resources can use for replication and scaling up. The function of the NGO here is akin to that of a research and development entity whose products are scaled up and commercialized by large enterprises. The NGO in this scenario may offer not only pilot projects but also training and other services needed by those responsible for scaling up, and perhaps even the personnel required for replication. The kind of indirect yet powerful role that a small organization can play in scaling up has been admirably demonstrated by the well-known farmer cooperative "Amul Dairy" in Anand, India, in working with the National Dairy Development Board of India (Paul 1982).

**What should public policies do for NGOs?**

As our contributors have noted, there is diversity among NGOs. Not all are interested in or capable of collaborating with governments or international donors. Some NGOs, given their history and value orientation, are primarily agents for policy advocacy; others are leaders of protest movements and champions of causes. There are NGOs that act as development catalysts but are averse to service delivery. The costs and benefits of the different types of NGO operation may vary greatly. The problems of scaling up and dilution of mission are less acute for NGOs that do not seek to collaborate with donors or governments in any program- or project-related sense. But whether the issue of collaboration is relevant to them or not, all NGOs are directly affected by the public policies of governments. How such policies impinge on NGOs has several implications.

First, the focus should be on creating an enabling environment for NGOs, not merely on public policies. The latter are only a part, albeit important, of the enabling environment necessary for NGOs to emerge, operate, and grow. Fiscal policies (taxes and subsidies) can be designed to encourage or discourage NGOs through tax incentives and disincentives. Grant-in-aid policies can be tailored to strengthen or neglect the core facilities and capabilities NGOs require to perform their functions. Regulatory policies can restrict or ease the flow of foreign assistance to NGOs, impose burdensome or easy reporting requirements, and influence NGO access to important resources such as bank loans. Clearly, public policies should be examined to see how they can help rather than hinder NGOs. What is often forgotten, however, is that while "good policies" can be designed on paper, they may be rendered ineffective by procedural and other bureaucratic barriers. Cumbersome procedures and delays in getting approvals from government can inhibit the work of small NGOs. Bureaucracies that function through connections, contacts, and corruption can leave NGOs far behind. Since nonpolicy aspects can be as critical to NGO survival as policies, attention to their reform should be a priority.

Second, the basic political values and systems that govern a society are an essential element in the enabling environment. This element may be even more important than public policies. A political system that does not respect the freedom of association of citizens or tolerate dissent and autonomy among organizations cannot offer an enabling environment for NGOs. An open and tolerant political regime is also a prerequisite for good public policies to be nurtured and sustained. It is possible, for example, for a country to be liberal on foreign exchange flows or tax incentives for NGOs, yet highly restrictive about freedom of expression and autonomy. NGOs will find it hard to survive in this environment. Policy reform should be informed by a realistic assessment of the political preconditions for its success.

Third, it is developing country governments that are ultimately responsible for creating an enabling environment for their national NGOs. The popular view of NGOs as agents for service delivery may limit government understanding of what it takes to create and sustain an enabling environment. Strengthening the professional and managerial competence of NGOs can often divert attention from the fact that the basic political foundation beneath NGOs is weak. The abuse of public policies and incentives by self-serving NGOs makes governments understandably cautious in moving toward reform of the environment. The elements of the enabling environment for the private sector recently proposed by the World Bank and several international donors are quite similar to those needed by development-oriented NGOs. International aid and policy dialogue can be the means by which donors kindle government interest in reform in those countries where the environment for NGOs is disabling.

## Directions for change in relations between donors and NGOs

The chapters that follow devote special attention to relations between donors and NGOs and to the importance of donors improving their understanding of the potential and limits of NGOs. An emerging issue in this area is the shifting role of international and developing country or indigenous NGOs. Donor-NGO collaboration in development projects began with international NGOs. Over time, indigenous NGOs grew in number and experience, at least in Asia and Latin America. While international NGOs have greater resources, foreign linkages, and professional competence, their indigenous counterparts have more local knowledge and adaptability, staying power, and possibly more capacity for local empowerment. Donors who prefer the wholesale approach in the project arena naturally have closer links with larger, international NGOs, but indigenous NGOs are demanding greater involvement in development projects (Elliot 1987b). The nature of shifts is ably summarized in the following statement:

> *Given the rapid expansion of indigenous NGOs in recent years, there are those (both in the North and the South) who feel that international NGOs should now play a less decisive role in priority setting, project approval and evaluation of performance, and allow their indigenous partners in the South a far greater deliberative as opposed to advisory role in decisionmaking. Such advocates believe that full and effective partnerships between international and indigenous NGOs require delegation by funding agencies in the North of authority to their counterparts in the South to make decisions regarding resource allocation, accountability procedures and project performance evaluation. In so doing, the argument goes, not only would indigenous NGOs be given the respect and full trust they deserve, but decisionmaking and oversight would be brought nearer to the local needs and realities of the grass-roots poor in developing countries. Moreover, international NGOs—freed from such administrative burdens—could devote more of their own time and energies to fund raising, development education and legislative advocacy work at home on behalf of developing country needs and priorities.* (Smith 1987, 87)

This assessment has important implications for future donor relations with NGOs. First, as indigenous NGOs grow in numbers and competence, the criteria of economic and social efficiency may require that they play a more active role in the initiation, design, and implementation of projects, replacing international NGOs. The latter will increasingly be intermediaries, facilitators, and providers of linkage and support. Donors, for example, could use them to evaluate and assess local NGO capabilities, strengthen indigenous technical and managerial capabilities, create accountability systems, and play other support roles.[6] Since country conditions and levels of development vary, the types and mix of roles to be played by international and indigenous NGOs must clearly be tailored to fit the circumstances.

Second, it is important that donors invest in the support institutions for indigenous NGOs, as our contributors note. Here again, international NGOs can be useful agents, provided donors and governments are willing to supplement their limited resources. Strengthening the technical and managerial competence of indigenous NGOs is a useful way to prepare them to assume greater responsibilities as international NGOs begin to phase out or shift to other roles. Building local capabilities must be undertaken with a long view. Donors should be willing to stay with institutions through ups and downs.

Third, international donors can assist developing country governments to work closely with their own NGOs. The importance of creating a healthy political space for development-oriented NGOs has already been stressed. Where governments are committed to collaborating with NGOs, the approaches and practices of donors in working with them will be instructive. The approaches used by donor staff in assessing local NGO capabilities, the contracting and monitoring arrangements they work out with NGOs, and the sensitivities they display in their relationships with NGOs are aspects of collaboration from which interested governments can learn.

## Need for balanced view of NGOs

The foregoing issues—and the proposals presented for dealing with them—have important implications for NGOs, international donors, and governments. Some of the proposed actions will require collaboration among agencies. Minimizing the risk of dilution of the NGO mission or dealing with scaling up, for example, calls for mutual understanding and cooperation to arrive at satisfactory arrangements between NGOs and donors and governments. Improving knowledge about NGOs—through sector studies and rigorous work to understand the contributions of different types—is an area in which NGOs, an international donor, or a government can initiate action. Collaborative endeavors can be difficult. They deserve to be undertaken, however, where donors or governments feel that costs and benefits favor interventions by NGOs over those of the market or state. Ideological beliefs or unverified claims about NGO competencies are not an adequate basis for investing in these more complex joint endeavors. Forums such as the NGO-World Bank Committee therefore have a useful role to play in identifying issues and finding creative, mutually acceptable answers.

To conclude: The need for a balanced view of the potential and the limits of NGOs in development cannot be overemphasized. While donors and governments are likely to base assessment on a variety of contextual factors, some general points that emerge in the following chapters have a direct bearing on the subject.

First, our discussion of the risks of dilution of the NGO mission and of the pressure for scaling up should foster realism about the capacity and willingness of the NGO sector to respond speedily to an ever increasing demand for development services. A significant conclusion of our contributors is that such rapid expansion is neither feasible nor desirable. The demand by some NGOs for greater participation in development projects and the unbridled enthusiasm with which some donors seek a wider role for NGOs in the countries they assist must be moderated by awareness of these risks.

Second, there is some evidence that the supply response of NGOs in the face of growing demand for their services tends to be slower than that of for-profit firms (Hansmann 1987). Limited access to capital, concern for quality, and the problem of incentives have been cited as likely causes. Similarly, some aspects of NGO behavior can make collaboration among donors, governments, and NGOs difficult and slow. As Salmen and Eaves point out, the antigovernment stance associated with the advocacy role of NGOs can spill over into donor-government relations in unpredictable ways. Their relative lack of familiarity with macroeconomic problems can be a liability. The severity of such limitations varies with country contexts and historical factors. Nevertheless, these are important problem areas that donors and governments should take into account in a realistic assessment of NGO potential.

Third, donors and governments should be sensitive to the fact that creating an enabling environment for NGOs, in many ways a positive step, can also lead to the entry of many NGOs that are self-serving and oriented toward the short term—NGOs that wish to take advantage of financial incentives and other related benefits. Given the limited knowledge of this heterogeneous sector and the difficulties in evaluating NGO credentials ex ante, some abuse and unethical practices by shrewd operators may have to be tolerated; the alternative is a highly restrictive environment for NGOs that may invite political victimization and limit their potential contributions to the good governance of the countries they serve. The important implication is this: those who support the NGO sector have a special responsibility. They must help countries improve their knowledge about the NGOs that can truly contribute to development, and they must help design public policies that can motivate those NGOs to perform well.

## Notes

1. The other two sectors are the market and the government. Market here refers to the sector of private, commercially oriented organizations. Government refers to state-owned or state-controlled organizations. Needless to say, the boundaries between these sectors are not always clear-cut.
2. This is by no means an adequate definition of NGOs. The World Bank's operational policy guidelines define NGOs as entirely or largely independent of government, and characterized primarily by humanitarian or cooperative rather than commercial objectives. Chapters 2 and 3 of this book offer more elaborate definitions. The range and focus of NGO activities are evolving and tend to vary across countries and sectors. It is not therefore easy to arrive at a definition that is acceptable to all.
3. The nomenclature used in the U.S. literature is "nonprofit organizations." We use the terms nongovernmental, voluntary, and nonprofit interchangeably throughout this book.
4. Some of these theories are further discussed in Chapter 3.
5. Economic and sector work refers to periodic studies of a country's problems that the

Bank undertakes jointly with a view to generating knowledge and findings of potential use to the latter.
6. This, of course, assumes that these ideas are acceptable to indigenous (developing country) NGOs, and to governments.

# 2

# The Role of Nongovernmental Organizations in Development: Changing Patterns and Perspectives

*David C. Korten*

## An introduction to NGOs

Long considered peripheral and largely inconsequential actors in development, NGOs became a focal point of attention for development thinkers and practitioners during the 1980s. This chapter reviews NGOs' historical role in development and international assistance and their current relationships with governments and official assistance agencies. It then examines forces that may shape NGO-government relations in the 1990s.

### *Diversity of NGOs*

Given that the term NGO defines a residual category—organizations that are neither governmental nor for-profit—it is not surprising that a wide variety of organizations can be so classified. NGOs can be large, highly visible organizations with long histories—the Catholic Church, Oxford University, the International Red Cross. NGOs can also be small neighborhood groups formed for community self-help, social, or charitable activities—village sports clubs, labor-sharing groups, rotating credit groups.

Other organizations that fit the broad definition include volunteer fire brigades, the parent-teacher associations of elementary schools, the Society for International Development, Friends of the Earth, the American Medical Association, Rotary International, the Self-Employed Women's Association of

Ahmedabad, Amnesty International, and the Ku Klux Klan. Simply listing types of NGOs could fill many pages.

The World Bank's Operational Directive on NGOs (No. 14.70, August 1989) defines them as:

> *groups and institutions that are entirely or largely independent of government and characterized primarily by humanitarian or cooperative, rather than commercial, objectives.*

In the Bank's Operational Directive, the term NGO is used to refer "principally to those private organizations that pursue activities to relieve suffering, promote the interests of the poor, protect the environment, or undertake community development."[1]

*Historical importance of NGOs*

Although NGOs have only recently emerged into the development limelight, they are not a recent phenomenon. Nor is their relevance to national development processes recent. If we accept that all nongovernmental, nonprofit organizations are properly classified as NGOs, we may safely conclude that they were the earliest form of human organization. Long before there were governments, people organized themselves into groups for mutual protection and self-help.

Roberto Unger (1987) discusses the important role of farmers' organizations in maintaining the vitality of early agrarian-bureaucratic empires.[2] Following the Meiji Restoration in Japan in 1868, farmers' organizations, especially seed-exchange societies, played a vital part in agricultural improvement. In 1937, 25 million farmers in Europe belonged to 25,000 rural cooperatives (Esman and Uphoff 1984). In the Western democracies, NGOs helped shape values, served as a counterweight to the accumulation of excessive power by the state, and developed many services essential to community well-being and economic growth (Bratton 1989; and Hall 1987).

*Number of NGOs*

Estimating the total number of NGOs is a difficult, perhaps futile undertaking. Because of the variety of organizations, the first challenge is simply defining the universe (see Gronbjerg 1989). Another difficulty is that while some NGOs have survived for centuries, others are small, unregistered organizations that form and disband almost overnight. There is no written record for many smaller, informal organizations even if they survive.

Most available estimates of the number of NGOs are probably too low. The *Yearbook of International Organizations (1984/85)* lists 7,109 international NGOs and 5,577 internationally oriented national NGOs.[3] A directory prepared by the Organization for Economic Cooperation and Development (OECD) lists more than 4,000 NGOs from Development Assistance Committee (DAC) member countries[4] that are engaged in international assistance, up from the 1,702 listed in a similar 1981 directory (OECD 1988). Even Japan, whose nongovernmental involvement in international assistance has been financially modest, has 174 NGOs thus engaged (JANIC 1988).

Most NGO activity in both developed and developing countries is oriented to domestic concerns. Independent Sector, a U.S. nongovernmental organization concerned with promoting nonprofit initiatives, estimated that there were 873,000 independent sector organizations or NGOs in the United States in 1986 (Independent Sector 1988). These organizations raised $82.2 billion in contributions from private sources (Independent Sector 1988, Table 7).[5] In 1985, 82.2 million adult Americans contributed 14,808 billion hours of volunteer work (Independent Sector 1986). The value of volunteer work contributed in 1986 was placed at $104 billion (Independent Sector 1988).[6]

For Sweden, there are estimates that even small communities (5,000 to 10,000 inhabitants) commonly have 100 or more NGOs of various types (OECD 1988). One study calculates that France had 300,000 to 500,000 nongovernmental associations in 1981, with some 100 new associations formed each day.[7] It has been estimated that in Brazil, 3 million people belong to 100,000 Christian Base Communities, and 1,300 neighborhood associations exist in Sao Paulo alone. Small farmers' groups in Zimbabwe are credited with 400,000 members (Durning 1989). In Bangladesh some 6,000 village self-help organizations are registered with the government for the purpose of receiving a small government subsidy. Three hundred fifty NGOs belong to the country's Association of Development Agencies.[8]

Individual grass-roots organizations may be small, but in the aggregate they can be a highly consequential development force. In the Philippines, for example, independent farmers' irrigator associations watered 640,000 hectares in 1986, 45,000 hectares more than government irrigation systems (Bagadion 1989).

## Involvement in international assistance

One of the many reasons for growing donor interest in NGOs is the realization that they control a large share of the funds committed to international assistance. While the number, size, and sophistication of NGOs grew significantly during the 1980s, their approaches to international assistance are rooted in a substantial historical experience. Understanding this history is essential to understanding their current diversity.

### *Resources*

According to the OECD, the NGOs of its Development Assistance Committee (DAC) member countries provided $3.3 billion in private contributions to developing countries in 1986. This was the equivalent of 9 percent of total official development assistance (ODA) for that year. In addition, the governments of DAC member countries channeled another $2.0 billion of their foreign assistance through NGOs (OECD 1988). All DAC countries now have active private sector involvement in international assistance. For 1986, the leaders in private contributions as a percentage of gross national product (GNP) were Ireland (0.09 percent), the Netherlands (0.08 percent), Norway (0.08 percent), and Sweden (0.07 percent).

Official U.S. government contributions to NGOs were only 0.04 percent of GNP in 1986, but in absolute terms they exceeded the total contributions of all other DAC governments to NGOs. In addition, U.S. private contributions were $1.8 billion, also more than half the total for DAC countries.[9] The United States is clearly the largest source of financing for NGO efforts in international assistance.[10] According to statistics compiled by the U.S. Agency for International Development, CARE USA alone reported annual expenditures in 1986 of $398.1 million.[11]

Japan, which now leads all countries in total overseas development assistance (ODA) funding, still has only limited NGO participation in international assistance. In 1986, private contributions to Japanese NGOs totaled $82 million, less than 0.01 percent of GNP. Official contributions to NGOs totaled $92 million, or 1.6 percent of Japan's ODA funding (OECD 1988).

Most official statistics, including those of the OECD, make no distinction between expenditures for humanitarian assistance (relief and welfare) and those for development. OECD figures for 1983, however, indicate that for seven reporting countries plus the European Community, 44 percent of ODA funding channeled to NGOs was for food aid and relief (OECD 1988).[12] The NGO division of the Swedish International Development Authority (SIDA) reports that of SEK 1,140 million in grants to Swedish NGOs in 1988/89, SEK 615 million was for disaster relief and SEK 525 million was for support of long-term development projects.[13] Of the $1.06 billion in official contributions from the U.S. government to U.S. private international assistance agencies in 1986, 52 percent consisted of donated food, related transportation, and excess property—predominantly relief and welfare assistance. Even indicative figures are lacking on the division of private contributions between welfare and development assistance. However, the appeals that generate private funds, especially in the United States, are heavily oriented toward relief and welfare needs.[14]

### *Historical evolution*

There is a long history of international voluntary action to assist the victims of wars and natural disasters and to provide welfare services to the poor. Religious groups have commonly taken the initiative. In 1647 Irish Protestants sent food aid to settlers in North America who were victims of the Indian wars. Private British charities supported missionaries and schools for Indians, blacks, and poor whites in America throughout much of the seventeenth and eighteenth centuries (Sommer 1977). In 1793 private groups in the United States provided voluntary assistance to refugees fleeing revolutionary turmoil in Santo Domingo. The American Red Cross was established in 1882. Major international relief and missionary societies sprang up in Europe and America in the nineteenth century.

Private international initiatives grew substantially during World War I. Food contributions to Europe from U.S. charities during the war totaled an annual $250 million (Sommer 1977). The oldest of the British international charities, Save the Children Fund, was founded in 1919 as an outgrowth of opposition to the Allied blockade of Germany (OECD 1988).

Many of the major international NGOs now assisting developing countries were established to help victims of World War II in Europe; these include Catholic Relief Services and CARE. Oxfam (U.K.) was started in 1942 to aid starving children in Nazi-occupied Greece. The Danish Association for International Cooperation was founded in 1944 to enable Danish youth to take part in war reconstruction in Europe and subsequently to work in Israel (OECD 1988).

As Europe's postwar recovery progressed, organizations increasingly turned their attention to developing countries. Particular effort went to assisting refugees from political conflicts in China, India, Korea, and the Middle East (OECD 1988). Under the Agricultural Act of 1949, U.S. voluntary agencies became qualified to distribute government surplus food stocks to the needy in developing countries (OECD 1988). This led in time to a substantial increase in the scope of American efforts.

In the early 1960s, international voluntary agencies became increasingly interested in development work. The impetus came from the recent independence of former colonies and the corresponding changes in relationships between churches in developed and developing countries.[15]

### *Diversity of contemporary orientations*

Multiple currents emerged in NGO assistance efforts from this time forward, revealing differing definitions of the development problem and differing degrees of political activism. These define the variety of approaches taken by contemporary NGOs.

**Relief and welfare**. The administration of food aid programs, including food-for-work and nutrition programs, continues to be the primary commitment of some of the largest international NGOs. For example, 87 percent of CARE's total resources in 1985 were for food aid and freight. Catholic Relief Services devoted 80 percent of its funds to food aid (OECD 1988).

**Human resources development**. Focusing on financial transfer for development, the World Council of Churches recommended in 1958 that industrial countries transfer 1 percent of income to developing countries. Many religious organizations committed themselves to contributing a portion of their own resources for local development activities in addition to their traditional support for more conventional church activities and social services. This commitment led to a substantial growth in privately funded micro-projects in developing countries.

Such efforts often focus on building local skills and capabilities (human resources development strategies). Some NGOs have established permanent training centers in developing countries (OECD 1988). Many NGOs provide services for small and micro-enterprise development. Inspired by the example of Bangladesh's Grameen Bank, small-scale credit programs have become popular among NGOs and their donors.

**Political activism and empowerment**. A different NGO current emerged in the 1960s, responding in part to the encyclical letters of Popes John XXIII and Paul VI. The letters articulated principles that ultimately became the shared values of much of the global NGO community, and especially of the emerging national NGOs. These values became strong themes of liberation theology and of much indigenous NGO activity in Latin America and in Asia—even among secular and non-Catholic NGOs (OECD 1988).

Specifically, the papal encyclicals stated that human beings must be both the agents and the goal of development, and that development should involve self-reliance, responsibility, human dignity, and freedom from oppression. Attention was drawn to extreme inequalities in the sharing of goods and power—identified as the underlying causes of persistent poverty.

**Policy advocacy.** With greater experience, many international NGOs, especially in Europe and Canada, came to question both the human resources development and community empowerment approaches. NGO involvement in these undertakings was too limited and too fragmented to make any lasting impact. Furthermore, the technical assistance approach assumed that the problem was primarily a lack of basic technical knowledge. This assumption was seldom valid; the problem often was that someone else controlled the technology, the necessary productive resources (the land, the fishpond), and the market.

Even empowerment-oriented local organizing—although it acknowledged the political dimension of poverty—often implicitly assumed that village organizations of the poor could mobilize sufficient political resources to change the relevant power structures. But in time it became evident that local power structures were embedded in protective national and international systems, against which even the strongest village organizations were relatively powerless. Many NGOs also realized that changes in official aid budgets could quickly alter total flows—and that fluctuations in export earnings had an even greater resource impact than official aid.

As a result, a group of NGOs concerned with broader issues of trade and development policy formed the International Coalition for Development Action (ICDA) in 1976; its purpose was to engage in public education and advocacy. Thus began the trend toward greater NGO involvement in education and advocacy that some observers expect will increase in importance in the 1990s (OECD 1988; and USAID 1988).[16] The trend is particularly strong in Europe and Canada. A growing number of national NGOs in developing countries are also becoming advocates in macro-issues.

U.S. NGOs have largely continued to concentrate on relief and on welfare and technical assistance efforts aimed at strengthening human resources; they have declined to join Canadian and European counterparts in directing attention to policy. Nor do U.S. NGOs seem to be serious critics of U.S. international assistance policy, beyond lobbying to protect and enlarge their own funding.[17] This may change. InterAction, the association of U.S. international assistance NGOs, has invited participation by developing country NGOs in its forums and policy deliberations, a move contributing to a new climate of critical self-examination.

## Developing country NGOs: Regional patterns

The most significant recent development among NGOs has been the growth in number, size, and sophistication of organizations indigenous to the developing countries. This growth has taken on several patterns loosely associated with geographical regions. While an attempt is made below to summarize some of these patterns, generalizations necessarily simplify complex social processes and differences among and within countries.[18]

### *Latin America*

Until the mid-1960s, NGO activities in Latin America, especially those connected with the Catholic Church, were oriented primarily toward charitable welfare. Much NGO effort involved transferring food surpluses from the developing countries as a stop-gap measure to relieve suffering among the Latin American poor until development efforts of official agencies could improve conditions. Most NGOs accepted the prevailing wisdom that the solution to underdevelopment would be found in the large-scale transfer of resources and technology, "securing investments for development that would yield results measurable in general indicators such as per capita income" (Landim 1987, 31).

Many key Latin American opinion leaders, however, began to question both conventional development ideology and the excesses of authoritarian military rule. A new breed of NGO—a fairly explicit political opposition force—began to proliferate. Particularly during the 1970s, NGO activity in Latin America became highly politicized. Newer NGOs had a strong commitment to strengthening civil society, styling themselves as a bulwark against political and economic oppression perpetrated by the state. Support for small-scale local development initiatives became part of a campaign to protect and strengthen resistance movements at the grass roots. The politically activist stance of the Catholic Church and of liberation theology provided inspiration and political protection (Landim 1987).

During the 1980s, the growing strength of democratization processes in Latin America thrust NGOs into a new development phase. Popular organizations, such as neighborhood and peasant associations, grew into important additions to the institutional fabric of Latin societies. Social movements, such as those supporting the causes of ethnic groups, women, and ecology, broadened the scope of participation and the issue consciousness of grass-roots groups (Landim 1987; and Annis 1987 and 1989).

Interestingly, these changes have had a bearing on the relationships between grass-roots organizations and the NGOs that assisted their development. In some instances grass-roots organizations have indicated that NGOs are no longer needed—their continued presence serves only to protect their staffs' jobs (personal communication with Mario Padron).

The deep antipathy of Latin American NGOs toward the state has been overcome only gradually. As democratization has made the state more responsive and accountable to the people, NGO leaders have tried to reduce the gap between the state and civil society. Cooperative initiatives are relatively common (Landim 1987).

Latin American NGOs demonstrate a growing interest in forming national and international networks through which they can coordinate their efforts in support of social transformation. An important theme is the collective commitment of the NGOs to pluralism and the strengthening of civil society. There is a self-conscious perception among the NGOs of their own importance in consolidating advances toward democratic rule (Landim 1987).

### *Africa*

Traditional village mutual self-help associations have a long history in Africa, though modernizing states have tended to play them down on the grounds that they present barriers to progress. Both trade unions and cooperatives figured prominently in Africa's struggle for independence, but many were later reduced to instruments of patronage politics and largely lost their ability to provide independent leadership (Hyden 1983).

Churches and missionary societies were important in Africa throughout the colonial era. Colonial governments were concerned primarily with maintaining law and order; the provision of basic education and health care services was left largely to church-related organizations (Bratton 1989). The churches generally remained neutral in the independence struggles; thus they emerged from the colonial era with weak political legitimacy. Even so, they have become one of the few African institutions, other than ruling parties, to have broad popular followings. The strength and legitimacy of the churches have been achieved through their activism on such matters as human rights and their expansion of activities into support of women's groups, environmental protection, agricultural productivity, and other issues bearing on the lives of the poor (Hyden 1983).

According to Bratton (1989), Africa's first modern NGOs emerged in the latter days of colonial rule as ethnic welfare associations. Through these associations, newly urbanized Africans were able to articulate their demands that colonial governments give more attention to essential services. The associations were the foundations of nationalist political parties, and the role they played vis-à-vis the colonial governments was clearly political (Bratton 1989).

NGO involvement in African development activities has grown rapidly since independence. Even more than in Latin America and Asia, this growth has been a response to the evident inability of governments to deliver basic services and to implement programs that strengthen the economic participation of the rural and urban poor. Indeed, the African experience has been particularly important in calling the attention of international assistance agencies to the potential of NGOs as alternative service providers.

The growing involvement of African NGOs in development and in the delivery of basic services has been a source of tension between them and their African governments. The governments have characteristically based claims for the legitimacy of authoritarian, one-party states on their ability to deliver essential services and to be the agents of national development. In this context, it is common for any competent NGO that demonstrates efficiency in service delivery to be perceived by government as a direct political threat. The weaker the legitimacy of the regime, the stronger this perception of threat (Bratton 1989). Even so, African governments have generally tolerated NGOs that provide only relief and basic services. Many have been less tolerant of NGOs concerned with civil, political, and economic rights; NGOs with those orientations have been slower to take root in Africa than in other regions (Bratton 1989).

In Africa, international NGOs remain an important, even a dominant, operational presence—much more so than in Asia or Latin America. This reality has generated considerable sensitivity among African NGO leaders, who have challenged international NGOs to give greater attention to the development of local NGO capacities.[19] In general, indigenous NGOs in Africa are fewer, smaller, and less inclined to engage in activities that go beyond conventional service delivery than NGOs in Latin America and Asia.

*South and Southeast Asia*

Asia's cultural heritage includes deeply ingrained values of shared responsibility for the well-being of the community and its members. There is a tradition of harmonious life within the community and with the natural environment. There is also a tradition of communities organizing to build irrigation systems, fish ponds, roads, public buildings, and canals using only local resources (Korten 1986).

In many instances complex and often highly effective structures of mutual self-help have been disrupted by modernization. Yet others survive to this day. The wet rice cultures of much of the region demanded irrigation and provided an incentive for farmers to organize themselves for the construction and management of sophisticated engineering structures. In one functioning irrigation system in Bali, for example, 54 farmers carved a 2 kilometer tunnel through a mountain to irrigate their 22 hectares—with no formal irrigation training and minimal government assistance (Satawan and others 1984). Equally impressive accomplishments are found in the Zanjera irrigation systems of Ilocos Norte in the Philippines; some cover 1,000 hectares or more and, although centuries old, have highly appropriate and systematic procedures for water allocation and system maintenance (Siy 1986).

In South Asia, the modern NGO movement traces its roots to the struggle for independence, and in particular to the response by thousands of young women and men in the 1920s and 1930s to the call by Mahatma Gandhi to work among the rural poor and the castes. According to Rajesh Tandon (1989):

> *This period witnessed the flowering of the spirit of voluntarism and the sacrifices of volunteers to the cause of socioeconomic upliftment of the poor and the weak. It was also the time when India became free of foreign rule.* (15)

Many NGOs in South India began in this experience. Others were founded for the relief and rehabilitation of victims of floods and wars. Between the mid-1960s and the mid-1970s many NGOs became innovators in areas such as appropriate technology, adult education, and health care to improve the conditions of the poor (Tandon 1987). There are examples of efforts by governments to replicate these innovations on a national scale.[20]

In the mid-1970s a new thrust emerged among NGOs disenchanted with conventional development theories and practices. They focused attention on organization building and consciousness-raising among the poor so as to empower them to struggle for their rights and to acquire the resources for development. In India, many tiny groups sprang up to undertake this work. More recently, specialized support NGOs have begun to provide training and technical services to other NGOs that in turn serve grass-roots groups (PACT 1984).

The empowerment theme has become central for the more activist NGOs throughout South and Southeast Asia. These NGOs draw inspiration from many sources, including Gandhi, Saul Allinsky, and Paulo Friere. Thinking has evolved beyond village-level organizing and consciousness-raising to a recognition of the need to work for democratization of institutions at the national as well as the local level. There is also a growing commitment to advocacy in support of the sustainable use of environmental resources (ANGOC 1988b).[21]

Indonesian NGOs give special attention to environmental issues. In the Philippines, land reform is a key issue. Malaysia's strong consumer affairs NGO has had a leading role in the international movement.

In general, Asian NGOs share with Latin American ones a commitment to empowerment and democratization in the service of the oppressed. But Asian NGOs have generally demonstrated greater willingness to maintain working relations with governments, even authoritarian ones.

## Relations between NGOs and government

Generalizations about NGO-government relations are complicated by the many NGO orientations toward government, even within one country. There are also differences among governments in both commitment to pluralism and ability to enforce their will.

### *NGO orientations*

At one end of the spectrum of NGO attitudes toward government are those NGOs created by government to serve its interests. These NGOs may be headed by government officials or members of their families and are sometimes referred to disparagingly as "governmental" nongovernmental organizations (GONGOs).[22] Other NGOs at the progovernment end of the spectrum may position themselves largely as nonprofit contractors to government.[23]

At the other end of the spectrum are NGOs that oppose any contact or collaboration with government. Some of the more conservative religious organizations see their role as nonpolitical and avoid contact with government on these grounds. Others see government as corrupt and ineffective beyond any hope and want nothing to do with it. Some NGOs have an anarchist orientation, viewing the state as inherently opposed to the interests of the civil society, or even as the active enemy of the people. Still other NGOs may be aligned with leftist revolutionary movements that seek to replace existing structures with a Marxist state.

Most NGOs fall somewhere between the extremes—skeptical if not suspicious of state power, yet accepting of government's necessary function. They are prepared to work with government when opportunities arise consistent with their social commitment.

*Government orientations*

Governments have their own spectrum of orientations. They also vary in their ability to enforce a preferred orientation. Thus some governments that might like to constrain NGO activities simply lack the political and administrative strength to do so (Bratton 1989).

Under dictatorial regimes that have banned opposing political parties and suppressed unions and other groups, NGOs may represent the only viable form of political opposition (Tandon 1987). In such situations, some NGOs may undertake relatively innocuous welfare-oriented, service-delivery projects as a protective cover for more political activities or as a holding action while waiting for an opening of political space.

NGOs in many Asian countries have demonstrated substantial adeptness in building alliances with those in government who are both influential and sympathetic to their cause. Alliance building is often a conscious political strategy aimed at securing political protection for the NGO and its activities. With time the alliance may become the basis of a coalition advocating constructive policy changes to which the NGO and the concerned officials have a mutual commitment.[24] Indonesian NGOs cultivate such relationships.

The most restrictive policy stance vis-à-vis NGOs is usually found in Marxist-leaning, single-party regimes. On the theory that it is the vanguard of the people, represents their aspirations, and leads their struggle, the ruling party commonly maintains that work with the masses must be done under its auspices, not that of others (Tandon 1987). The result is commonly a repression of independent NGO activities even more severe than that found under authoritarian governments of the right.

An interesting recent phenomenon, however, is the emergence of NGOs in the changing socialist countries and the roles they are taking in the reform process. The Catholic Church and Solidarity have been particularly key in the reform process of Poland.

Overall, government's stance toward NGOs is likely to be most complex under liberal democratic regimes. These commonly profess commitment to both populism and pluralism, but they are subject to the pressures of many interest groups, including those of elite factions that may not fully share such commitment. Under these regimes, NGOs may work with government while bringing alternative perspectives to bear and challenging the authorities when they stray from stated commitments. Especially where political parties represent factional politics rather than competing political ideologies, NGOs may be one of the more important sources of alternative policy ideas.

## Official assistance agencies and NGOs

The recent upsurge in attention to NGOs by official development assistance (ODA) agencies has tended to obscure the fact that some bilateral and multilateral agencies have been directing ODA to NGOs for many years. Most of these relationships feature grant-funding mechanisms specific to NGOs.

### *Bilateral assistance agencies*

In the early 1950s, the United States became the first country to channel official development assistance through NGOs. Germany and Sweden followed in 1962. Australia, the Netherlands, Norway, and Canada also established programs in the 1960s, and the remaining DAC countries in the 1970s (OECD 1988).

The first step usually taken by a national development assistance agency is to provide funding to or through NGOs of its own nationality. As experience is gained, increasing portions of available funds may go to NGOs of assisted countries, either directly or through one or more of the donor-nation NGOs (OECD 1988). The United States has created two public foundations—the Inter-American Foundation and the African Development Foundation—specifically to channel funds to developing country NGOs.[25] The private Asia Foundation plays a similar role in Asia using both public and private funds.

In 1975, the Canadian International Development Agency (CIDA) took what remains a distinctive initiative by establishing a separate division devoted exclusively to supporting true international NGO bodies engaged in strengthening developing country NGOs (OECD 1988). Many of the DAC countries have established formal mechanisms for regular consultations between NGOs and government on official aid policies. The European Economic Commission has an NGO Liaison Committee that allows a continuing dialogue between some 600 European NGOs and the European Parliament's committee on development and cooperation. The Development Assistance Committee of the OECD sponsored a meeting between official aid agencies and NGOs in November 1988 on measures to strengthen NGO partners in developing countries.

*Multilateral assistance agencies*

Article 71 of the United Nations Charter makes provision for qualified NGOs to be granted consultative status to the United Nations Economic and Social Council. Many U.N. specialized agencies make similar provision in their constitutions (OECD 1988). Several organizations in the U.N. system have had active relationships with NGOs since their founding. The Food and Agriculture Organization (FAO) has had a long history of promoting NGO involvement in the global effort to end hunger (OECD 1988). The U.N. Children's Fund (UNICEF) has sought NGO help in fund raising, development education, and project implementation; it has demonstrated a unique ability to work flexibly outside the normal framework of intergovernmental relationships. The Office of the U.N. High Commissioner for Refugees (UNHCR) contracts with NGOs to assist in the care and resettlement of refugees. The U.N. Fund for Population Activities (UNFPA) has contracted with NGOs for project implementation since its inception in 1969 (OECD 1988).

The experience of NGOs in implementing World Bank projects is examined in detail in Chapter 4 in this volume. NGOs played only an incidental role in some Bank projects before the 1980s, but since then their role has steadily grown.

Among the regional development banks, the Inter-American Development Bank has operated a program for the "Financing of Small Projects" since 1978; it extends loans of up to $0.5 million each to government organizations, and to intermediary NGOs (cooperatives, foundations, and producers' associations) for relending to low-income groups and individuals (OECD 1988).

In July 1987, the directors of the Asian Development Bank (ADB) approved a policy paper calling for ADB cooperation with NGOs, especially in providing help to the poor and in environmental protection. Since then the ADB has carried out several studies to identify opportunities for collaboration with NGOs, has consulted with a number of NGOs, and has begun building NGO involvement into some new project designs. According to the OECD (1988), the ADB is the first regional development bank to establish an explicit policy of cooperation with NGOs.

The U.N. Development Program (UNDP) and the International Fund for Agricultural Development (IFAD) are relative newcomers to the ranks of agencies with an active interest in NGOs. Beginning in 1988, the UNDP committed $1 million a year for cofinancing grants to NGOs in 40 countries; one stated purpose is to sensitize staff to the potential for collaboration with NGOs in mainstream UNDP projects. IFAD initiated an NGO cofinancing program in 1987 with annual global funding of $350,000 (OECD 1988).

Important issues must be addressed when large international assistance agencies attempt to work with NGOs, especially the smaller, more fragile ones. As these are central concerns of other chapters in this volume, they are not discussed here.

*Grant funding*

Bilateral agencies commonly make a distinction between the grant financing of NGO activities conceived and planned by the NGO and the contracting of NGO services for implementation of donor-designed projects. While the use of NGOs as contractors has been increasing, ODA financing of NGOs by DAC member countries continues to concentrate on grant financing in support of NGO-led initiatives. This approach is intended to recognize the special role of private voluntary initiative in development.

Five issues are actively debated in discussions of ODA grant funding for NGOs.

• *Cofinancing requirements*. It is common for official assistance agencies to provide funding on a cofinancing or matching grant basis. Normally the intent is to augment demonstrated private support for the work of the NGO through a matching contribution of government funding. Policies on the ratio of government to private financing vary substantially among governments, as do policies on whether the government should calculate the match against the overall budget of the NGO or on a project-by-project basis (OECD 1988). The latter involves more detailed scrutiny and control by the grant-making agency.[26]

• *Administrative costs*. Most governments allocate a certain amount of the budget of cofinanced NGO projects for administrative costs. This varies from the 5 percent allocated by Belgium and the United Kingdom to the 15 percent authorized by Italy. Critics have noted that donors fault NGOs for inadequate attention to administration and financial management but are often unwilling to make adequate allowances for such costs of assisted NGOs (Smillie 1988).[27] While donors routinely pay overhead rates of 100 percent and more to for-profit contractors, they seem to assume that NGOs either have no overhead costs or that NGOs should pay these out of contributions from private sources.

• *Multiyear funding*. The early practice of many aid agencies of providing funding to NGOs only on a budget-year basis created serious problems. It was seldom possible to attain consequential development results with a one-year commitment. Financial planning became nearly impossible. Delays in project approvals almost insured major gaps in funding. In consequence, many countries moved toward multiyear funding arrangements that assure greater continuity (OECD 1988).

• *Managing small grants programs*. The amount of funds committed in many individual government grants to NGOs is minuscule relative to the size of most ODA-funded projects. Agencies that fund NGOs sometimes find themselves involved in the review and administration of hundreds or thousands of individual small grants. This has led some donors to use block grants to fund an entire program of an approved NGO. Sometimes the NGO itself becomes a retailer of the funding, making smaller grants to other NGOs. Some donors have encouraged the creation of umbrella organizations that receive large block grants and retail them to other NGOs for individual projects. The umbrella organization assumes much of the oversight responsibility.

• *Direct versus indirect funding of developing country NGOs.* Funding for the NGOs of recipient countries has increased in recent years. There is controversy over whether this funding should be made directly to the recipient NGO by a donor country embassy or aid agency or should be channeled through a developed country NGO. By and large, developed country NGOs see their roles diminished by direct funding relationships. This is a special problem for developed country NGOs that yield to pressures from developing countries to reduce or eliminate their direct field operations; without an intermediary funding role they fear they may play no legitimate part.

Developing country NGOs often object to indirect funding on the ground that it is difficult to establish true partnership with developed country NGOs while depending on them for funding. Yet there are advantages in indirect funding; it can create a buffer between developing country NGOs and the onerous administrative requirements imposed by some official donors. Usually what developing country NGOs really want is greater control over their own funding sources, a concern that has led to experimentation by the Canadians and others with the creation and funding of grant-making mechanisms controlled by developing country NGOs (CCIC 1988).

## Development and NGOs: Contrasting perspectives

How one looks at NGOs and their development roles often depends on deeper questions of how one looks at development and the role of the state. A simplified, perhaps exaggerated, contrast between two points of view is helpful in illuminating the issues. The first approaches development primarily as a technical and financial problem involving the transfer and allocation of economic resources. The second approaches it more as a political and institutional problem involving the redistribution of power and the creation of new human and institutional capacities. Adherents of both perspectives will be found within the NGO community and within government.[28]

### *The development technocrats*

Those who see development as primarily financial and technical are commonly focused on achieving (1) the appropriate allocation of resources to maximize growth in economic output and (2) the efficient delivery of public services that enhance the welfare and productivity of the poor. They generally look to government, as the sovereign representative of the national interest, to be the responsible agent of development. They may accept authoritarian rule as a necessary interim measure to curb the dominance of factional interests that might distort resource allocation decisions.

Those of this persuasion are generally interested in NGOs only to the extent that they are more cost-effective than government or for-profit businesses in the delivery of basic services. They think of cooperation with NGOs primarily in terms of contractor relationships and are likely to be leery of the tendency of some NGOs toward political activism.

*The political activists*

Those who see the development problem as primarily political and institutional are commonly focused on the need to achieve a more equitable allocation of political and economic power that will allow the people, especially the poor, to control their own development. They generally view the government as the instrument through which the rich and powerful control the coercive power of the state to maintain their advantaged position, using the veil of national sovereignty to deflect challenges to their authority. NGOs affiliated with the radical left may support revolutionary groups seeking to gain control of authoritarian structures on the theory that they will use them to correct the abuses.

NGOs oriented to the democratic left or center normally reject authoritarian rule, whether of the left or the right, as inherently corrupting and exploitive. They embrace the democratic principle that sovereignty resides in the people. They are likely to see NGOs as a political and social force for strengthening pluralism and curbing the power of the state vis-à-vis civil society. They stress the role of NGOs as catalysts of social and institutional innovation and the importance of maintaining NGOs' independence. They tend to be leery of formalized contractual relationships between NGOs and government that reduce the inclination and ability of the NGO to act independently.

*Efficiency of service delivery: The development technocrat's question*

The bottom-line question for the technocrat is whether NGOs are more cost-effective than government in the delivery of basic services. By contrast, some social activists may argue that the question is irrelevant and reflects a lack of understanding of the real business of NGOs, which is to serve as catalysts of social change.

Many claims have been made about the cost-effectiveness of NGOs, both pro and con.[29] The general consensus of the evaluation literature seems to be that NGOs that receive official development assistance funding are reasonably efficient, often effective in reaching remote areas and the poor, but characteristically weak in management and planning.

Certainly an NGO can be highly cost-effective. Peter Drucker, one of the world's foremost management authorities, has written in the *Harvard Business Review* that the Salvation Army and the Girl Scouts of America, among others, demonstrate program performance and advanced concepts of management from which the better-run corporations might gain useful lessons (Drucker 1989). But not all NGOs are such models of efficient performance and sophisticated management.

NGOs come in all sizes and competencies. A few are large and able to implement national-scale programs that are highly cost-effective. Others have the potential to do so if the capability is developed. Still others do not consider themselves in the business of service delivery. The appropriate questions in dealing with NGOs engaged in service delivery are: How can their capability and potential be assessed? How is the capability best utilized when available? How is existing potential most effectively developed?

*Power redistribution: The social activist's question*

Social activists are generally not concerned with testing whether NGOs are an important instrument for advancing political and economic democratization; they take this as a given.[30] While they may seek innovative approaches to service delivery that are indeed more effective and efficient, their primary aim is to realign control over resources and decisionmaking in ways that broaden the power base within the community.

Long focused on the issue of equity, the social activists are increasingly interested in the issue of sustainability—environmental, financial, and organizational. The debt crisis, the social and environmental effects of related structural adjustment policies, and growing awareness of the global environmental crisis are pressing the social activists to extend their concerns beyond village-level interventions to address macro-policy choices (Padron 1988). They are thus taking greater interest in policy advocacy.[31]

## Voluntarism and professionalism: One or both?

In recent years the official development assistance agencies have placed considerable pressure on NGOs engaged in relief and development to "professionalize." Commonly this means enhancing technical and managerial capabilities and installing improved control systems so that NGOs can function more like the technical agencies of government. Professionalism in this context is sometimes treated as the antithesis of voluntarism.

NGOs in the United States and in India and some other developing countries commonly refer to themselves as "voluntary" organizations. But the meaning of this term has become unclear among NGOs that engage in international assistance and development. A few NGOs specialize in placing volunteers overseas.

The vast majority, however, depend on full-time paid staff to carry out their work. Staff members may be paid below their market value, but most depend on their NGO salary as their main source of livelihood.

Many relief and development NGOs have unpaid volunteer boards whose roles are often fairly limited. Development NGOs that raise money through individual private contributors commonly refer to those people as their volunteer constituency. In a few organizations, such as Oxfam (U.K.), volunteers may play a direct and consequential role in generating funds for overseas activities. It is rare, however, for even such volunteers to have direct involvement with the organization's field programs. An important criticism of some NGOs is the claim that what they do with their contributors' funds often diverges from what is suggested by their fund-raising messages; perhaps they prefer donors not to be well-informed on how funds are used.[32]

Many NGOs grew out of true volunteer traditions. A group of people decided to commit their uncompensated time to righting a social wrong. Eventually they became strong enough to raise the funds to hire a small paid staff to support their volunteer efforts. As the organization gained credibility it was able to attract further funding and hire more paid staff. Eventually the paid staff displaced the volunteers, in part on the theory that volunteers cannot be expected to meet necessary performance standards. With time the organization became increasingly "professionalized" and "bureaucratized" (Brodhead, Herbert-Copley, and Lambert 1988, 33). Perhaps it took on the characteristics of a tax-free business, organizing around "profit centers" and divesting activities that did not carry their weight financially.[33]

When NGOs have completed this "professionalization" process, the extent to which they retain the distinctive quality given by voluntarism may vary substantially. But there is no reason to expect that a fully "professionalized" NGO will necessarily vary significantly in behavior from a public agency, especially if it is heavily dependent on public funds. It may also be similar to a business, especially if organized around "profit centers."

The theoretical advantage of an NGO over a public agency or business in the cost-effective delivery of services to the poor is found in a combination of the flexibility of nonbureaucratic structures, an ability to mobilize volunteer labor, and an independent social commitment. The process of "professionalization," as that term is commonly understood by relief and development NGOs, will tend to displace these qualities.

In the following chapter, Brown and Korten discuss the distinctive nature of the true voluntary organization and the importance of voluntarism in development. They maintain that the commonly presumed trade-off between voluntarism and professionalism is false. So is the presumption that good management (not synonymous with bureaucratization) and voluntarism are antithetical.

Peter Drucker, drawing on the experience of the domestic programs of such U.S. NGOs as the Salvation Army, the Girl Scouts of America, and the American Red Cross, strongly affirms the point made by Brown and Korten. Each of these organizations operates efficient national-scale programs built on the unpaid volunteer work of thousands of Americans, many of them highly educated professionals. According to Drucker, these NGOs attract such commitment because they have innovative, socially important programs backed by sound management practices that provide the volunteers with challenge and satisfaction that many fail to find in their regular jobs.

Each of these successful NGOs is driven by a well-defined social mission and a strong performance orientation that focuses energies and produces results. Reliance on volunteer labor holds down costs. No claim is made that all NGOs, or even all voluntary organizations, have these qualities. But the outstanding examples demonstrate the potential of true voluntary initiative that only a few mainstream relief and development NGOs have attempted to nurture.

## Forces shaping the future

The past three or four years have been a particularly dynamic period of critical self-examination and change among NGOs involved in development and international assistance. This process can be expected to continue in the 1990s. The following are suggested as likely directions of future movement.

### *Large-scale service delivery*

Although NGOs have been criticized for their inability to undertake and sustain large-scale service delivery, they are no strangers to such programs. The Red Cross runs thousands of blood banks around the world. In Bangladesh, CARE supports the construction of nearly 10,000 miles of roads a year with its food-for-work program, and the Bangladesh Rural Advancement Committee (BRAC) has reached some 90 percent of households with oral rehydration training. Sarvodaya programs reach more than 5,000 villages in Sri Lanka.

Both NGOs and donors, however, generally operate on the presumption, often wrong, that they are engaged only in temporary relief or in development interventions that address self-liquidating needs. NGOs have no means of sustaining large-scale service-delivery efforts without continuing financing. In part because of these false presumptions, international assistance agencies provide NGOs primarily with small amounts of short-term project funding. These conditions work against NGOs becoming large-scale service providers.

Pressures are growing in support of creating large-scale NGO service-delivery and support structures in health, family planning, education, small-scale credit, social forestry, and the like. More NGOs will develop their abilities to support large-scale service-delivery structures in the future, using creative combinations of fee for service, volunteers, local contributions, and sustained commitments from international donors.

Public assistance agencies may need to rethink their policies on NGO funding if their goal is to establish sustained service delivery. Since NGOs are not governments and have no taxing authority, they cannot be expected to take over the expenses of a service-delivery project with their own resources. And NGOs also need to become clearer about how the services they provide are to be sustained.

We must bear in mind, though, that service delivery is only one NGO role. Perhaps the most important trend to be expected during the current decade will be substantially greater NGO involvement in advocacy and development education.[34]

*Advocacy and development education*

Developing country NGOs are questioning the appropriateness of developed country NGOs' continuing to engage in direct field operations in developing countries; they argue that, besides channeling money to developing country NGOs, developed country NGOs should devote attention to advocacy and development education among their own constituencies (Drabek 1987). NGOs in developing countries call for particular focus on the reform of policies that contribute to maintaining authoritarian governments and to the deepening of poverty and environmental destruction in the developing world.

Awareness is growing among NGOs of both developed and developing countries about the structural determinants of poverty and environmental destruction that conventional development practice does not address. NGOs are increasingly sensitized to the importance of macro-policy choices, including those concerning foreign assistance, trade, and investment. Many believe that the prevailing wisdom guiding the recommendations of the IMF and the international assistance agencies is grounded in false premises.[35]

As these trends gain momentum, it is likely that active alliances will be forged among development, environmentalist, human rights, women's, and peace groups—among others—to support significant reforms. International assistance agencies will come under growing pressure to come to terms with these groups.

*Interaction with developing country governments*

NGOs from both developed and developing countries are coming to recognize that actions to improve the lives of the poor and to correct environmental abuse necessarily involve government. In some instances NGOs may reach agreements with government under which the NGOs assume responsibility for the delivery of certain services, possibly with public funding, or for the implementation of certain aspects of a program. In the Philippines, for example, NGOs have an important role in implementing the government's land reform and social forestry programs.

NGOs may also work with governments on the introduction of new services or on helping develop capabilities to reach less accessible elements of the population. For example, Helen Keller International has assisted the Ministry of Health in Sri Lanka in introducing a program of cataract care as part of the national rural health service.

NGO efforts in advocacy and public education almost invariably involve government. While advocacy activities may place NGOs in an adversarial relationship with government on certain policies, more progressive regimes may welcome their input as a means of improving public policy. In some instances there may be active cooperation. NGOs in Indonesia, for example, work closely with the Ministry of Population and Environment on environmental policy and public education efforts.

*People-to-people cooperation*

One of the more important observations made during the OECD DAC meeting on NGOs held in Paris in November 1988 was that many development problems are shared by both developed and developing countries. Often these problems can be resolved only through voluntary citizen action supported by enlightened public policy. Awareness of this reality is expected to lead to a growing number of direct international citizen-to-citizen initiatives oriented not to financial transfers but to sharing experience and solving problems jointly. The critical flow of experience is expected to be between developing and developed countries—in both directions—as well as among developing countries and among developed countries.[36] Aiding this flow will become an increasingly important function of international NGOs during the coming decade. More than money managers, they will become information managers, facilitating exchanges of experience and forming international citizen advocacy networks.

## Notes

1. The Bank's statement notes that in the United States these organizations may be called "private voluntary organizations," and that in most African countries they are called "voluntary development organizations." The terminology for dealing with the types of organizations included under the general label NGO has long been in dispute and has been criticized on many grounds. For example, Brown and Korten, in Chapter 3 of this volume, argue that it is so broad as to be meaningless. Some say it suggests that NGOs are antigovernment. Still others say it implies that government is the central actor and everyone else is peripheral. In the United States NGOs are commonly called private voluntary organizations (PVOs). Other terms in common use are voluntary organizations, nonprofit organizations, third sector organizations, self-help development organizations, and independent sector organizations.
2. See Chapter 3 in this volume for a summary of the Unger thesis.
3. As quoted by Nerfin (1986).
4. DAC member countries are members of the OECD that have official programs of financial assistance to aid developing countries. They include virtually all industrial countries with foreign assistance programs.
5. It has been noted by a number of research studies that though philanthropic giving in the United States is often labeled "charity," only about 30 percent of philanthropic organizations serve a clientele of which the majority are poor. Furthermore, less than 10

percent of philanthropic giving is directed toward persons who have fewer resources than the contributor (Ostrander 1989).

6. Independent Sector estimates the annual dollar values for volunteers by multiplying the total aggregate number of full-time equivalent volunteers (1,700 hours per year) by average gross hourly earnings for private, nonagricultural employees, increased by 12 percent to approximate the cost of supplements to wages and salaries (pensions, unemployment and health insurance, and so on) for that year, as reported in the *Economic Report of the President* for the appropriate year. See Independent Sector (1986, 14, footnote b to Table 1.1).

7. Solange Passaris, "Les Enjeux de la Vie Associative en France," *IFDA Dossier 24*, pp. 15-24, as quoted by Nerfin (1986).

8. Many of these are substantial organizations. In 1988 the largest of the Bangladeshi national NGOs, the Bangladesh Rural Advancement Committee, had 2,500 staff active in 1,800 villages and an annual operating budget of $8 million.

9. This reflected a rather steady upward trend from 1981 on.

10. All figures are data for 1986 from the OECD (1988).

11. Figures reported by the Office of Private Voluntary Cooperation of the U.S. Agency for International Development. In this same year United Jewish Appeal reported total expenditures of $350,573,000, Catholic Relief Services reported $334,679,000, and the American Red Cross reported $216,924,000.

12. This includes $24 million in U.S. assistance for ocean freight reimbursement and refugee assistance as food aid and relief.

13. According to SIDA, these figures do not include an additional SEK 18.8 million granted to NGOs for information activities.

14. Many studies of NGO activities make no distinction between humanitarian and development assistance, erroneously labeling both development assistance. Smith (1984) notes that the predominant emphasis of U.S. NGO effort is on relief, though official mission statements of U.S. NGOs commonly emphasize long-term development.

15. For a thoughtful, comprehensive, and authoritative review of the evolution of development thought and action within the Christian religious communities, see Elliot (1987a).

16. This was also an important theme underlined by the OECD DAC meeting on cooperation with NGOs held in Paris in November 1988. See also Chapter 3 in this volume and Korten (1987 and 1990).

17. From an excerpt of Brian H. Smith, *More than Altruism: The Politics of Private Foreign Aid* (Princeton, NJ: Princeton University Press, forthcoming) in InterAction (1989, 11).

18. Brown and Korten demonstrate the importance of intraregional differences in the final section of Chapter 3 in this volume. For example, India has one of the most highly developed NGO communities in the world, yet in some states of India it is reportedly difficult to find any active NGO. Among India's neighbors Bangladesh is noted for the size and competence of its NGOs, while Pakistan and Nepal are noted for their lack of NGO development.

19. This demand has been articulated by NGOs from throughout the developing world. See Drabek (1987). Generally, however, African NGO leaders have been the most outspoken on this issue. See Ziswa (1988); and Adam and Brown (1987). The dominant focus of international NGOs on the direct implementation of their own programs is evident in a report prepared by InterAction (1985), the U.S. NGO consortium body. The 50-page report describes in detail the range of goods and services being provided to

Africans by American NGOs. There is only one brief reference to U.S. NGOs working to strengthen African NGOs and another to their work through African churches. There is a strong message that U.S. NGOs work directly with the people in Africa, not with African NGOs. The watershed NGO Conference held in London in March 1987 sensitized the leadership of InterAction to this issue, and numerous important initiatives have since been taken to change this orientation. The U.S. Agency for International Development has also encouraged U.S. NGOs to address this issue.

20. These efforts face substantial barriers. The difficulties in replication are examined in Pyle (1984), which explains the failure of the Indian government to replicate some of the highly successful community health programs developed by Indian NGOs in Maharashtra.

21. The concluding chapter of ANGOC (1988b), "Democratizing Asian Development," presents the conclusions of a major workshop of Asian NGO leaders.

22. See Chapter 3 in this volume. The situation is not necessarily as clear-cut as this statement might suggest. Some GONGOs are formed by government with the intent of capturing donor resources otherwise directed to NGOs that might take a more independent stance, or of otherwise competing with or disrupting what some refer to as "legitimate" NGOs. Other NGOs may be created by government officials or politicians solely to capture resources from donors for personal use. Yet there are other instances in which government officials committed to helping the poor create their own NGO as a means of circumventing government policies and procedures. There are examples of local government officials doing this in both Indonesia and the Philippines, with good intentions and good results. There are also examples of government officials who choose to serve the government during office hours and to serve as a volunteer outside office hours. One Indonesian NGO that plays an important role as convener of network meetings of the independent Indonesian NGOs is chaired by an individual who happens to be a senior government official. The integrity of this individual and his commitment to the cause of the NGO community is above question and fully accepted—even by those NGO leaders who disparage the GONGOs and look with suspicion on any government action that infers exerting control over NGOs.

23. Other chapters in this volume discuss the role of NGOs as nonprofit contractors.

24. To fully understand such relationships, it is necessary to recognize that no government is truly monolithic.

25. For further background on these foundations see Hellinger, Hellinger, and O'Regan (1988).

26. It has been argued that providing the matching funds only on individual projects that must each pass donor review against its policies and be implemented according to its procedures produces the direct opposite of the intended result. Rather than supplementing private initiative, it converts flexible private money that might be used for experimentation and advocacy outside of official policy into the equivalent of an official aid dollar subject to all the limitations and restrictions of conventional ODA funding.

27. In some instances, donor administrative requirements are responsible for a substantial inflation of NGO overhead expense.

28. For further discussion see Bratton (1989).

29. See Robert R. Nathan Associates (1982); Ellis (1984); Kramer (1981); Morss and Morss (1982); Tendler (1982); Brodhead, Herbert-Copley, and Lambert (1988); and Kanter and Summers (1987).

30. For a discussion of the role of voluntary action in relation to democracy see Sasono (1989); ANGOC (1988b); Van Til (1988); Diamond, Linz, and Lipset (1988); and Dia-

mond (forthcoming). John Clark, Policy Advisor for Oxfam (U.K.) and a member of the NGO-World Bank Committee is presently preparing the manuscript for a book to be titled *Democratizing Development—The Role of Voluntary Organizations* that promises to be the definitive treatment of this theme.

31. Elements of the emerging alternative vision are articulated in Drabek (1987). The themes are developed further in ANGOC (1988b). One of the more fully developed statements of the macro-issues posed by the alternative people-centered development vision is found in "Manila Declaration on People's Participation and Sustainable Development." The declaration emerged from the Inter-Regional Consultation on People's Participation in Environmentally Sustainable Development, which involved 31 NGO leaders from Africa, Southeast Asia, South Asia, the South Pacific, Latin America, the Caribbean, North America, and Europe. This consultation was a prelude to a series of regional NGO consultations that are expected to continue the dialogue on the alternative vision and its implications for development action. Copies of the Manila Declaration and a meeting report are available from either of the cosponsors of the consultation: Asian NGO Coalition, MCC P.O. Box 870, Makati, Metro Manila 3117, Philippines; and Environmental Liaison Centre International, P.O. Box 72461, Nairobi, Kenya.

32. Berg (1987) speaks of the "parallel duplicity" (37-38). He notes that international NGOs, particularly in the United States, raise their money as relief agencies, but with the intention of doing development projects. NGOs in recipient countries commonly accept money from the international NGOs to implement development projects, but with the intent of using the funds to empower the poor.

33. This phenomenon is outlined by Van Til (1988). For a well-documented case study demonstrating this phenomenon see Foley (1989).

34. As development NGOs become more concerned with advocacy and development education they will likely move toward a greater concern with advocacy. One of the more interesting U.S. development NGOs is an organization called Results that devotes its energies entirely to development education and policy advocacy. It is especially active in lobbying the U.S. Congress on behalf of the interests of the poor of developing countries. Results is built on committed and dynamic volunteer networks that have been developed throughout the United States. It is extending its membership to Europe, Canada, and Japan and considering establishing chapters in developing countries.

35. These were central themes of the recent Inter-Regional Consultation on People's Participation in Environmentally Sustainable Development, described in note 31.

36. One example is the technical assistance being provided by the Grameen Bank to groups in the United States seeking to implement similar programs in small-scale credit.

# 3

# Working More Effectively with Nongovernmental Organizations

*L. David Brown and David C. Korten*

The 1980s saw a rapid increase of interest in organizations that are nongovernmental and nonprofit within the international development community.[1] These organizations command growing attention as possible alternatives to government in addressing the needs of populations otherwise unreached by official development programs.

The reasons are many, including:

- Growing interest among donors and national governments in strengthening the developmental roles of institutions outside the public sector
- The demonstrated capacity of some nongovernmental organizations (NGOs) to reach the poor more effectively than public agencies
- A sharp decline in public development resources, causing governments to search for more cost-effective alternatives to conventional public services and development programs
- The fact that NGOs mobilize $3 billion a year in development resources from private sources and manage another $1.5 billion from official aid agencies (OECD, Development Assistance Committee 1986)
- An awareness that some NGOs are sophisticated and influential organizations able to carry out programs on a national scale and to influence national policies and institutions. Organizations such as the Bangladesh Rural Advancement Committee (BRAC), Philippine Business for Social Progress (PBSP), and the Peruvian Institute for Liberty and Democracy are leading examples.

The search for new options reflects a painful realization that despite a few "miracle economies," such as the Republic of Korea, Singapore, and Taiwan, China, the incidence of debilitating, dehumanizing poverty persists at unacceptable levels in most developing countries and regions. The advances achieved through economic modernization have bypassed large segments of the population.

In many countries, the development gains of earlier decades evaporated in the 1980s. The World Bank's *World Development Report 1988* reports that poverty in developing countries is on the rise, estimating that the number of people with inadequate diets in developing countries (excluding China) increased from 650 million to 730 million between 1970 and 1980. Declines were reported in life expectancy, per capita calorie supply, and real wages in the 1980s (World Bank 1988). The countries of Sub-Saharan Africa experienced an annual decline of 2.9 percent in per capita income from 1980 to 1987. Declines in real per capita income were also experienced during this period by oil-exporting and heavily indebted countries (World Bank 1988).

It is little wonder that thoughtful development theorists and practitioners are searching for new approaches to deal with poverty in developing countries. In this search, a growing number of aid donors and national governments have turned to NGOs as potential instruments for implementing official development projects, especially those intended to channel public resources to the poor.

We share this interest in organizations that are neither governmental nor commercial and in their distinctive potentials for supporting national development. But we are concerned that these organizations are too often viewed through conceptual lenses that miss important aspects of their nature. Their developmental roles and performance have most often been assessed through theoretical frameworks shaped to review organizations in the commercial and government sectors. The resulting analysis offers only a partial view and often leads to working with these organizations in ways that diminish rather than enhance their contributions to solving critical development problems. In this chapter we propose a conceptual lens for analyzing such agencies that offers a more complete and accurate picture of their special development roles.

## The NGO: A residual category

The labels "nonprofit" and "nongovernmental" say more about what organizations are not than about what they are. The terms define organizations that are residuals of more standard classifications. Many diverse, structurally and functionally unrelated organizations fall into the nonprofit and nongovernmental category.

Prevailing analytical classifications reflect the lack of a social science discipline that specializes in the study of this group of organizations, in the sense that political science specializes in the study of governments and economics specializes in the study of market-oriented institutions (Montgomery 1988).

When social scientists do turn their attention to the "residual" organizations, they tend to apply analytical perspectives developed for other sectors. The following brief characterizations of commonly applied perspectives seek to capture their essential elements. These perspectives are useful and accurate, as far as they go.

### *The lens of economic analysis*

The lens of economic analysis has often been applied to explain why NGOs exist and what motivates their behavior.[2] Economic analysis tends to focus on the implications of their nonprofit status. Of particular concern to the economist is the question of how the productive efficiency of nonprofit organizations differs from that of for-profit and governmental organizations.

**Public goods.** One common explanation for the presence of nonprofit organizations parallels the economic argument for governments. Economists argue that certain "public goods," such as clean air, can be enjoyed by everyone whether they have paid or not. Economists note that there is no economic incentive for a consumer to pay for products from which others benefit equally at no cost. This "free-rider" problem explains why markets seldom produce public goods—use cannot be restricted to those who pay for them.

Governments, in contrast, can use their power to tax and regulate to compel shared support for producers of public goods. Provision of public goods is generally considered to be one of the major legitimate functions of government.

But some segments of the population may want more of the public good than the government is willing to provide. They can obtain additional quantities through a nonprofit agency by conducting a community clean-up campaign, offering public education, or pressing the government for more action. The action of the nonprofit organization is explained as a private response to market failure.

**Contract failure**. Many nonprofit organizations produce services that do not meet the definition of public goods. In many instances, such as the delivery of medical or child care, their services may be indistinguishable from those of a for-profit agency. The economic explanation for such nonprofit providers is that when the quality of the service provided is difficult to assess, the consumer will prefer a nonprofit provider that has less incentive than a for-profit firm to take advantage of their ignorance (see Hansmann 1987; and Salamon 1987). A variation of the contract failure argument suggests that purchasers of services (for example, donors "purchasing" relief assistance from an NGO) will prefer nonprofits if the services are provided to other parties with whom the donor is not in direct contact and the donor cannot directly evaluate service quality. For example, in development work donors can feel more confident that their resources will be used by nonprofits to benefit their intended beneficiaries, since it is difficult for the "owners" of a nonprofit to appropriate surpluses. A nonprofit agency such as Oxfam America may be seen by donors as more likely to deliver donations to intended recipients than a for-profit agency that might be tempted to convert the donations to profits.

**Consumer control.** Some nonprofits may be created by consumers to achieve greater control over the services rendered, thereby insuring quality and avoiding exploitation by for-profit agencies. Thus marketing or consumer cooperatives may be designed to reduce the capacity of middlemen to exploit monopsony or monopoly positions (Hansmann 1987).

The above are all explanations for the emergence of nonprofits as a result of various forms of market failure. Market failure analyses ask what niche can be filled by nonprofit organizations that is not served by the for-profit sector. Markets tend to be especially vulnerable to failures in developing countries,[3] where much of the population lacks the basic purchasing power to participate, so organizations that are remedies for market failures may be particularly relevant there.

In addition, those who apply the lens of economic analysis commonly note that tax exemptions provide nonprofit organizations with a competitive advantage in market situations and that this advantage in itself motivates their formation. Governments are often understandably concerned that many nonprofits are nothing more than commercial enterprises that use the legal form of nonprofit to avoid the tax collector.

### *The lens of political analysis*

Much as economic analysis tends to focus on the role of nonprofit organizations in filling niches created by "market failure," the lens of political analysis tends to focus on their role in filling niches created by "government failure," particularly in the production of public goods. Political scientists share with economists a concern with the free-rider problem as a major rationale for the existence of both government and NGOs.

In general the tools of political analysis assign a natural role to NGOs in the provision of public goods that serve the needs of relatively small groups that can be brought together in face-to-face organizations. The members of such organizations are best able to see the results of their individual contributions, and the group is in a position to exert social pressures that minimize the free-rider problem (Olson 1971). This focus on the small group leads to a particular interest in the role of NGOs in local development (Cernea 1988).

The political analyst finds the main arguments for the existence of NGOs in the reality of social diversity and in otherwise unmet needs for experimentation and flexibility.

**Social diversity.** Societies are characterized by a wide variety of views of the public good. Formulation of consistent policies normally requires governments to make choices among these views. It is difficult for governments to respond effectively to social diversity that results in different constituencies making different or contradictory demands for services (Douglas 1987). For example, public policy in the United States precludes the teaching of religion in the schools. Groups that believe strongly that religious teaching should be integrated into the school curriculum can establish their own schools to accommodate their need.

This role of nonprofit organizations is considered particularly crucial in political systems where the people are sovereign but diverse—with competing and sometimes contradictory wills. The response of the NGO, of course, is not limited to providing the desired services. It might also engage in policy advocacy and political action.

**Experimentation and flexibility**. A widely recognized failure of large-scale government bureaucracies is their inflexibility and conservatism. Bureaucratic rules and attention to procedures can be justified for reasons of equity and accountability. But these institutional characteristics do not encourage flexible or innovative responses to novel problems (Douglas 1987; and Salamon 1987). Furthermore, many governments have difficulty introducing innovations before a degree of political consensus has been achieved. But consensus is unlikely to emerge until the concept has been successfully demonstrated, a sort of Catch-22.

Nongovernmental agencies, less subject to such political pressures, are able to experiment more easily with politically sensitive programs. The Ford Foundation, for example, can take on innovative projects that are not politically feasible for the U.S. government. NGOs can test innovative programs that governments would not undertake until the programs are proven politically feasible—or act as policy advocates of innovations.

Political analysts have observed that vital nongovernmental sectors are common features of pluralistic and democratic political systems (Diamond, Linz, and Lipset 1988; and Diamond forthcoming), and that they are one of the first casualties of a shift to a more authoritarian regime (Bratton 1989; and Douglas 1987). This has important implications for our subsequent argument regarding the distinctive nature and role of these organizations.

*The donor perspective*

While the lens of economic analysis focuses primarily on economic efficiency and incentives, the political analyst emphasizes the political and institutional role of NGOs. Many development donors have chosen to view NGOs through the lens of economic analysis, asking how the efficiency and reliability of NGOs compare with that of private contractors or government in the provision of specified services. For donors, the lens of the political analyst raises issues they have generally preferred to ignore in their desire to avoid being accused of meddling in the internal politics of the countries they assist.

Consistent with the choice of the economist's lens, development donors have generally concerned themselves primarily with NGOs that might assume roles in the implementation of specific development projects or in the transfer of financial resources, that is, with NGOs engaged in roles that would otherwise be assumed by governments, private contractors, or other organizations with well-defined roles.

Donors have been less attuned to the more distinctive contributions of NGOs in a dynamic society. This is an important oversight. These distinctive contributions include their roles as innovators and advocates; their contribution to the balance of power between the state and civil society essential to a dynamic economy and a participatory political system (Diamond forthcoming; Frantz 1987; Douglas 1987; and Jenkins 1987); their ability to tap otherwise inaccessible social energy; and their capacity to link with one another to become self-organizing systems responsive to a range of human needs.[4]

We agree with the growing list of observers who have concluded that the most important development roles of NGOs are organizational and political rather than financial and economic (Cernea 1988; and Bratton 1988).

## Three institutional sectors

It has been relatively rare in development circles to treat NGOs as constituting a sector with a distinctive identity and features of its own.[5] This is in fact appropriate, as the diverse collection of organizations classified as NGOs does not define a sector in a way that has conceptual meaning.

### *Defining three sectors*

We believe, however, that development theorists and practitioners do face an institutional reality comprised of at least three distinct organizational sectors, appropriately defined as government, commercial, and voluntary. Each sector so defined has distinctive and conceptually meaningful characteristics.

The term "voluntary" refers here to actions taken by the free will of the actor. We will argue that voluntary organizations (VOs) represent a distinct class of organizations that depend on energy and resources given freely by their members and supporters because they believe in organizational missions, not merely because of political imperatives or economic incentives.

Conceptually we can define the three sectors in terms of the three primary options available to organizations to mobilize the resources on which their function depends: coercion and legitimate authority in hierarchical systems, negotiated exchange in market systems, and shared values in consensus-based systems. Table 3.1 summarizes some of the differences among the three sectors so defined. These differences will be discussed in more detail below.

**Table 3.1 Sector differences**

| *Category* | *Commercial sector* | *Government sector* | *Voluntary sector* |
|---|---|---|---|
| Primary concern | Produce goods and services | Preserve social order | Actualize social visions |
| Implicit organization | Market | Hierarchies | Clan/consensus |
| Coordination mechanisms | Negotiated exchange | Authority and coercion | Shared values |
| Enforcement mechanisms | Contracts and reciprocity norms | Supervision and rules | Moral obligation; professional ethics |
| Prototype | Corporation | Army | Church |

Government organizations mobilize resources through the mechanisms of authority and legitimate coercion, consistent with government's primary role of preserving social order and social control. This pattern of resource mobilization is particularly evident in the power to tax or the power to draft an army, requiring individuals to provide resources despite their preferences to the contrary.

Commercial organizations produce goods and services through the mechanism of exchange. They offer financial incentives to gain access to the materials, information, and human resources required for their activity.

Organizations in the voluntary sector (VOs), in contrast, mobilize resources and social energy through the mechanisms of shared values and expectations. Most people have some basic values—interpersonal, religious, political—that are so deeply held that they guide behavior even in the face of countervailing coercive sanctions or material incentives. These values can be invoked to mobilize voluntary contributions of labor, cash, or kind to activities that give expression to the values.

Shared values can be powerful guides to behavior because they offer actors a sense of efficacy in molding the world to fit a collectively desired vision. Organized action to supplement or counteract the activities of government and commercial organizations often depends on mobilizing resources through such shared values. There is growing evidence that the economists' free-rider hypothesis does not hold up well empirically: people do in fact contribute time, energy, and money to agencies seeking to produce public goods even if they receive back less in material terms than they contribute.[6]

Conceptually the distinction we are making is quite simple. The three sectors focus on different concerns and employ quite different mechanisms to mobilize resources and human energy.[7] Empirically, of course, the world is a good deal more complex than our model suggests. Most organizations have multiple concerns and utilize a variety of mechanisms to pursue them. VOs utilize financial incentives in the form of salaries, and they employ hierarchical authority to guide activities.

But we will argue that true VOs are driven primarily by shared values. This distinction is critical to understanding the development potentials of NGOs that are truly VOs.

Note that not all NGOs are VOs by this definition. NGOs that are legally nonprofit but in fact primarily concerned with market and financial incentives are better classified as commercial agencies. NGOs that are largely dependent on and subordinate to governmental authorities are better understood as part of the government sector despite their nongovernmental legal status. We will elaborate on this later.

### *Defining development*

We believe that development is most usefully and accurately defined as:

> *a process by which the members of a society develop themselves and their institutions*[8] *in ways that enhance their ability to mobilize and manage*

*resources to produce sustainable and justly distributed improvements in their quality of life consistent with their own aspirations.*[9]

We further believe that many development failures can be explained as the consequence of focusing too heavily on the financial transfer dimensions of development and neglecting the institutional and political transformation dimensions essential to constructive sustainable improvements in human well-being. Defining development in institutional terms helps to avoid such errors.

Financial transfers will have developmental consequences only if institutional structures to manage available resources effectively are in place.[10] The Marshall Plan in Europe and Japan, for example, was successful because it channeled resources into settings in which the necessary values, skills, and institutional capacities to use them were present, despite widespread physical destruction.

In the developing world, by contrast, development assistance has commonly been fed into institutional systems devised for feudal or colonial expropriation, so new resources are too often converted by elites into current consumption or capital flight. Consequently, the anticipated economic renaissance has failed to materialize in many countries.

Where the necessary values, skills, and institutions for effective resource management are not in place, the developmental impact of financial transfers should be assessed largely by their contribution to creating them.

### *Differentiating development roles*

Now we are ready to look at the natural development roles of each of the three sectors. Historically, in many countries, government has assumed the primary responsibility for development leadership. Legitimate authority and coercion offer effective means for accessing existing wealth. If the central task of development is to gain control over existing financial and physical resources, the government sector must play a very central role. But authority and coercion are more limited tools in the creation of value added and in the promotion of social innovation.

The commercial sector has the advantage in the efficient production of goods and services, while voluntary agencies have greater potential for mobilizing voluntary social energies and innovative problem-solving. Consequently, development is difficult to achieve in a society in which the state maintains total dominion over civil society. While the state must set the rules and the framework, the civil society must ultimately drive the development process, a fundamental truth now acknowledged even in the U.S.S.R. and China.

From this perspective, it is an important advance that development analysts have turned their attention to the potentials of the commercial sector as an engine of development, after years of focus on centralized economic planning and production through public enterprise. Much of the current concern with privatization, for example, can be understood as an effort to separate the functions of the commercial and the governmental sectors so that each sector may perform those functions for which it is best suited.

But the development task is not limited simply to increasing the value of economic transactions, which is what gross national product measures. Development has failed unless the society has increased its capacity to transform available resources into justly distributed improvements in human well-being.

The commercial sector has evident advantages in the pursuit of market-induced innovations that increase the value of economic transactions. However, the innovations that insure that these increases in value are translated into justly distributed improvements in well-being must normally come either from government or from the voluntary sector. Between the two, NGOs have important advantages over government organizations as catalysts of the types of social and institutional innovation required.

Governments depend for their function on a broadly based political consensus fashioned through negotiation and compromise among numerous existing power holders and interest groups. Their ability to innovate is constrained by the necessity of first achieving a reasonably broad consensus, at least among key power holders who may have a substantial commitment to maintaining existing inequities.

The constituencies of VOs are generally much smaller than those of governments and are built around a more coherent consensus on values. Consequently, the VO is able to define positions more clearly than government, and to press for innovative solutions and experiment in ways that governments find difficult. This gives VOs a distinctive role as catalysts of change in systems—in defining, articulating, and advocating positions that are outside the established political mainstream and therefore not supported by existing public policy.

Driven by values rather than by the quest for economic or political power, many VOs focus their attention on the needs of the poor and disenfranchised more naturally than do governments. In countries with a mature voluntary sector, VOs are constantly calling attention to and acting on perceived opportunities for improving public well-being.

The role of the voluntary sector in social innovation is far more varied and pervasive than its commonly recognized role in implementing pilot projects for replication by governments and donors. For example, VOs have had key roles in the civil rights, environmental, and women's movements, and in focusing world attention on population issues. These efforts have changed global perceptions and policies on fundamental social issues.

In a world dominated by the government and commercial sectors, VOs may lose sight of the centrality of values to their existence. In their quest to strengthen their funding base through proving their professionalism many VOs have been inclined to deny their voluntarism, which some have come to view as an embarrassment. But voluntarism is in fact their distinctive asset. If VOs are to realize their full potential as a distinctive development force it is important that they become more conscious of the centrality of values and voluntarism to their distinctive nature and role.

*Pluralism and the voluntary sector*

Our definition of development focuses attention on distributive justice as a major development issue. This recognizes that poverty is as much a political as it is an economic condition. In many developing societies, attaining broadly based sustainable development depends on achieving a more broadly based distribution of economic and political power, while strengthening incentives and values that support the use of that power to make productive use of available resources. This requires strengthening the role of the civil society vis-à-vis the state. It must be recognized in turn that democratic pluralism is a sine qua non for a strong and dynamic civil society.

The voluntary sector has a special role in contributing to the development of pluralistic civil societies and in awakening a socially conscious work and investment ethic. Indeed, this may well be the sector's most important and distinctive development role.

The grass-roots organizing work central to the agendas of many VOs in developing countries is an important contributor to democratization and to the strengthening of civil society. It facilitates the breakdown of residual feudalistic structures and value systems by realigning power structures and improving access of the actual producer to productive resources. Producer organizations in turn reinforce new values that support socially conscious productive work and investment.

In their political role VOs supplement political parties as mechanisms through which citizens define and articulate a broad range of interests and make demands on government. In their educational role VOs provide training grounds for democracy, develop the political skills of their members, recruit new political leaders, and stimulate political participation. In their watchdog role they serve, as does the press, as checks on what Diamond (forthcoming) recognizes as a powerful tendency of the state to centralize power and evade accountability and control.[11]

## Voluntary energy as a development resource

Voluntary energy—an almost wholly neglected development resource—is the life force of the voluntary NGO. It is important that we better understand its nature and application.

*Special characteristics of voluntary energy*

Voluntary energy has several characteristics that distinguish it from the energy generated by financial exchanges or governmental authority. These characteristics are important to the role of the voluntary sector in development.

First, voluntary energies are low in cost, at least in financial and political terms, and exist in potentially inexhaustible quantities. Many powerful voluntary movements do not have access to much financial capital or political power—indeed, part of their appeal may be their relative poverty and powerlessness, as in Gandhi's independence movement. This is not to say that voluntary movements do not need financial and political resources; they do. But their lifeblood is in their appeal to values to which people will commit energy, time, and often their lives.

Second, voluntary energies are not easily controlled by the mechanisms used to control other forms of social energy. Furthermore, they are difficult if not impossible to buy and cannot be stored. Leadership by appeal to values demands skills different from those learned in market or bureaucratic organizations. Although some public and private leaders develop charismatic leadership styles that serve them well in mobilizing voluntary energies, others are mystified by the demands of mobilizing and guiding voluntary energies. Not surprisingly, voluntary energy has proven to be a development resource largely inaccessible to development planners, bureaucrats, and technicians.

Third, voluntary energies may be subject to self-reinforcing escalation. National and international social movements can grow from minuscule beginnings, as most of the world's major religions illustrate. Norman Uphoff (1987) has argued that the combination of shared values, new friendships, and new ideas about how to accomplish common goals can interact to produce a self-regenerating positive escalation of social energies with broad effects. He offers the example of a Sri Lankan project to rehabilitate an irrigation system in which the voluntary energy of participating farmers astonished the project organizers and led to development activity far beyond expectations.

There are also instances of negative reinforcement cycles that produce "burnout" of voluntary energies and a failure of enduring commitment. Greater understanding of the circumstances that lead either to positive or to negative reinforcement cycles in the generation of voluntary energy is badly needed.

*Voluntary energy in public and commercial sectors*

The importance of voluntary energy is not limited to the voluntary sector. Public and commercial agencies may also seek to mobilize voluntary energies in the service of government or corporate goals.

Much of the literature on "excellent companies" is focused on how to develop "strong cultures" that mobilize employee values and goals in the service of company strategies (Peters and Waterman 1982; and Kanter 1983).

Similarly, many governments seek to mobilize the voluntary commitments of their citizens in the service of public goals. When governments are seen as legitimate and the goals are consistent with popular concerns, enormous outpourings of energy may result. For example, thousands of young Iranians went forth to fight the Iraqi invasion; thousands of idealistic young Americans joined the Peace Corps in response to John F. Kennedy's call. When government actions are not seen as legitimate, the same energies may be turned against them, as in the United States when large segments of the population actively resisted the Viet Nam War and in the Philippines when election fraud led the people to oust their government.

### *Mobilizing voluntary energy*

While most organizations in practice utilize several approaches to mobilizing and organizing their resources, they often depend on one primary approach. Thus Etzioni (1961) argued three decades ago that organizations could be divided into three types quite similar to the sector descriptions we have proposed. In his typology, utilitarian organizations, like commercial firms, promise material rewards to their members in exchange for their calculative involvement; coercive organizations, like prisons and armies, secure alienating involvement through coercive control; normative organizations, like churches or social movements, mobilize members for moral involvement through shared values and norms.[12]

If voluntary NGOs in fact mobilize people around shared values, we would expect their members to see their jobs in quite different terms than members of primarily commercial or governmental organizations. There is evidence that they do.

One recent comparison of work force characteristics in the three sectors in the United States found that voluntary sector employees reported significantly more meaning in their jobs and significantly fewer experiences in which job requirements violated their consciences. They also were paid two-thirds as much. The authors of the study concluded:

> *Third sector employees bring to their jobs a greater commitment and nonmonetary orientation and find more challenge, variety, and autonomy in their jobs and more influence, and, perhaps, mystique in, their work roles. Nonprofit workers also find more intrinsic rewards in their jobs. The majority would prefer to continue in their present work.* (Mirvis and Hackett 1983, 10-11)

The dominance of value-based motivation in the voluntary sector has implications for leaders of VOs. Leadership based on hierarchical authority or financial incentives is less likely to be effective in VOs than leadership grounded in shared visions and adherence to common norms. A growing body of research on the characteristics of the charismatic leader concludes that leaders able to articulate shared visions and mobilize their followers around them are more successful than others in sparking high levels of performance in individuals, teams, and even national governments.[13]

### *Organizing around shared values*

Organization to use voluntary energy effectively requires structures and processes in some ways quite different from those familiar in other sectors. Recent conceptual analyses suggest that there may be organizational forms that are particularly appropriate to different forms of social energy. The analyses of "transaction costs" theorists, for example, have identified three fundamentally different patterns of organization that are efficient under different conditions.[14]

• *Markets* are highly efficient for making decisions provided certain assumptions about competition and the availability of information are met. Prices provide a coordination mechanism; decisions are made through negotiations about prices; agreements are formalized in contracts and if necessary enforced through the court system.

• *Hierarchies*, in contrast, are efficient organizational forms when the assumptions of a frictionless market are invalid. Formal authority is the fundamental coordination mechanism in hierarchies; decisions are made or legitimated by commands; authority can be formalized in rules and procedures and in the assigned responsibilities of individuals. Hierarchies are particularly useful when the transactions costs of repeated negotiations in an imperfect market outweigh the administrative costs of creating and maintaining a bureaucratic hierarchy.

• *Clans* are organizational forms that are coordinated by shared values and norms rather than authority or price mechanisms. Decisions in such organizations are grounded in consensus about values and goals; expectations are enforced by moral obligations or professional ethics. Clan organization has higher costs in terms of the socialization of its members for agreement on core values and expectations, but they cope efficiently with market imperfections that would undermine markets and with task uncertainties and ambiguities that would overwhelm bureaucratic hierarchies.

Clan forms of organization are equipped to innovate in the face of high levels of uncertainty and ambiguity. Their members are integrated around shared understandings of the organizational mission, so they can adjust their behavior to fit changing conditions—rather than follow outdated rules and procedures.

There are drawbacks to value-driven organizations. Experience in voluntary development organizations indicates that the value commitments that are their strength can also be the source of considerable difficulty. Disagreements within value-driven organizations are easily interpreted in ideological terms, for example, and so lead to explosive internal and external conflicts that can disintegrate the agency (see Brown and Brown 1983; and Brown and Covey 1987b).

*A mix of values and structures*

It is worth reemphasizing that most effective organizations in any sector will use a mix of values and structures to motivate and coordinate the activities of members. While voluntary NGOs are organized around and dependent on values for the definition of core activities and the mobilization of key resources, most also make use of authority and exchange.

In some NGOs it is possible to identify two distinct systems that operate side by side. One represents a sort of leadership core of the individuals who carry and interpret the values of the organization, providing it with its energy, continuity, and direction. This is the group that will be found working nights and weekends, that stays with the organization through good times and bad. There may also be a parallel system, comprised perhaps of the administrative and possibly the operational personnel, that performs somewhat like a conventional bureaucracy. This system is staffed with persons who have been attracted to the organization as a source of employment and remain as long as the pay and benefits are more attractive than alternative offers.

The Rural Development Trust in India, for example, hires many village-level workers whose primary reason for joining the agency is employment and regular pay. In return for employment these workers are expected to follow the dictates of authorities in the organizational hierarchy. Yet at the top of the RDT organization is a leadership group, the members of which are committed to a common vision, are the carriers of the organization's values, and remain with the organization to pursue that vision despite opportunities for more pay in other agencies. As long as members of the leadership team maintain the organization's value commitment, opportunities presented to the organization for increased funding and political power will be rejected if acceptance would threaten the organization's core vision of empowering the rural poor.

In the rest of this chapter, the term "NGO" will be used to refer primarily to voluntary NGOs—organized around shared values—unless otherwise indicated.

## Nongovernmental organizations and development

Generally the NGOs of concern to development donors have been those engaged in such functions as:

- *Disaster relief* for people suffering from famine, drought, war, and other natural and man-made catastrophes
- *Provision of services,* such as health care, family planning, agricultural extension and credit
- *Community organizing, technical and educational assistance* to enable local groups to organize, solve local problems, establish local enterprises, and influence other agencies to provide better services
- *Grant making* to people's organizations and to service-provider and community-organizing NGOs
- *Training and technical assistance support* to other NGOs performing development functions
- *Research and information exchange* for the formation of development policies and programs
- *Networking* for experience sharing, program coordination, and joint action on sector issues
- *Development education* to increase public and opinion leaders' understanding of key development issues
- *Advocacy* in support of critical policy and institutional changes.

Our experience suggests that the order in which this list is presented roughly coincides with the allocation of donor resources to NGOs under foreign assistance programs. In other words, disaster relief receives substantially more donor funding than any other NGO activity; advocacy receives the least.

All of the above activities involve international assistance. However, not all can be considered developmental by the terms of our definition. For the same reason, not all NGOs assisted by donors are properly classed as development agencies.

*Service versus development-catalyst organizations*

Welfare and development interventions differ in a way that is important in distinguishing between voluntary service-delivery organizations and voluntary development-catalyst organizations.

**Voluntary service-delivery organizations**. Many organizations that provide disaster relief and welfare services in developing countries are organized around shared values and visions, often tracing their roots to religious traditions.[15] NGOs that deliver disaster relief or social services perform important social functions, but unless they are developing the capacity of indigenous organizations to replace them in these functions on a self-sustaining basis after their departure they cannot claim to be doing development work. When these are foreign or foreign-funded NGOs they may unintentionally be creating an antidevelopmental dependence.[16]

For disaster relief agencies, it is clearly difficult in the midst of a catastrophe to work seriously on building local systems to respond to future crises. In nonemergency situations, however, attention should be given to reducing dependence on foreign charity.

Some NGOs, such as Oxfam America, have a clear commitment and approach to diagnosing local institutional capacities and to working to support and build these capacities rather than focusing on relieving immediate symptoms of a problem. Yet many NGOs that deliver services needed in a local setting, such as medical assistance or education, find that it is easier to provide the needed services than to build local capacity.

Sustainability and accountability to beneficiary populations are critical concerns in assessing the appropriateness of service-delivery arrangements. Sustainability requires building systems with reasonably secure sources of ongoing resource support, such as service fees or access to public finances raised in the jurisdiction served. Accountability can be achieved by developing competing fee-for-service providers that offer the consumer a choice, or through structures of governance that allow the service users to hold service providers directly accountable—for example, parents electing a governing board that hires the teachers for the local school.

Where services are funded by a foreign donor and delivered through an organization that has no accountability to beneficiaries, it is difficult to establish that the tests of sustainability and accountability have been met.

Foreign voluntary relief and service organizations can assist development when they make explicit efforts to create local capacities to support or provide services that can be locally sustained. They are not development agencies when their effect is to create continuing dependence on themselves by the populations they serve or when they compete so successfully with local institutions that they in effect destroy local capacity for self-reliance.

**Development-catalyst organizations**. Thirty Asian NGO leaders who met in Bangkok under the auspices of the Asian NGO Coalition in March 1988 to discuss NGO strategy focused their attention on the importance of NGOs working as development-catalyst organizations, defined as:

> *organizations that use temporary interventions to promote the creation of sustainable locally accountable institutions that improve the quality of life.*

Development-catalyst NGOs differ substantially from NGOs that undertake to deliver services for an indeterminate period. The role of the development catalyst is temporary. Its actions are directed toward catalyzing changes that produce self-directing, self-financing local institutional arrangements that can survive its departure. For example, Seva Mandir is a voluntary organization that works with small farmers in rural villages in India. In the late 1970s, village workers became frustrated with the minimal effects of training small farmers in agricultural methods. With the aid of an outside consultant they developed a program to help farmers' leaders and village groups analyze their circumstances, plan initiatives, and organize themselves to carry out their plans collectively.

The farmers' groups became extremely active, undertaking locally chosen projects such as building schools, reducing alcohol consumption, demanding more attention from agricultural extension agents, and building coalitions to elect new representatives to local government bodies. The results of the workshops and village follow-up activities were so successful that Seva Mandir staff soon began extending them to dozens of other villages (see Tandon and Brown 1981).

Some NGOs that believe themselves to be catalysts are surprised to realize on reflection that they are not. Even NGOs committed to organizing local communities for empowerment and self-reliance often find that they have unintentionally allowed the beneficiary groups to become dependent on them for services such as credit or health. Such dependence is increasingly being recognized by NGOs as counterdevelopmental.

Development-catalyst NGOs face constant pressures from donors to move into welfare-oriented service-delivery roles that may compete with their distinctive catalytic functions. Service delivery is easier, produces results more quickly, and is more likely to please donors who want their resources matched with clearly measurable outputs. Both donors and catalyst NGOs must be alert to these forces and resist them.

Another dilemma that well-meaning donors pose for the catalyst NGO is the expectation that it should demonstrate its ability to become self-financing. The expectation commonly reflects the donors' lack of understanding of the catalyst NGO's basic nature and function.

First, the catalyst NGO is neither a government dependency nor a business. So unless a donor gives it an endowment to fund its operations in perpetuity, the NGO must depend on a continuing flow of external contributions from donors willing to allow it the autonomy essential to carrying out its mission.

Second, the true catalyst NGO performs temporary functions. For this reason there is no inherent contradiction between its reliance on external funding and its commitment to sustainability—as long as it maintains its independence in defining its agenda and strategy.

The task of the catalyst NGO is to build self-reliant sustainable institutions that are accountable to the people, rather than to become self-reliant and sustainable itself. Because the catalyst role is by nature temporary, the donor's concern therefore should not be whether the catalyst NGO is becoming financially self-reliant, but whether the NGO is developing self-reliant, self-sustaining organizations and structures able to survive its departure.

Effective performance as a catalyst requires the NGO to maintain substantial independence in defining and interpreting its mission so that it does not fall captive to power holders in government or business who see their interests as better served by maintaining the status quo. At the same time, its survival and effectiveness often requires that it maintain credibility and legitimacy with a wide variety of external constituencies, including donors. Effective development-catalyst NGOs become adept at articulating visions and values that strike resonant cords among diverse external constituencies, as well as in their own members.

### *Voluntary sector-support and networking organizations*

As a voluntary sector matures, there is normally an increasing differentiation of functions among its component organizations, some of which undertake to become specialized service providers either to other members of the sector or to people's organizations. Similarly, growing numbers of networks will emerge.

**Sector-support organizations.** Sector-support organizations provide technical assistance, training, research, advocacy support, and other services to NGOs that cannot allocate resources away from their primary activities to create in-house expertise. As the voluntary sector grows in size and complexity, increasing numbers of such specialized organizations can be expected to emerge to serve its expanding needs. In India, for example, the voluntary sector has grown to the point where it requires the support of many high-quality technical service organizations. The Society for Participatory Research in Asia (PRIA) is an NGO that provides participatory research, training, and consulting support to a wide range of grass-roots organizations in India and Asia. Its staff members typically have backgrounds in community organizing and management, and they work in half a dozen sectors ranging from women's development to adult literacy to wasteland reclamation.

PRIA has pioneered the theory and practice of participatory research and evaluation, developing in cooperation with grass-roots NGOs ways of diagnosing and solving their problems of organization and management. The agency has developed a program of educating NGO staff in experiential training methodologies adapted to rural organizing work. PRIA staff have also utilized their experience to develop manuals and literature on participatory organizing. Through linkages with similar institutions in other countries, these materials have been disseminated worldwide.

**Networks.** Networks are self-help support systems, often with secretariats that provide services for their members similar to those provided by the sector-support organizations described above. But unlike other sector-support organizations, the network secretariat is commonly responsible to a board representing the members the secretariat is intended to serve. Most networks also link like-minded organizations to share information, plan joint activities, and make a united response to political pressures from governments and the demands of international development agencies.

As development-catalyst NGOs become more concerned about the sustainability of local development initiatives, they also become more conscious of the detrimental consequences of many existing development policies and institutions and the need for collective advocacy efforts. This is leading network organizations to take on increasingly important roles. There is a new interest among members of NGO networks in defining shared visions, so that resources can be used in mutually supportive ways to pursue national development agendas beyond the reach of any single member organization.

Some networks attempt to link all voluntary agencies within a country or geographic region. An example is the Association of Development Agencies of Bangladesh (ADAB), which includes in its membership the major NGOs working on development projects in Bangladesh. Other networks are organized around specific issues or areas of joint interest. The International Council on Adult Education (ICAE), for example, includes regional and national networks concerned with adult education and literacy. At ICAE World Assemblies, adult educators from all over the world share experience, learning, and support.

While these associations seldom speak for a very integrated constituency, they do serve as important channels for the diffusion of ideas and technologies for local development initiatives. The "participatory research" movement, for example, which has advocates and practitioners on virtually every continent, has grown largely out of networks inspired by ICAE and its members.[17]

## Other types of social action NGOs

As indicated earlier, some NGOs of interest to development donors are not voluntary organizations. Two types deserve special mention: public service contractors and people's organizations.

*Public service contractors*

Many NGOs are highly market-oriented, evaluating their overall performance on such criteria as total funding level and market shares of particular types of funding. Though nonprofit, they function largely as businesses within the development industry, selling services to governments or private donors, much as firms in the United States accept contracts from government to provide a range of municipal services. We refer to these organizations as public service contractors (PSCs). The more competitive PSCs feature substantial technical competence, elaborate management systems, and concern with cost-efficiency. Where resources are available they may operate on a considerable scale.

It is important to address PSCs as a special category of NGO, because they often represent what donors are really seeking when they contract with NGOs for advisory services and project implementation. Donors that want a contractor service should be aware of the difference between voluntary NGOs and PSCs, both to increase the chances that they will get what they want, and to reduce the chances that they will treat a voluntary NGO like a PSC and unintentionally reduce its ability to function in its distinctive role.

Conceptually, the difference between a voluntary NGO and a PSC is clear. A value-driven NGO defines its program based on its social mission, and then seeks the funding required to implement it. The market-driven PSC starts with an assessment of prospective funding sources and defines its program on that basis.

In reality it is sometimes difficult to distinguish between the NGO and the PSC, particularly as NGOs come to rely heavily on government support, and as a growing number of NGOs establish PSC units or affiliates as a means of generating income.

The PSC may in many respects look much like an NGO in its structure and its formal statement of purpose and have the same type of legal registration. Many PSCs combine a market orientation with a social commitment and have mission statements that emphasize a social agenda—as is true of many socially progressive for-profit businesses. Many also operate on the basis of high ethical standards—as again do many for-profit businesses.

However, the value-driven NGO is likely to be more clearly focused than the PSC in the pursuit of its particular social mission. It is more likely to challenge conventional practice and to be openly critical of government and of public policy. It will be more selective in its choice of funding sources, attempting to limit its reliance on donors that might redirect its mission. It will strive to accept contracts only when they offer a clear opportunity to advance its own mission.

We will look more closely at the issues raised by the PSC in a later section.

*People's organizations*

People's organizations (POs) are commonly classified as NGOs. They represent a special form of NGO that differs from PSCs in ways that make them of special importance. For an organization to qualify fully as a PO it must meet three criteria:

- It must be *self-reliant* in that its continued existence must not depend on outside initiative or funding.
- It must be a *mutual benefit association* in that it exists to serve its members.
- It must have a *democratic structure* that gives its members ultimate authority over its leaders.

The fundamental importance of strong POs in maintaining the dynamism of a society has been demonstrated throughout history, even in the early preindustrial empires. Studies by Unger (1987) concluded that periods of decline in the great preindustrial empires were triggered by elites gaining control over peasant land and labor. This control enabled them to reduce smallholders, independent tenants, and wage laborers to serfs on great estates. According to Unger, empires that avoided decline were characterized by vigorous, independent, local organizations of agriculturists who were sufficiently politically conscious and organizationally skilled to mount a collective self-defense against these ultimately self-defeating and antidevelopmental forces.

As development-catalyst NGOs articulate their visions, they commonly define as one of their central tasks the economic and political empowerment of people through the formation of grass-roots organizations to assume key roles, including exerting influence over decisions of other agencies—public and private—that affect the people. An increasing number of the more visionary NGOs see this work as part of a larger commitment to democratizing the economic and political structures of societies.[18]

People's organizations are training grounds for democratic citizenship, and institutional building blocks for the democratization of otherwise authoritarian societies. They broaden the distribution of political and economic power, which most development-catalyst NGOs believe is an essential step to more broadly based development participation. They create demands for greater responsiveness to grass-roots concerns, providing the collective bargaining power that can enable landless people, small farmers, or urban squatters to negotiate on more equal terms with representatives of government bureaucracies or wealthy private corporations.

Self-reliant cooperatives, landless associations, irrigator associations, burial associations, credit clubs, labor unions, trade associations, elected local government councils, and political interest groups with accountable leadership—all are examples of POs. Some POs might also be classed as voluntary NGOs, if shared values are the primary basis on which they acquire resources and the commitment of their members. However, POs by definition exist to serve their members, while a voluntary NGO is generally committed to values that transcend its members' immediate interests.

People's organizations are commonly difficult to classify according to our resource-acquisition scheme because of the mixed basis on which they acquire their resources. Take the example of a cooperative, an important form of people's organization. The cooperative may have highly motivated leaders who volunteer substantial uncompensated time to insure the success of the enterprise. Its members may be committed to shared values of cooperation that cause them to direct their business to their cooperative even when better prices are available elsewhere. And these same members may grant their leaders the authority to impose penalties or levies (taxes) on members, much as citizens in a democratic society vest this authority in their government. Yet successful cooperatives are generally highly market-oriented in their external exchange transactions.

A number of studies of NGO development roles deal almost exclusively with POs, reflecting their special importance (see, for example, Esman and Uphoff 1984; and Cernea 1988). But strong POs able to help members broaden their economic and political participation are relatively rare in most developing countries. The donor that chooses to work directly with and through POs to benefit the poor may therefore find that investments must first be made in the institutional development of the POs. Such investments are usually best made through NGOs.

Government efforts to promote the development of POs usually result in something quite different. An organization may be formed, but its leadership will more likely be accountable to the government than to its members, and its existence is likely to depend on continued government patronage.

In many countries it is becoming clear that for village-level POs to become truly effective economic and political forces, they must be federated into larger structures that give their members a political voice and provide services that strengthen their participation and bargaining power. This federating process has been occurring in Latin America, often through the leadership of the POs themselves. In Asia, more and more NGO leaders are encouraging the POs they have assisted to form federated structures.

POs offer important opportunities for institutionalizing sources of credit, production inputs, marketing services, technical support, education, health, and other essential services in ways that insure accountability and responsiveness to the people served. Building such support structures becomes an important concern of the development-catalyst NGO.

The differences between the catalyst NGO and the PO have important implications for their funding that donors commonly overlook. We argued earlier that it is neither realistic nor appropriate to expect NGOs performing temporary catalyst functions to become self-financing, unless donors are prepared to provide endowment funds.

By contrast, a strong PO is normally expected to survive as a permanent institution serving important functions for its members. It is therefore necessary and appropriate that the PO work seriously toward making its activities largely self-supporting and locally sustainable. Any external funding should be consistent with this outcome, primarily supporting capacity building, and possibly capital investments. Excessive outside generosity in subsidizing POs to provide routine services and to cover their core costs will create dependence and work to the detriment of the organization over the long term.

## Strengths and weaknesses of NGOs

Many who have written about NGOs have been particularly interested in enumerating NGOs' special strengths and weaknesses, commonly using government or commercial organizations as a basis for comparison. While these assessments differ, there is a general consensus, which we attempt to summarize below. In each instance we have indicated the characteristics of NGOs that give them the special strength or debility in question. The NGO community is highly diverse. Not all NGOs reflect the strengths noted here. Nor do all suffer from what are widely perceived to be typical weaknesses.

### *Strengths of NGOs*

In general evaluators agree that NGOs have a special ability:

• *To reach the poor* and other populations not served by public or commercial agencies.[19] This capacity is often a function of their special commitment to helping the poorest and most neglected groups.

• *To facilitate local resource mobilization and the development of POs* through which the poor can participate in their own development. NGOs have demonstrated their ability to promote local participation and their willingness to adapt to local needs and conditions in the support they provide to these groups.

• *To deliver services* at a relatively low cost. This is derived from the NGO's ability to mobilize voluntary energy and resources.

• *To find innovative solutions* to novel problems and to support successful innovation in government programs.[20] The capacity grows from their small size, administrative flexibility, and relative freedom from political constraints.[21]

### *Weaknesses of NGOs*

NGOs are commonly criticized for having limited:

• *Technical capacity for complex projects.* This is a function of their small size and budgets. They have limited staff, and their modest pay scales affect their ability to attract people with advanced technical and professional qualifications.[22]

• *Ability to "scale up" successful projects* to achieve regional or national impact. This is a function of small size and resources, limited administrative systems, intensive focus on a few communities, the difficulty in maintaining their essential value consensus as the staff expands, inattention to developing real efficiency and expertise in a well-defined technology,[23] and even their own commitments to their initial beneficiary populations.[24]

• *Ability to develop community organizations that are able to sustain themselves* once the NGO withdraws its special staff and resources. This is a function of the fact that NGOs depend on short-term, soft-funding sources, commonly define their interventions as short-term, and work in isolation from or even in competition with other institutions whose support is required for long-term viability. NGOs also seldom give adequate attention in project planning to sustainability questions.

• *Strategic perspective and linkages with other important actors.* NGOs often ignore the larger context in which they operate, focusing only on the micro-level and failing to recognize the extent to which the communities they serve are parts of systems strongly influenced by other agencies and forces (see CEE 1981; Hursh-Cesar and Associates 1986; and Tendler 1987). This weakness may stem from a combination of commitment to locally specific interventions and a sense of moral superiority that leads to the undervaluing of the ability and intentions of other organizations.

• *Managerial and organizational capabilities.* This stems from a combination of their lack of the necessary skills, reluctance to spend their scarce resources on functions that seem unrelated to beneficiary needs, donor unwillingness to fund administrative expenses, and values that equate administration with inflexible bureaucracy.

### *Rethinking strengths and weaknesses of NGOs*

To summarize, voluntary development organizations have demonstrated substantial comparative advantages, especially their ability to innovate, adapt to local conditions, and to reach and work with the poorest and most difficult-to-reach populations in developing countries. These capacities are a function of their values, special skills, small size, limited resources, flexibility, and freedom from political constraints. NGOs also commonly demonstrate serious weaknesses, especially in achieving sustainable outcomes on a consequential scale. It is important to note that many of these weaknesses are a function of the same characteristics that give voluntary NGOs their distinctive advantages.

One important implication is that it may not be possible to eliminate all the weaknesses in NGOs without simultaneously eliminating their strengths. For example, the larger the organization, the more difficult it is to sustain the value consensus that is critical to sustaining the flow of voluntary energy that gives the NGO its special quality. Emphasizing professional qualifications in staff recruiting can undermine the voluntary character of staff motivation as well.

On the other hand, some NGO weaknesses are not inherent, that is, they can be corrected without eliminating the qualities that give the voluntary NGO its distinctive strength. However, corrective action must take into account the distinctive nature of these organizations. Otherwise, well-intentioned interventions may eliminate the very qualities that made the NGO an attractive partner in the first place.

Ultimately, it is the commitment to values and social mission that defines the distinctive strengths and weaknesses of the sector. The voluntary energy that drives such NGOs is self-directing within the parameters set by organizational values and visions. It supports innovative problem-solving behaviors of a type and intensity that is difficult to achieve through coercion or even market forces.

Development planners and donors who recognize the special power of voluntary energy as a development resource face a frustrating dilemma. They see the potentials of NGOs. Yet they need to operate on a large scale, while NGOs tend to be small and scattered, with accounting systems that do not meet the standards of donor auditors. The primary tools of planners and donors are the conventional government tools of coercion and money. The use of either is more likely to suppress than to elicit voluntary social energy. Furthermore, their planning and management tools call for adherence to project blueprints and fixed schedules. The social processes through which voluntary social energy is generated and released simply do not conform to these types of blueprints and schedules.

The first temptation of planners and donors is to remake the NGO to conform to their administrative and programming requirements—something akin to killing the goose that laid the golden egg. It is likely to destroy the NGO's ability to generate the very resource—voluntary social energy—that a planner/donor wants.

A particular danger is that a planner/donor will create incentives that will encourage voluntary NGOs to assume more of the characteristics of PSCs. Or the planner/donor may unintentionally encourage the formation of new market-driven NGOs, or PSCs, primarily in response to the availability of funds. The availability of funds from foreign donors for family planning services in Bangladesh, for example, has inspired the emergence of agencies that are legally organized as NGOs but that appear to be responding more to market incentives than to voluntary commitment.

Differences inherent in the nature of organizations in each of the three sectors—government, commercial, and voluntary—give organizations in each sector a natural advantage in some tasks and a natural disadvantage in others. Thus, for example, it is equally inappropriate to criticize:

- Voluntary organizations for limited ability to provide routine services to large populations on a sustained, self-financing basis
- Government organizations for limited ability to innovate and to adapt responsively to the needs of many different groups
- Commercial organizations for limited ability to provide services below cost to persons who cannot afford to pay.

Donors and planners accomplish little by treating voluntary NGOs in ways appropriate to commercial or government agencies. Indeed, doing so may inadvertently limit their ability to make their more distinctive contribution by creating incentives and structures that move them in the direction of being commercial enterprises or government dependencies. When a donor identifies a task suited to government or commercial sector organizations, it should not look to NGOs as a cheap substitute.

## Improving the performance of NGOs

There are important opportunities for improving the performance of NGOs without losing their distinctive assets. Many of the past limitations of NGOs have been largely self-imposed, partly due to their own acceptance of the prevailing belief that development leadership can come only from large organizations with substantial financial resources.[25] As NGOs reexamine their development roles, many see with increasing clarity the extent to which their limitations are largely self-imposed. Growing numbers of NGOs are thinking beyond charitable action in a few communities and giving greater attention to the underlying causes of poverty, injustice, and environmental destruction.

This means thinking beyond defined project areas. It means thinking and acting in terms of people's movements, and shaping national policies and institutions. This requires gaining access to top-level technical talent, thinking strategically about issues of scaling up, and building organizations that mobilize and use resources effectively. In turn, large-scale sustainable changes require building alliances with other organizations—voluntary, commercial, and government—to solve problems that are intractable to any one of them alone (Brodhead 1987; and Korten 1987).

*Enhancing technical capacity*

NGOs have the capacity to tap highly sophisticated technical talent either as employees or as volunteers—when they set their minds to doing so.[26] There has been significant growth over the past two decades in the number of highly qualified and socially committed specialists, researchers, lawyers, and economists on the staffs of NGOs (Cernea 1988).[27] Of course, when adding such people, it is important to take care that they not only bring technical expertise but also share in the value commitment of the organization.

When NGOs are criticized for lack of technical capability, it is important to ask what kind the critic believes they should acquire. Many NGOs demonstrate the ability to undertake projects that are highly complex from a social or political perspective. But one would not normally turn to an NGO to build a dam or implement a major reclamation project. These capabilities are readily available from commercial firms, which would be technically ill-suited to mobilizing community organizations.

*Expanding scale and sustainability*

Not all NGOs have difficulty in increasing the scale of their operations. The Bangladesh Rural Advancement Committee and the Sri Lankan Sarvodaya Shramadana, for example, operate programs and projects of national scale and employ thousands of staff members. The difficulties of sustaining voluntary commitments and value consensus in such large organizations are serious but not insurmountable.[28] At the same time there is reason to question whether NGOs operating on this scale are most accurately classified as voluntary NGOs or as PSCs.

More to the point, however, is the question of whether NGOs should operate programs of such scale, given their special strengths and weaknesses. We would argue that the scaling-up issue has generally been improperly defined, at least in relation to NGOs. It is not evident that it is in the nature of the voluntary NGO to operate services on a large scale. There are other, possibly more appropriate, ways for them to contribute toward large-scale social and economic programs. Following are some of the appropriate NGO roles and strategies in support of "scaling-up."

• *Demonstration and transfer to government or commercial sectors.* The NGO may prove a service concept to be politically and economically viable on a pilot basis and then facilitate its transfer to the government or commercial sectors through technical support. This was the chosen strategy of many of the local affiliates of the International Planned Parenthood Federation that pioneered the development of family planning services. Helen Keller International (HKI) used a variation on this approach in working with the Ministry of Health in Sri Lanka to develop a program of primary eye care and cataract treatment. Rather than running its own pilot, HKI helped the ministry develop the new service on a pilot basis and then supported expansion on a national scale.

• *Small-scale development on a large scale through the networking of NGOs and POs.* In Indonesia WALHI has promoted environmental action on a national scale by working to develop a network of independent local environmental organizations.[29] The Association of Development Agencies of Bangladesh (ADAB) has brought together a number of major NGOs engaged in rural development to formulate a joint strategy for building federations of landless people's organizations that can take over many of the functions of the catalyst NGOs, including efforts to influence national policy. This will allow the assisting NGOs to redirect their attention to organizing landless groups in new areas of the country with the expectation that these groups will eventually join the federated structure.

• *Promotion of national policies that enable self-help action.* This may be effective where legal barriers seriously constrain decentralized self-help action. The Institute for Liberty and Democracy in Peru has identified legal and procedural constraints that limit the productivity of self-help employment in the informal economy and has mobilized broad political support for key legislative changes (see de Soto 1987).

The strength of the voluntary sector as a development agent is not found in the size of its individual organizations so much as in their number and variety, their ability to evolve, and their ever-shifting networks and coalitions. To focus on the performance and scale of individual NGOs is to risk losing sight of the aggregate phenomenon that they represent—a movement attempting to return the control of development to the people through the creation of what Annis (1988) describes from the Latin American experience as a "thickening web of grass-roots organizations" (210; see also Korten and Klaus 1984; and Korten 1986).

Cernea (1988) describes this movement as:

> *a growing stream which gradually gathers its waters from innumerable affluents of various origin, location, and content, at every turn running into barriers or being constrained by straits, but nevertheless converging into an ever wider flow with multifaceted strength.* (11)

Although it is probably inappropriate to look to NGOs as large-scale service providers, nothing precludes their pursuit of strategies aimed at large-scale consequences, as demonstrated by a rich experience.

### *Improving the management of NGOs*

We see no inherent reason why an NGO should be poorly managed. But the management procedures and styles chosen must be appropriate to the NGO's nature and task.

Too often, criticism of NGO management capabilities is substantially motivated by donors' concern with meeting their own auditing and reporting requirements. There is little evident relation between performing these tasks well and actual effectiveness in development, particularly in the more innovative roles of the NGO.

The control-oriented styles of management common to government, and generally favored by donors, are not effective when the goal is innovative problem solving and the mobilization of voluntary energy. The contemporary literature on corporate management demonstrates that the most effective forms of management, even for large, market-oriented corporations, are those that seek to mobilize the self-motivation and self-direction of staff through the development of value consensus regarding the firm's social role (see, for example, Peters and Waterman 1982; and Kanter 1983).

These forms of management emphasize self-directing, problem-solving teams. They also feature well-developed accounting and information systems, but these systems are designed to provide information useful in self-directed problem solving rather than to assure close adherence to budgets and blueprints (Korten 1984). These forms of management are well suited to NGOs.

As NGOs take themselves and their development roles more seriously, they are also becoming more interested in improving their managerial capabilities. The barriers are increasingly found in (1) the lack of adequate sources of assistance in developing appropriate management systems and skills[30] and (2) donor resistance to funding administrative overhead and staff development expenses.[31]

## Intersectoral relations

Balanced development is a complex undertaking that cannot be achieved by any one sector alone. Each sector—market, government, and voluntary—is subject to failures inherent in its nature. These failures can often be compensated by strengths of organizations from other sectors. Pluralistic societies that foster the strength of all three sectors thus gain institutional advantages. But in practice such collaboration is often difficult to start and even more problematic to sustain.

The differences among the sectors are both the source of potential synergies and the cause of serious misunderstandings.

*Development partnerships*

Cooperation across sectors is an attractive means of using the special capacities of different sectors in development projects. The importance of public-private partnerships between government and business is increasingly recognized in some settings. For example, in the United States there has been a dramatic rise in the use of public service contracting as a substitute for direct delivery of public services through government. The resulting competition among service providers is expected to result in increased efficiency (see Salamon 1987).

Many development questions have the characteristics of social "messes," in which interacting problems reinforce one another and frustrate single agency's efforts at solution (see Ackoff 1974). Multisectoral partnerships of institutions that utilize the special strengths of each may help solve such problems.[32]

The potentials for joining forces with other organizations within or beyond the voluntary sector are being discovered by a growing number of NGOs. In Zimbabwe, the Savings Development Foundation (SDF) works with government ministries and private firms to support increased agricultural production among smallholders, particularly women. SDF pioneered a simple method of encouraging weekly savings of small amounts of money by households organized into neighborhood groups and devised a financial recordkeeping system accessible to illiterate people. As a result, group members—by 1985 numbering about 250,000 persons in more than 5,700 clubs—now save enough money to place bulk orders for fertilizer and seed. Rural women thereby increase their financial independence and modernize their farming skills.

The partnership involves the Ministry of Community Development and Women's Affairs, whose field staff are trained by SDF to teach the savings methodology, and the Ministry of Agriculture, whose extension agents are linked by SDF to groups that require technical services. The partnership has also brought in a private fertilizer company to finance the production of training materials. The company's sales to peasant farmers have increased as a consequence of greater savings. By the 1980s this innovative, low-cost, and participatory approach to raising agricultural production among the rural poor had become firmly institutionalized in Zimbabwe as a trilateral partnership among the public, private, and voluntary sectors.

NGOs have natural advantages in helping such partnerships form among potential partners with histories of conflict or mistrust.[33] NGOs' independence gives them a degree of neutrality and flexibility,[34] and sometimes confers credibility that other participants lack—particularly in dealing with poverty groups. At the same time, the experience of NGOs in relating with POs, donors, and government can be a critical input to the sensitive negotiations required to launch and maintain cooperative activity among very diverse agencies (see Brown forthcoming).

*Uneasy relations between governments and NGOs*

For those who hold state power, NGOs and POs may represent more than a source of competing ideas. NGOs are commonly training grounds for alternative leadership, and sometimes the temporary haven of out-of-power opposition politicians. Consequently, there are good reasons for politicians in power to look with a wary eye on the emergence of a dynamic voluntary sector.

For these reasons, governments of developing countries are inclined to assess NGOs and their contributions more from a political perspective than from the economic-efficiency perspective that tends to preoccupy donors[35] and to make decisions regarding their regulation on this basis. The less secure a government is about its political legitimacy, the greater its reason to fear a populace mobilized in autonomous organizations—and the more likely it is to seek to control, even suppress, the voluntary sector (see Bratton 1989).

Michael Bratton has identified four categories of control mechanism used by African governments to control NGOs and POs, ranging from the relatively subtle to the outright coercive.[36]

- *Monitoring/registration.* To transact business, and particularly to receive foreign funding, in most countries, an NGO must be registered. This can be a pro forma procedure or a serious barrier to NGO formation.[37] Requiring government approval of foreign contributions also provides opportunities for harassment and delay.[38]
- *Coordination.* Haphazard patterns of rural development can lead to official coordination of NGO activities. At local levels NGO activities may be subject to approval by a local agency or official, which affirms that development activities are a monopoly of the state.
- *Co-optation.* In some countries all development NGOs are required to become members of a government-sponsored coordinating body. The body may be registered as an NGO but often has a board of trustees documented by senior government officials; its work may include review and approval of operating plans or control of all foreign funding. Co-optation is particularly popular with authoritarian governments of the political left.[39]
- *Reorganization, dissolution, and imprisonment.* Less subtle measures of control include forced reorganization (in which the government replaces the existing leadership—often in the name of correcting some financial abuse), dissolution of the organization, or imprisonment of its leaders.

Many governments of developing countries have been particularly preoccupied with controlling POs, especially labor unions and cooperatives. Throughout much of the developing world, government control of cooperatives is so complete that they are more accurately described as government agencies.

NGO leaders in India have recently expressed concern that their government may follow the same regulatory path with NGOs that undermined the cooperative movement as an independent force. The first Cooperatives Act was introduced in India in 1904 "to encourage thrift, self-help, and cooperation among agriculturalists, artisans, and persons of limited means, and for that purpose to provide for the constitution and control of cooperative societies." This 10-page document left management matters to cooperative members. The Registrar of Cooperatives was to provide for their legal registration, audit their accounts free of charge, and perform certain fairly minimal regulatory functions.

Subsequent versions of the law dropped the statement that the purpose was to encourage thrift, self-help, and cooperation; increased the involvement of government; and all but eliminated members' control over organizations. The act in force in the state of Andhra Pradesh in 1985 was more than 80 pages long and gave the Registrar of Cooperatives the power, among others, to divide and consolidate cooperatives, amend the by-laws of any cooperative, postpone management committee elections and appoint a "person-in-charge" to assume the management committee's functions, supersede the decisions of elected committees, and issue instructions that all cooperatives were required to follow—irrespective of members' wishes.

Due to the application of these provisions, all cooperatives in Andhra Pradesh were for several years managed by persons-in-charge who had no accountability to members. Free election of management committees by cooperative members was restored only as the result of a successful court action brought by Samakhya, an NGO committed to restoring the independence of cooperatives.

This extension of regulatory control sometimes proceeds in small incremental steps—each of which is relatively innocuous. The cumulative impact of many small steps can devastate the independence needed for effective operation of both NGOs and POs.[40]

The threat that some governments perceive NGOs to pose does not arise purely from their efforts to spawn political competition. The legitimacy of many governments of developing countries is based on their ability to deliver services. Any NGO that delivers services more efficiently than government may be perceived as a political threat.

There are basically three options open to the regime so threatened. One is to position itself to claim credit for NGO accomplishments. A second is to hinder NGO operations to the point that they become ineffective. A third option is to displace the voluntary sector by creating captive organizations to assume the apparent functions of NGOs, but as instruments of the regime.

### *Captive organizations: GONGOs and DONGOs*

NGOs created as captives of government to substitute for true NGOs are commonly referred to as "GONGOs," government-organized NGOs. GONGOs are created and registered as NGOs by governmental agencies to be instruments of government policy. An example is the national women's organization in an Asian country. Its national chairman is the wife of the Minister of Home Affairs. Each provincial organization is chaired by the wife of the governor, and so on down through the hierarchy. It is made clear to wives of government officials that they are expected to participate.

The formation of a GONGO seldom reflects a spontaneous expression of a shared value commitment, and participation is often less than voluntary. The motives in forming such organizations may be positive, and they may serve useful social functions. But they are less likely than truly voluntary agencies to serve as agents of social innovation.[41]

As donors become more interested in NGOs, they also find themselves tempted to create NGOs suited to their own perceived needs. Such agencies might be called "DONGOs," or donor-organized NGOs. The mission of a DONGO will normally be defined by its sponsoring donor. Such organizations may serve useful functions for the donor, while offering a degree of flexibility in administration and funds disbursement that the donor's own procedures might not allow.[42]

Since donors are particularly preoccupied with the disbursement of funds and usually find their own procedures and modes of working ill-suited to making grants to dozens—or even hundreds—of small scattered organizations, the DONGOs they create are most often funding bodies. This does not create a particular problem in itself, unless a number of donors should decide to pool their funds and channel them through a single DONGO—creating one control point for funds, in violation of the pluralism principle we outline later. Ultimately, those who control this organization gain inordinate control over the sector.[43] Such an organization also becomes a natural takeover target for a government that feels threatened by independent NGOs.

Concerns with the coordination, size, and technical capacity of NGOs may encourage donors to support the idea that NGOs should be brought together under coordinating bodies that can absorb and retail large blocks of donor funds, insure proper accounting standards, and coordinate responsibilities for service coverage. This concern may lead a donor to suggest that a government form an NGO coordinating body; or the donor might decide to act directly to form or co-opt a national-level NGO or consortium body to serve as a coordinating agency.

Such initiatives may appear to suit the needs of the donor, but they carry considerable risk of disrupting or co-opting the organizations they are intended to assist. The distinction between voluntary NGOs, POs, and PSCs becomes important here. There is no contradiction in a donor effort to coordinate activities of PSCs through centralized contracting mechanisms. But any external effort to impose coordination on NGOs and POs denies their essential nature.

The donor conscious of such issues may seek to avoid the imposition of external coordination by channeling its funds through an existing autonomous NGO consortium body governed by its own members. This too can have unintended consequences. Consortium bodies normally exist to be responsive to the needs and interests of their members. When NGO consortium secretariats become involved in judging members' proposals for the purpose of allocating limited funds, it inevitably changes the relationship between the consortium body and its members. It may also politicize elections for the board of the consortium body by enticing politically ambitious members to compete for control over the consortium's fund.[44]

If donors and governments are to build an effective partnership with NGOs, it is important that they recognize the distinctive social roles of the NGO and the extent to which these roles turn on the NGO's independence. They must also be able to recognize the nature of such NGO variants as DONGOS and GONGOs.[45]

## Guidelines for donor action

There are important dilemmas in any effort to forge partnerships between NGOs and major donors. As articulated by Michael Bratton (1988):

> *Big donors and small NGOs make uncomfortable bedfellows by virtue of unbridgeable differences of scale, ethos, and capacity. In an asymmetrical power relationship driven by the movement of money, the goals of the dominant agency will invariably displace the goals of the subordinate partner.* (21)

The differences between voluntary NGOs and large donors are important and often difficult to bridge. In general, official donors deal in money and technology; NGOs deal in values, people, and institutions. Donor agencies usually work with central governments, NGOs with grass-roots organizations. Donors engage in large projects, NGOs in small projects. Donors fund contracts; NGOs depend on grants. Donors emphasize preplanning; NGOs engage in adaptive learning.

There are many opportunities for complementarity; there is also much potential for conflict and mutual damage. There are no easy rules for donors. We believe, however, that two basic tests of available choices—pluralism and voluntarism—provide useful guides to action.

### *The test of voluntarism*

Commercial organizations are driven by market demand for goods or services. In working with commercial organizations it is appropriate for donors to say what goods and services they want, and for vendors to present their bids. In the development "business," donors contract with agencies that demonstrate their ability to meet required quality standards at the least cost. The contract specifications and the donor demand that they be met as a condition of payment constitute the relevant control mechanism.

In contrast, the donor's guarantee of a voluntary NGO's performance is the NGO's demonstrated commitment to its mission and values. If the NGO is to exercise its distinctive competence as an agent of innovation, the relationship between the donor and the NGO must allow for flexibility. It is entirely possible that outputs cannot be known in advance or contracted in the conventional sense.

In a value-driven organization, the value commitment is the source of motivation and discipline. With such an organization, grants with broad terms of reference are appropriate, especially when the donor is more interested in investing in the organization and its mission than in purchasing a specific service or product. Under such grants NGOs are answerable to donors more in terms of faithfulness to espoused values than in terms of contracts and outputs. Of course donors have to be well-informed about what values are; there can be unpleasant surprises.[46]

This leaves the donor with a difficult question. How does it know whether it is working with a voluntary NGO, when many organizations may be GONGOs, DONGOs, or PSCs? Whether an organization is nongovernmental or nonprofit is easily established. Whether it is an NGO by our definition is less easily determined and very much a matter of judgment.

As public funding for NGO activities increases, so do reports of retired bureaucrats, unemployed local touts, and other opportunists rushing to form NGOs to qualify for funding. These organizations are formed more as an entrepreneurial response to opportunities than as a value commitment. Donors should not expect that such NGOs will act like voluntary organizations, or even like responsible PSCs.

The test of voluntarism, asking questions such as the following, can be helpful:

- Does the organization have a well-defined sense of its mission, and has there been continuity over the years?
- Is there evidence that the staff, and especially the leaders, work for the organization primarily because they believe in its mission?
- Has the staff accepted adverse working conditions, when necessary, to pursue that mission—including working at salaries below the market rate?

The track record is critical. Substantial differences in commitment and capability will have a major bearing on NGO performance. An effective NGO commonly has a program that has evolved on the basis of learning from its own experience (Korten 1980). When an organization has a program consisting of partial, short-term commitments that coincide with shifting donor fads—women in development one year, and small enterprise development the next—one might ask whether it is more market-driven than value-driven.

### *The test of balanced pluralism*

When choosing interventions that bear on the development of the voluntary sector, balanced pluralism among the sectors is a useful guide. By balanced pluralism, we refer to development of different sectors consistent with effective use of their complementary strengths. A key issue in the evolution of balanced pluralism is the distribution of power among the sectors. While equality among them is not practical in most countries, some degree of mutual influence is critical to using their complementary strengths well. The test of pluralism involves one basic question: Does the proposed intervention enhance institutional pluralism and mutual influence in the society?

When the intervention would be more likely to create monopoly control over a particular institutional space, reduce the independence of existing organizations, or create a control point that might be used to limit freedom of independent association, it fails the test.

The issues involved are complex. Take the case of funding for voluntary activities. Many donors are interested in increasing the flow of funding to NGOs and POs. There are also calls for greater local control of such funds, on the grounds that funding decisions should be made by indigenous organizations.

The range of possible mechanisms for financing voluntary activity is quite broad, a subject we touched upon above. What guidance is provided by the "test of pluralism" in choosing among them? To illustrate the underlying issue, we can put forward a worst-case scenario:

> *It is required that all financial contributions to NGOs, whether from government or private, foreign or domestic sources, must pass through a single government-controlled agency with sole power to decide on their allocation.*

In this scenario there is a single decision point, a total monopoly on voluntary financial resources. Decisionmaking would be in the hands of a single individual or group, virtually eliminating the possibility that the sector will serve multiple perspectives and values. The interests served would almost certainly be those of the persons who control the state.

An alternative scenario with respect to pluralism might look like the following:

> *A strong prevailing norm of voluntarism encourages individuals in the society to contribute 10 percent of their income and time to voluntary causes of their choice. The state supports voluntary funding of NGOs through tax exemptions for contributions to qualified organizations. Qualifying for tax-exempt status is simple, and freedom of association and expression is protected by the courts.*[47]

In this scenario the state sets the basic framework. The choice of priorities in the allocation of funding resides entirely with individual citizens according to their individual value preferences.

These two scenarios represent the extremes of the spectrum from unitary central control to the ultimate pluralism of individual choice. The second scenario is generally limited as an option because of both lack of governmental commitment and insufficient development of an ethic of charitable giving. We would argue, however, that among policy options, donor preference should be toward those that represent greater pluralism—more broadly distributed choice making. Thus, for example:

- Public financial support of NGO activities should give preference to tax incentives for individual contributions over direct government funding.
- Direct public funding of NGOs should be dispersed across multiple ministries and levels of government rather than centrally controlled.
- Blocks of funds contributed to indigenous organizations to allocate should be distributed to several independent agencies rather than through a single conduit organization.

Donors should decline to participate in or endorse any scheme that calls for channeling all foreign contributions to the voluntary sector through a single government-controlled agency. Such schemes are, by their nature, a direct denial of the pluralism that represents the foundation of the voluntary sector.

## Modes of donor support for NGOs

What are ways in which large donors can work effectively with NGOs? On the basis of the discussion so far, we can identify at least five possibilities.

### *Giving direct financial support*

Most donors are primarily funding agencies. It is natural for them to think first in terms of providing NGOs with increased financial support for their activities. There is no question that NGOs require financial resources. But there are several dangers involved.

- Too much money can undermine voluntarism. Those who carry the values of the NGO must remain clear on the organization's mission and their own reason for participating. Money must remain secondary to mission.
- The easiest relationship for donors is to enlist NGOs as contractors to implement projects and to deal with them essentially as commercial firms. NGOs that respond to this invitation may find themselves reorienting their basic nature to become PSCs rather than social catalysts.
- Donors that seek to support NGOs through earmarked government-to-government transfers, with funds to be reallocated by the recipient government to NGOs, risk undermining NGO independence by giving the state control. Grants administered through the recipient government can inadvertently compromise pluralism.

We have argued that the distinctive role of NGOs comes in strengthening civil society and people's capacity to participate. The alleviation of poverty depends as much on the strengthening of institutions for political participation as on the strengthening of institutions that guarantee economic competition. Both forms of initiative depend on institutional pluralism. If donors accept this perspective as the basis for their relationships with the NGO community, they must recognize that on many issues NGOs have more relevant expertise than donors. Where the NGOs have greater expertise, it is appropriate for them to take the lead in defining the relationship.

This will not be easy for either party. Few NGOs have given serious thought to the possibility of such a relationship. Neither have donors. The donors would have to learn to listen and to play a supportive role, seeking ways to respond constructively to the needs and agendas of the NGOs. The NGOs would have to learn to grapple with issues and concerns on a more national scale.

Avoiding the hazards of directly financing NGOs will require new mechanisms for making funds available in amounts and through procedures that will not overwhelm or pervert their special capacities. Appropriate guidelines might include the following:

- Direct aid for NGOs, particularly from large public donors, should generally be limited to two types of organization:
  - Large and well-established NGOs whose track record demonstrates their capacity to handle large blocks of funds without being overwhelmed or co-opted.
  - Organizations that function in the role of private foundations in making small grants to NGOs and POs. These might be quasi-governmental organizations, such as the publicly funded German foundations or the U.S. Inter-American Foundation. They might also be entirely private foundations geared to this purpose, such as the Foundation for the Peoples of the South Pacific or Philippine Business for Social Progress. The Canadian International Development Agency has created several foundation-like mechanisms for channeling assistance to NGOs in Asia.
- Funding should take the form of broadly defined grants tied to mutually agreed-upon "program missions" that are evaluated in terms of general development and objectives rather than contracted outputs.
- Reporting systems should be standardized across donors and not require or reward the commitment of substantial NGO resources to satisfy special needs of individual donors.

Providing direct assistance to key NGOs is a potentially important role for donors. But mechanisms are needed to provide that support without undermining the distinctive nature of the sector. Without adequate safeguards, it is better for large donors to focus on other approaches.

POs are also subject to co-optation, and donor support for them can be even more problematic. POs ideally are permanent community organizations that mobilize local resources to meet continuing local needs. Their strength depends even more than that of NGOs on their becoming financially self-reliant.

### *Financing sector-support institutions*

Our review of the weaknesses of NGOs suggests that they often need support other than increased financial resources. Donors may well contribute, for example, to the improvement of NGO technical or management capacities. This might be accomplished by providing resources to promote the emergence and effectiveness of institutions to support the voluntary sector, such as the following:

- Regional, national, and subnational NGO consortium bodies that enable individual NGOs to share experience and effective innovations, to undertake cohesive action to resist destructive pressures from international agencies or government, and to create strategic networks and integrated national sector strategies for development.
- Institutions offering training and consultation services to NGOs, especially in priority areas such as strategy formulation, organization development, management training, community organizing, and various technical areas.

• Research institutes that offer the voluntary sector access to high-quality technical advice and research support. Such information can be critical in helping NGOs influence policy decisions that require analytical sophistication that individual NGOs seldom possess.

• Advocacy centers that make available to NGOs and POs expertise in developing policy positions, planning advocacy strategies, and lobbying legislatures. As more NGOs and POs become interested in shaping the larger policy context, such advocacy and legislative skills will be more in demand.

The more the voluntary sector moves from work at the grass roots to asking questions about how to influence institutional and policy contexts, the more important specialized institutions characteristic of a strong voluntary sector will become.

Donor agencies may be able to support the work of grass-roots organizations indirectly by making resources available to institutions that serve the sector as a whole, even when direct financial aid to operating NGOs is not practical for the reasons discussed earlier. Mechanisms that allow NGOs to choose among support services can encourage their providers to remain responsive to the needs of NGOs.

*Increasing political space*

Our analysis leads us to conclude that some of the most promising opportunities for donor support of the voluntary sector lie in the realm of policy dialogue with national governments rather than in direct financing. There are few natural incentives for governments to encourage NGOs, even though NGOs can play an important role in the long-term development process. Donors had to assume a lead role in gaining recognition for the importance of the market, and they may have to provide similar leadership in promoting policy and operating space for NGOs.

There are three areas to which particular attention should be directed:

• *Guarantees of freedom of association.* For the commercial sector to function efficiently, legal and procedural barriers that constrain the market must be minimized. Similarly, for the voluntary sector to perform its social role effectively, legal and procedural barriers to free association and expression must be minimized—in accord with the universal declaration on human rights. Registration procedures should be simple and easily negotiated by any legitimate group that meets the basic standards. Reporting should similarly be simple and limited to routine annual reports of activities and finances appropriate to the public record. Recognized organizations, so long as they are not convicted of illegal activities, should not have to obtain prior approval for ordinary activities and financial contributions.

Just as donors have developed expertise in advising on policies, laws, and procedures for a productive market sector, so might they develop the expertise required to advise national governments about the promotion of a strong and constructive voluntary sector. A first step might be to develop an inventory of relevant policies and procedures in countries at differing stages of development and with differing political systems, to better understand the range of options and consequences.

• *Policies encouraging private philanthropy.* As middle classes emerge in developing countries, the potential for generating significant resources for voluntary sector activities increases. The contribution of such resources to voluntary development activity can be encouraged by legislation that provides tax or other incentives.

Donors might consider building the capability to advise countries on how to structure incentives that will encourage private voluntary financing of NGOs. Considerable experience has been gained around the world with such tax incentives. As a starting point it may be appropriate to survey this experience for lessons. Examination of how the philanthropic ethic develops in a country and how traditional charities can be encouraged to support development-oriented activities is also worth attention.

• *NGO participation in policy processes.* Governments commonly require that NGOs obtain prior permission for activities to insure that the activities are supportive of the governments' priorities. Less common have been decisions like that of the Aquino government in the Philippines to invite NGOs to participate in the deliberations of planning councils, to help insure that development plans are responsive to public needs. Openness in governance and citizens' access to information on government development plans is essential. It should be encouraged by donors, and donors themselves should set a positive example by making their documents readily available to the public.

In general, development policy deliberations have suffered from lack of effective feedback from the grass roots. Even the introduction of locally elected councils has only partially addressed this problem, because local elites have often controlled those councils to serve their own interests. In a number of countries NGOs have been addressing this problem by helping the poor organize themselves to support the election of their own candidates. But effective feedback channels from NGOs or representatives of the poor remain the exception rather than the rule.

Donors can do much to help recipient governments explore mechanisms for expanding popular participation in a variety of policy forums. Again, a first step might be to compile an inventory of experience with efforts by NGOs and POs to provide substantive input to public policy processes.

### *Creating feedback links from NGOs to donors*

Donors need the kind of feedback that NGOs can provide. NGOs concerned with development and the environment have become increasingly active in providing donors with feedback on the negative environmental and social consequences of projects. Some donors have taken such feedback seriously and have built mechanisms for continuing the dialogue. This is a positive step. But donor mechanisms for obtaining and acting on needed feedback are still limited.

As NGOs become more comfortable in dealing with donors as partners, they will probably seek greater involvement in early project planning in the hope of reducing negative social and environmental consequences. Donors might find the establishment of national NGO advisory groups to be useful, just as some have experimented successfully with international NGO advisory groups.

One important issue that donors will need to face is the secrecy of their own proceedings and documentation. Donors typically treat their own planning documents as privileged information to be shared only with authorized representatives of the recipient government. It is the rare representative of a donor agency who is prepared openly to share such information with individuals or groups that might be critical of their content. There are reports of Asian NGOs being able to obtain documentation on World Bank projects being planned or implemented in their countries only by working through U.S. NGOs that could acquire the documents by exercising the U.S. Freedom of Information Act.

It is appropriate for NGOs of all countries to demand that donor documentation be treated as a matter of public record accessible to any citizen of either donor or recipient country. The greatest resistance to this is likely to be found among recipient governments. But it must be remembered that it is ultimately the people who are borrowing the money, not the government. They have a right to know what is being borrowed in their name, and how it is being used.

Some donors are becoming more forthcoming, but there is a long way to go before critical information on plans and projects becomes public information. NGOs need open access to donor records and technical data.

*Building development partnerships*

In the type of development partnerships that we are advocating, NGOs are equal participants in planning, solving problems, and taking action—not simply implementors of projects initiated, designed, and funded by others. This gives maximum scope for the NGO to perform its institutional catalyst role.

An Indonesian case that involved collaboration between an Indonesian NGO, three government ministries, the Ford Foundation, and the World Bank, in support of programs aimed at strengthening the role of farmer/irrigator associations, illustrates the potential of development partnerships. The Ford Foundation, itself an NGO, had an important role in helping the Indonesian NGO establish itself as a credible member of the partnership and in funding its participation.

The operating modes of large donors generally do not allow them to play the kind of supporting role the Ford Foundation played in this instance. Large donors that lack such capability might find it useful to ally themselves with organizations, such as the Ford Foundation, that are better suited to nurturing. Foundations or international private NGOs like Oxfam or the World Council of Churches might also be good allies.

Further efforts to identify and document examples of development partnerships should be undertaken so that the conditions for their success can be better understood and their implications for donor strategy and practice explicated.

## Issues for further study

We have proposed a conceptual lens for examining the voluntary sector that emphasizes its special capacities for social innovation and responsiveness to relatively deprived and unserved populations. There has been little theoretically grounded research on NGOs. With the benefit of a conceptual lens, we can define a range of research needs that have important bearing on donor policy formulation and programming action. Among the important topics for research are the following:

*NGO sector development*

NGO sectors have developed quite differently in different areas. Voluntary sectors in Asia, Latin America, and Africa each have their distinctive characteristics. In Asia and Latin America the voluntary sectors are generally strong. In Africa the indigenous voluntary sector is less well established. In Asia NGOs have been inclined to seek out opportunities for collaboration with government. In Latin America they have been more politically active, often seeing themselves as in fundamental opposition to government.

Differences within regions are sometimes even more striking than differences among regions. In the Asia region the Philippines is known for the variety and density of its VOs. Yet within India, it is reportedly difficult to find a development VO in any of the three northern states of Punjab, Haryana, and Himachal Pradesh. Pakistan and Bangladesh were once part of the same predominately Islamic country, with few if any NGOs. In less than two decades, Bangladesh has become home to some of the largest and most effective development VOs in the world. In contrast, Pakistan may have fewer development VOs on a per capita basis than any other non-Communist country in Asia.

NGOs in Nepal are limited to a few charities working under the supervision of the Queen. The largest VO in Indonesia is barely a tenth the size of the largest VO in Bangladesh, though Indonesia is larger, more populous, and generally more developed. In Bangladesh, VOs tend to become all-purpose community development generalists providing similar services. VOs in India, Thailand, and the Philippines are often more specialized.

There are also important differences among countries in the extent to which the legal framework guarantees freedom of association and encourages the voluntary sector's involvement in development. There are similar differences in the number and strength of support institutions offering educational, consultancy, research, and advocacy services to the voluntary sector.

Little attention has been given to mapping and understanding these differences and the forces that have created them. For example, how have NGOs and POs developed differently under authoritarian and democratic regimes? What have been the consequences of various types of regulatory and incentive policies? Such knowledge is basic to government and donor policies and to action intended to strengthen voluntary sector development.

Approaches to supporting voluntary sector development will need to be very different in the Philippines or in Andhra Pradesh (India) than in, say, Pakistan, Nepal, or the Indian Punjab. Yet donors have few frameworks available for understanding these differences and their implications.

What are the characteristics that define a healthy and effective NGO community? Does Bangladesh provide the model, with its large generalist NGOs substituting for government in offering nearly identical services to large rural population? Or is the appropriate model something more like the Philippines, with its diversity of NGOs of differing political ideologies, operating styles, and policy and program commitments? Are there identifiable evolutionary stages in the development of an NGO community? What types of support are most important at each stage? These are vital questions for donors if they are to avoid creating distortions through well-intentioned but possibly misguided application of their resources.

Since development-catalyst organizations commonly define their own performance in terms of the creation of strong, self-reliant POs, no study could be complete without serious attention to NGO contributions to the promotion of POs.

The questions involved are most amenable to analysis on a comparative basis. They are also questions that many NGOs and NGO-coalition bodies need to be asking themselves. Therefore, a participatory type of research process might prove appropriate. For example, the draft study report for an individual country might serve as the basis for a national conference of NGOs to review the report in a kind of sectoral self-assessment exercise.

Several country studies might form the basis for a regional conference devoted to a comparative assessment that would help to sharpen the frameworks for comparative analysis. An international conference might then examine patterns of regional differences. The result would be a much refined set of frameworks for assessing NGO development in any given country, and a heightened self-awareness within the voluntary sectors of the participating countries of the issues they face as a sector.

### *Small-scale development on a large scale*

Conventional concepts of replication and scaling up reflect a top-down bias in their underlying presumption that the task involves defining a blueprint for project action and then engaging a large development bureaucracy to stamp out replications of projects.

Sheldon Annis (1987) puts a different twist on the conventional formulation by asking: "How large can small become?" Or, to put it differently: "Can small-scale development be a large-scale policy?" His questions put the problem in proper context. The genius of the NGO approach is found in its people-sized units of action and its local problem-solving focus, in contrast to the imposition of an externally defined blueprint. Yet so long as this is accomplished in only a few communities, the consequences will be severely limited. The proper answer is to do it on a large scale.

The questions posed by Annis are best addressed on a case study basis. The research task is to identify examples of both successful and unsuccessful efforts to accomplish small-scale, locally controlled development on a large scale. Normally the focus should be on reasonably mature efforts that yield clear and easily documented lessons, rather than on incipient efforts in which it is only possible to speculate about prospective results. Each effort selected should be documented and analyzed as a case study to yield lessons and insights that might be translated into other efforts to make small-scale development large-scale policy.

Particular attention should be given to questions such as the following: Is there a point at which a critical mass of small POs sets loose a new dynamic that supports the spontaneous generation and linkage of such organizations? What are the conditions conducive to such an outcome? Reports on the Latin American experience suggest that important insights into these questions may be found in that region.

The proposed documentation should be done from a social learning perspective. The most useful lessons are likely to address the question of how to create and manage the learning process by which a functioning set of institutional relationships emerges in support of large-scale local development action. Efforts to find blueprints for cookie cutter replication are likely to contribute only to more large-scale, top-down failures.

In many instances the successful examples of large-scale coverage that provide useful lessons may not be limited to NGOs of the type described in this chapter. A study of livelihood programs done by Judith Tendler (1987) for the Ford Foundation identified six initiatives that had influenced the lives of large numbers of the poor. One was sponsored by a public sector enterprise, three by trade unions, one by a bank, and one by a private consulting firm. Tendler's study provides an important caution in such a research undertaking: it should not look only for examples in which the chief sponsor is an NGO.

*Mechanisms for NGO/PO funding*

The potential dangers of public donors channeling large blocks of funds to NGOs and POs have been examined in this chapter. But simply sensitizing donors to the potential dangers of inappropriate action does not provide them with a solution to their problem. We have yet to answer the key question: Are there demonstrated ways to channel such funds that are consistent with enlarging the scale of impact while simultaneously strengthening the funded organizations in their distinctive roles?

Again a comparative case study approach is the research method of choice. There is a need to pull together the available data on a variety of different approaches to public funding of different types of NGOs, applying the conceptual framework proposed by this chapter to discriminate between development and welfare interventions, as well as among voluntary NGOs, PSCs, and POs. There should be no presumption that a funding mechanism appropriate to one of these will prove equally satisfactory for others, because both the nature of the organization and the task are likely to differ.

A first step would simply be to do an inventory of the many mechanisms presently in place. These include specialized organizations such as the Inter-American Foundation, the partnership funding mechanisms being established by CIDA in a number of countries of Asia, the efforts of USAID to expand the coverage of family planning service in Bangladesh through grants to NGOs, and the experience of European governments in channeling public resources through international NGOs to indigenous organizations.

Once the inventory is complete, experiences that represent a range of approaches and outcomes should be documented and analyzed from a comparative perspective in relation to the issues identified in this paper. Much of the necessary information might be compiled from existing evaluation and assessment documents.[48] The resulting cases should provide a basis for a contingency analysis suggesting the circumstances under which different funding mechanisms are appropriate. It will be important to assess these mechanisms from a variety of perspectives. Those that are effective at fostering NGOs as a dynamic force for social innovation may not be the same ones that demonstrate effectiveness in contributing to small-scale development on a large scale.

### *NGO/PO policy participation*

There is growing interest among donors in the roles of NGOs and POs as sources of grass-roots feedback in the design, implementation, and evaluation of projects. Here again documentation and comparative analysis of experience, particularly of successful experience, is likely to result in useful lessons.

At the macro-level it might be helpful to examine the role and strategies of environmental NGOs in reshaping the environmental policies of the World Bank and the Asian Development Bank. Going back in history, the same questions might be asked regarding NGO roles and strategies during the 1960s and 1970s in reshaping global policy and programs on population and family planning.

At the micro-level it would be helpful to examine the use of formal mechanisms for achieving direct grass-roots input and feedback into both donor and host government policy and programming. Examples might include MYRADA's role in improving the design and implementation of World Bank-funded projects in India involving resettlement of displaced populations and the Philippine experience with the participation of NGOs on regional and provincial planning councils.

One output of the country studies suggested earlier might be an assessment of the extent to which NGOs and POs in the country in question have played useful roles in shaping development policy and programming, and why.

*Development partnerships*

There are numerous experiences that may lend themselves to documentation and analysis to achieve better understanding of the dynamics of development partnerships, the special role of VOs in their formation and maintenance, and the conditions conducive to their formation. Examples include the LSP initiatives in Indonesia described in note 34, and the collaboration of Philippine Business for Social Progress with the government, the banking system, and a variety of VOs in Negros Occidental.

The interest is in cases that involve joint, intersectoral problem solving, often in situations that demand considerable voluntary energy. This is not the same as the case of the multisectoral project-implementation committee charged with implementing a project blueprint.

Although most NGOs are quite small by donor standards, they are not simple, either in organizational form or in the roles they play in development. And they are particularly complex in the aggregate, in part because the term NGO does not define an organizational type.

NGO defines only a broad range of types of organizations that have little in common with one another except that they are nongovernmental and are legally registered as nonprofits. They include market-oriented PSCs, value-driven VOs, and POs accountable to their members.

Even within the more precisely defined category of VOs, there are differences. Some organizations function purely on voluntary commitment, with no budget. Others have well-paid, full-time professional staffs. Their commitments span the range from pure relief operations to development advocacy and the mobilization of politically active people's movements. The participants range from saints to scoundrels.

The most important development contributions of VOs will often be overlooked if attention is focused on individual organizations. Only in the aggregate is it possible to appreciate fully the sector's contribution to mobilizing voluntary energy in support of a broad range of social agendas; its role in serving as a marketplace of ideas and innovations; and its function in the promotion and preservation of democratic institutions, in part as a counterweight to the state. These contributions are best appreciated within the context of the broader political and institutional dimensions of development that have so often been overlooked.

The strongest NGOs and POs respond to a good deal more than financial incentives. Their distinctive development contributions are found in the fact that they are not the same as government organizations or businesses. At the same time they are not immune to financial incentives, which, if wrongly applied, have the potential to destroy the voluntary nature of all but the most strongly self-aware NGOs and POs. The issues are complex, the necessary data elusive, and the potential for damage substantial if partnerships are not planned with a full understanding of these issues.

If there is one central message of this analysis, it is that no responsible donor should undertake to "assist" or "use" NGOs as a part of its development programming unless it is prepared to make a substantial investment in understanding their nature and their distinctive roles. Donors cannot automatically assume that their existing staff's experience and training prepare them to play a constructive role in helping NGOs become more effective in their essential roles in national and global development.

## Notes

1. One indicator is the number of recent studies of voluntary organizations' performance, many commissioned by major international donors. For U.S. experience, see Hursh-Cesar and Associates (1986). For an overview of many studies, see OECD (1988). The Club of Rome has also focused on the role of voluntary nongovernmental organizations as major actors in the development process; see Schneider (1988).
2. This summary is based on Hansmann (1987); Douglas (1987); and Salamon (1987).
3. The impact of market failures on activities in developing countries is examined in Jorgensen, Hafsi, and Kiggundu (1986).
4. For an excellent treatment of this potential as it is emerging in Latin America, see Annis (1987).
5. For an important exception, see Esman and Uphoff (1984). Esman and Uphoff argue for defining local membership organizations as a third sector. We share their concern for the need to give special recognition to the development roles of local membership organizations, termed people's organizations in this chapter following the convention of many voluntary organizations. However, we believe that our scheme offers a stronger conceptual basis for a division of the institutional territory into three sectors, and that people's organizations constitute not a distinctive sector so much as a special type of organization that may assume characteristics of all of the government, commercial, and voluntary sectors as we define them below.
6. We are indebted to Michael Bratton for much of the language of these two paragraphs that describes value commitments. Research on voluntary associations in the United States suggests that the free-rider hypothesis—that people will not contribute resources to causes from which they will not receive private benefits—does not stand up empirically. Knoke (1988), for example, found that "normative incentives" grounded in agency efforts to influence policy and create public goods were more powerful predictors of member behavior and contributions than utilitarian or social incentives.
7. See Fowler (1989) for further discussion of distinguishing characteristics of the three sectors.
8. *Institutions* in this definition refers to the enduring systems of structures, rules, customs, and values that shape the behaviors and relationships of people within a society.
9. This definition is the latest in a series of development definitions focused on institutional aspects of the societies involved, beginning with the definition articulated in Korten (1988).
10. It is a fundamental error to assume that a society that is not making productive use of its own resources will make productive use of concessional foreign resources. This insight has resulted in a basic reorientation of the programs of the Institute for Development Studies (LSP) in Indonesia toward a focus on forming development partnerships including

government, banking, and private commercial sector groups aimed at improving the utilization of major blocks of existing national resources and talent in ways that would benefit the poor.

11. The roles described here are a dual function of VOs and people's organizations.

12. Etzioni's formulation roughly parallels that of the "transaction costs" theorists who have identified three primary patterns of organization: markets, hierarchies, and clans. The government sector tends to be organized primarily around hierarchies, the commercial sector around markets, and the voluntary sector around clans. See Williamson (1975) for the initial development of the transaction costs perspective. His analysis has been extended to include the operations of "clan" forms of organization, in part to explain the exceptional efficiency of Japanese organizations. See Ouchi (1979 and 1980); and Williamson and Ouchi (1981).

13. For a series of reviews of recent research on charismatic leadership, see Conger, Kanungo, and Associates (1988).

14. See Williamson (1975); Ouchi (1979 and 1980); and Williamson and Ouchi (1981) for the analysis underlying these distinctions.

15. Mother Theresa's work with the dying poor in Calcutta, for example, grows out of a religious vision. The Sarvodaya Shramadana in Sri Lanka has drawn on the Buddhist tradition to inspire voluntary commitments to work on behalf of poor villages by persons from all socioeconomic strata, from the poor to the affluent. See Macy (1983). Cross-cultural studies of the voluntary sector, such as James (1987), have noted the prevalence of religious traditions, especially Christianity, in the antecedents of the voluntary sector.

16. For illustrations in the African setting, see Morss (1984).

17. See the ICAE journal *Convergence* for a review of the literature on participatory research in development; and Brown and Tandon (1983).

18. See ANGOC (1988a), a report of the conclusions of a workshop of 30 top Asian NGO leaders held in Bangkok under ANGOC auspices in March 1988; a similar theme is presented in ADAB (1989), a report on a series of workshops of Bangladeshi NGO leaders organized during 1988 by the Association of Development Agencies in Bangladesh (ADAB).

19. See, for European experience, CEE (1981). For an assessment of U.K. experience, see Osborne and Armstrong (1982). For U.S. experience, see Hursh-Cesar and Associates (1986). For an overview of many studies, see OECD (1988).

20. Although many governments regard NGOs as a nuisance or as a threat, in some circumstances NGOs and governments have joined together in creating development strategies that build on the comparative strength of the NGO in piloting innovations and the comparative strength of government in broad-scale implementation. In Thailand, for example, an adult education program developed in one area by World Education, a small international NGO, has been adopted by the Ministry of Education, which worked closely with the NGO during the pilot tests. The potential for shaping government policies and programs has been assessed by an evaluation of USAID projects in small enterprises, health and nutrition, water and sanitation, agro-forestry, and livestock. In the first two sectors NGOs had marked impacts on national policies: they demonstrated the effectiveness of community-based primary health care as a vehicle for improving the health status of underserved populations, and they encouraged more favorable government policies toward small and informal enterprises. See Hursh-Cesar and Associates (1986).

21. Government agencies must answer to many constituencies, any one of which may wish to block a particular initiative. The interlocking structures of their own bureaucracies also serve to block innovations considered to be against some bureaucratic interest. The

fact that NGOs are answerable only to their own boards and possibly to the funder of a particular project gives them much greater flexibility to experiment and to demonstrate the viability of innovative programs.

22. In Senegal, for example, NGO efforts to irrigate desertified lands with wind and solar power have failed because of inadequate technical analysis or limited capacity to maintain the installations required. Note that this limitation is similar to the problem of "amateurism" identified as a "voluntary failure" in studies of the U.S. PVOs.

23. The importance of developing a narrow and well-understood technology that is suited to replication over a wide area with relatively little training and funding has been underlined by Judith Tendler's study (1987) of VOs that serve large numbers of clients, a report prepared for the mid-decade review of the Ford Foundation's programs on livelihood, employment, and income generation.

24. The Women's Health Coalition in Bangladesh, for example, has expertise in reproductive health and has created clinics for menstrual regulation badly needed by Bangladeshi women. But the agency is now offering other services in their clinics that potentially dilute their special expertise in order to respond to patient requests.

25. The myopic view that many NGOs have had of their roles is revealed in the common practice among NGOs working in South India of referring to themselves as "projects," essentially defining themselves not as an organization, but as the project they are implementing in some defined set of villages. A common response to the question "What influence has your work had beyond your project area?" is a blank stare. A number of these NGOs are becoming aware of the problem and are taking steps to correct it.

26. PROCESS, a Philippine NGO, recognized a need to develop the capabilities of its assisted fishermen's organizations to deal with the courts and the legislature on matters relating to fishing rights and fisheries resource management. It recruited two lawyers to develop legal manuals and training appropriate to the needs and educational levels of the fishermen and convinced several Congressmen, including the Speaker of the Philippine House of Representatives, to coach association leaders in how to lobby the Congress.

27. Chambers (1986) describes this joining of technical expertise and commitment to the poor as the "new development professionalism."

28. Sarvodaya has been accused within the NGO community of having become a state within a state—a sort of parallel government operating a vast bureaucratic apparatus engaged in nearly every aspect of Sri Lankan village and national life—that so dominates the scene that it inhibits the development of a dynamic, pluralistic voluntary sector. BRAC has been engaged in a fundamental reexamination of its strategy in an effort to reduce its direct operational presence and serve in more clearly catalytic roles in the transformation of national credit, poultry, health, and education systems. BRAC is a leading candidate to demonstrate that it is possible for a NGO to be big and to be an innovative social catalyst.

29. Sheldon Annis (1988) describes the processes by which grass-roots people's organizations in Latin American are forming themselves into networks that are gradually transforming the institutional structures of numerous countries in the region.

30. The availability of knowledge and expert resources in the field of NGO management is growing rapidly. Research centers like the Program on Nonprofit Organizations at the Yale Institution for Social and Policy Studies, the Management Division of Independent Sector, and the NGO Management Network of the International Council of Voluntary Agencies are potential resources for improving the management of voluntary organizations. More research on the special strategic and organizational problems of

development-oriented voluntary organizations is also becoming available, such as Brown and Covey (1987a and 1987b).

31. The Bangladesh Rural Advancement Committee insists that each project grant or contract routinely allocate 7 percent of the budget for staff development. We believe this is a sound policy responsible donors should honor and encourage other voluntary organizations to emulate. Ian Smillie (1988) has written an illuminating paper on the perverse funding policies of donors regarding NGOs and the debilitating consequences of the policies. This set of issues received extensive attention at a November 1988 meeting of the Development Assistance Committee of the Organization for Economic Cooperation and Development in Paris, resulting in recommendations that donors should be more willing to fund administrative overhead and staff development. See OECD (1989).

32. Another example comes from the Philippines, where Philippine Business for Social Progress (PBSP) has been engaged in a partnership with the Provincial Government of Negros Occidental and the National Bank of the Philippines in a local land reform initiative. Negros Occidental is a sugar-growing province that suffered economic devastation as a result of a drop in sugar prices. Hardest hit were the families who worked on the sugar estates. They were among the poorest families even before the decline. After the decline their conditions were truly desperate. Many of the estate owners who had mortgaged their lands during better times were not able to meet mortgage payments after the fall. Large tracts of land were foreclosed by the National Bank. PBSP was invited by the provincial government to form a development partnership with itself and the bank to transfer these foreclosed lands to otherwise landless laborers. PBSP is responsible for developing the procedures and training the provincial development staff, as well as the staff of other voluntary organizations in Negros.

33. For further discussion of development partnerships, see Brown (forthcoming).

34. The Lembaga Studi Pembangunan (LSP), an Indonesian voluntary organization, served as a catalyst for a market development project in Samarinda, Kalimantan, Indonesia, involving local government, a private developer, and an association of small traders. Concerned that a new market development might displace a group of small traders, the LSP brought together the key actors in an arrangement involving what the LSP refers to as multistrata (social strata) land use. Local government responded with a zoning requirement that obligated the developer to allocate a portion of the land to small traders. The commercial developer financed and implemented the project. The LSP assisted the developer with the design and organized the vendors to negotiate their contract and manage their space in the development. The LSP has subsequently promoted a variety of other such urban development partnerships in housing and commercial projects that benefit the poor, all on a commercially viable basis using local public and private financing.

35. This holds at least for donor assessments regarding support for recipient country NGOs. Developed country NGOs present a somewhat different situation. To the extent that they are perceived by the donor as a political constituency able to influence legislative action on the donor's own budgets, the donor's interest in NGOs is also likely to be conditioned by unspoken political criteria that may equal or outweigh its professed concern for economic efficiency.

36. See Bratton (1989) for extensive documentation. Each of these forms of control are widely observed in Asia as well.

37. In this situation the interests of pluralism are likely to be best served where responsibilities for the registration and monitoring of different categories of NGOs and

POs is divided among a number of different agencies. This often gives the NGO or PO more than one option if a particular agency proves overly restrictive.

38. At the time of this writing delays of many months in government approval of some foreign donor-funded NGO grants was threatening the very survival of the prospective recipient organizations in Bangladesh.

39. Tandon (1987) notes that Marxist political parties commonly believe that any organizing for the poor and powerless should be done under the party's banner on the theory that the party is the vanguard of the people. Since the party represents the interests of the masses, there is, by the Marxist logic, no need for any other autonomous, independent structure to represent their interests.

40. Witjes (1987) provides a detailed description of how this process has progressed in various sectors in Indonesia.

41. The YPPSE in the Banjarnegara District of Central Java in Indonesia was formed by local government officials who found that working within governmental procedures and budget constraints made it all but impossible to respond in effective ways to actual community needs. They formed an NGO that could receive external donor funds specifically to give themselves needed freedom of action outside the constraints of government. The people involved were in fact value-driven and used the resulting freedom well. Yet in a workshop exploring the experience and its implications for local government-NGO collaboration, even some government officials expressed concern that YPPSE's special position with government may have resulted in its attempting to coordinate the work of other NGOs in the region and may possibly have inadvertently limited their freedom of action. See Iffrig and Korten (1988).

42. Depending on the nature of their charters, DONGOs may enjoy more independence than do GONGOs—if the donor understands the true nature of the voluntary sector and as a consequence takes measures to ensure such freedom. For example, LDAP in Thailand, a DONGO created by the Canadian International Development Agency (CIDA), seems to enjoy considerable freedom in defining a mission consistent with the value commitments of its leadership and with a social catalyst role.

43. Even when the DONGO handles only the funds of a single donor, problems can arise, not so much from the exercise of donor control as from the fact that inordinate influence over the indigenous NGO community may be placed in the hands of the local individuals who control the DONGO and its funds. This can create substantial destructive dissension within an NGO community, as resulted from a well-intentioned USAID initiative in Kenya.

44. This situation has arisen in Bangladesh, with serious consequences for the functioning of the NGO consortium body there.

45. Donors can do true voluntary organizations a great disservice if they fail to recognize the difference between these organizations and true NGOs. Two U.N. donor agencies named the Indonesian government-sponsored women's GONGO described earlier the outstanding NGO in Indonesia. Such actions send a signal to governments that international donors cannot tell the difference between a GONGO and a real NGO or that they applaud government's action in filling that institutional space with government-controlled organizations, therefore clearing the way for governmental control of the sector free from any fear of external repercussions.

46. Some donors in the Philippines have been shocked to find that some of the more "liberal" NGOs they were funding were channeling a portion of their finances to the armed insurgency attempting to topple the post-Marcos democratic government. These organizations were driven by values—but not necessarily values the donors shared.

47. We have been asked: Will this ensure that funds will flow where they are required, as with the market? The issues here are complex and the answer must be no, there is no such assurance. Yet at the same time, the question can really be answered only with another question: "Required" by whose definition or assessment? It is commonly assumed that governments represent the public interest in answering such questions. That is a demonstrably false premise. Governments represent the interests of the people who control them, and in nondemocratic countries the interests so represented may be quite narrow. It is also relevant to the argument that governments have numerous options for action on their priorities. For government to pursue those options by setting the priorities for the voluntary sector is to deny the distinctive nature of that sector. At the same time there is no contradiction in government choosing to fund nonprofit public service contractors to pursue government's definition of the public good. But that action should not be confused with providing support and encouragement for the voluntary sector.
48. This is not to negate the need for first-hand data collection as well. Situations are changing at a rapid rate and it would not be desirable to base conclusions only on historical data.

# 4

# Interactions between Nongovernmental Organizations, Governments, and the World Bank: Evidence from Bank Projects

*Lawrence F. Salmen and A. Paige Eaves*

With growing awareness of the limitations of government has come an increasing recognition of the contribution of NGOs to development. As World Bank President Barber Conable observed in his address to the Bank's Board of Governors in Berlin:

> *Government policies and public programs play a critical role in poverty alleviation. But governments cannot do everything. Nongovernment organizations in many developing countries have enormous potential for flexible and effective action. I have encouraged Bank staff to initiate a broadened dialogue with NGOs....I hope and fully expect that this collaboration will continue and flourish.*[1]

Bank Senior Vice President for Operations Moeen Qureshi stressed the importance of Bank-NGO collaboration for "more effective...efforts to eliminate mass poverty" in the keynote address to the 1988 annual conference of the Washington Chapter of the Society for International Development.[2] Increased interest in NGOs is evident in the work of bilateral and multilateral donors. In 1988, the OECD published *Voluntary Aid for Development*, a survey of NGO activities (OECD 1988). In July 1987, the Asian Development Bank approved a policy paper to enable cooperation with NGOs (OECD 1988). Independent research centers such as the North-South Institute and the Institute for Development Research also study NGOs (Brodhead, Herbert-Copley, and Lambert 1988;

Brown and Korten 1989). And a supplementary issue of *World Development* in 1987 was devoted entirely to NGO issues.

Within the Bank, Michael Cernea's *Nongovernmental Organizations and Local Development* was one of the first published attempts to deal systematically with NGOs as development institutions. He concluded that "the essence of the NGO approach is not to induce development financially, but to mobilize people into organized structures of voluntary group action for self-reliance and self-development" (Cernea 1988,7). This recognition has contributed to subsequent Bank efforts to develop effective partnerships with NGOs.

In August 1989, the Bank issued Operational Directive 14.70 on collaboration with NGOs. Its purpose is to set out a framework for involving NGOs in Bank-supported projects. The Directive defines NGOs as being "entirely or largely independent of government, and characterized primarily by humanitarian or cooperative rather than commercial objectives." After listing advantages and constraints of working with NGOs, the Directive sets forth types of collaboration with NGOs organized primarily by phase of the project cycle, as follows:

- *Analysis of development issues.* Bank staff and governments can learn from NGO assessments of official development programs, especially when NGOs relate concerns of low-income groups. (Adviser)
- *Project identification.* NGO knowledge of intended beneficiaries and appropriate technology can be tapped. (Adviser) Small NGO programs may become models for large-scale Bank-sponsored projects. (Adviser/Designer)
- *Project design.* NGOs may work as consultants to the Bank-financed project during planning stages. (Adviser/Designer)
- *Project financing.* NGOs may cofinance a project, or activities complementary to the project. (Cofinancier)
- *Project implementation.* NGOs may serve as brokers between government and local beneficiaries, organize communities, make project-financed credits available to low-income groups, be contracted by the Borrower to implement a project component, and so on. (Implementor)
- *Monitoring and evaluation.* As outside observers NGOs can often provide assistance as objective project evaluators. (Evaluator)

The International Economic Relations Division of the External Affairs Department (EXTIE) has primary responsibility for developing the Bank's policy toward NGOs. EXTIE also serves as a general liaison between NGOs and the Bank and as Bank Secretariat to the NGO-World Bank Committee. The Public Sector Management and Private Sector Development Division of the Country Economics Department (CECPS) resolved in discussions with EXTIE to undertake this review of Bank project experiences with NGOs with a particular focus on the institutional perspective. The objective is to assist Bank staff by contributing to the refinement of policy and the provision of operational guidance for future NGO-related work.

This chapter presents the universe of Bank projects with NGO involvement. It introduces a typology of NGOs delineated along a public-private continuum. It next presents issues that arose in analysis of a sample of 24 projects, based on information drawn primarily from reviews of the files, interviews with Bank and NGO staff, and, for four case studies, field visits. The last sections discuss experiences with coordinating Bank-borrower-NGO relationships and offer conclusions and policy recommendations.

The definition of NGOs warrants greater attention. Bank staff did not express a consensus on what defines an NGO. Until 1983, there was no Bank statement that clearly and comprehensively defined NGOs. A review of the literature reveals that the majority of analysts conclude, with Michael Cernea (1988), that "the term itself offers such a broad umbrella for a kaleidoscopic collection of organizations that attempts at simple definitions are quickly rendered meaningless" (9). While we concur with the definition quoted above from the Bank's Operational Manual Statement on collaboration with NGOs, we offer this refinement: NGOs are institutions in neither the public nor the private sectors whose goals are primarily value-driven rather than profit-driven.

This definition parallels one line of current thinking on NGOs, which highlights the particular importance of value-driven organizations. Such entities can be considered to constitute the voluntary sector and distinguished from both the governmental organizations that comprise the public sector and the profit-driven organizations of the private sector. As L. David Brown and David C. Korten explain in Chapter 3 of this volume, voluntary organizations "are driven primarily by shared values" (50). This value distinction is crucial to appreciating the kind of contribution NGOs can make to development work. The values of those NGOs of interest to development need to be consonant with bettering the opportunities of people, particularly the poor, for self-fulfillment.

This chapter is concerned with NGOs that work with the Bank, their roles, contributions, and limitations. The framework for discussion, formulated from a review of operational work, is oriented toward the more pragmatic issues associated with involving NGOs in Bank-sponsored projects.

## Survey of the universe

This review provides an analytic overview of the 218 Bank projects involving NGOs, classifying them by sector, region, and form of collaboration (Table 4.1). The universe of 218 Bank projects involving NGOs was taken from early records of the Bank-NGO liaison office in EXTIE, six progress reports of the NGO-World Bank Committee,[3] and other referrals made to CECPS during research.

Based on the known universe, Figure 4.1 shows the number of Bank projects involving NGOs from fiscal 1973 to fiscal 1988. With no discernible trends, Bank-NGO collaboration seems to have depended on the work of particularly motivated staff, the winning of an International Competitive Bidding contract by an NGO consulting firm, or personal connections between Bank and NGO staff. However, the 1988 progress report on Bank-NGO cooperation notes a trend of expansion in Bank-NGO relations: there was a sharp rise in the number of projects

**Table 4.1 World Bank projects involving NGOs, by sector and region, 1973-88**

| *Sector* | *Asia* | *Africa* | *Europe, Middle East, and North Africa* | *Latin America and the Caribbean* | *Total* | *Percentage* |
|---|---|---|---|---|---|---|
| Agriculture | 30 | 47 | 7 | 19 | 103 | 47 |
| Education and training | 2 | 13 | 1 | 4 | 20 | 9 |
| Population and health | 8 | 11 | 2 | 5 | 26 | 12 |
| Industry and energy | 5 | 10 | 4 | 3 | 22 | 10 |
| Infrastructure and urban development | 6 | 27 | 2 | 6 | 41 | 19 |
| Relief and compensation | 0 | 3 | 0 | 3 | 6 | 3 |
| Total | 51 | 111 | 16 | 40 | 218 | .. |
| Percentage | 24 | 51 | 7 | 18 | .. | 100 |

*Source:* World Bank data.

under preparation in which Bank staff see potential for NGO involvement. And the quality of NGO involvement in some current activities has improved.

Discussions held with more than 50 Bank professional staff during this review revealed some imprecision in this universe. Many projects recorded by the former (pre-reorganization) Bank-NGO liaison office as involving NGOs had in fact only peripheral association with NGOs, and the office makes no claim of completeness. Other projects with significant involvement were not reported to any central office; there was no requirement for Bank project officers to do so. In addition, there has been widespread confusion among Bank staff as to what constitutes an NGO. For example, staff who considered community associations to be para-government bodies, or contractor NGOs to be private, profit-generating firms, would not have reported their projects as having NGO involvement. Thus, because of the nonsystematic reporting and the problem of definition, the universe of NGO-Bank collaborative projects, while useful, is only approximate.[4]

## *Regional distribution*

NGOs have worked with the Bank in just over half of all countries with Bank-sponsored projects. A breakdown by country (Table 4.2) shows that five held one-third of the projects: India (23), Indonesia (14), Zaire (10), Kenya (nine), and Cameroon (eight). The list includes projects in which NGOs took part (often at their own initiative) as policy advocates; thus not all projects involved formal contractual agreements between borrower and NGO. For example, at least two projects in India (Narmada/Sardar Sarovar and Singrauli Power) and one in

Indonesia (Transmigration) attracted critical international attention generated by advocacy NGOs. Since these NGOs ultimately affected project implementation, and since informal Bank-NGO dialogue continues, such projects are said to have NGO involvement.

*Sectoral distribution*

Nearly half the 218 projects reviewed were in agriculture. NGOs work to design and implement low-cost credit schemes in more than 30 rural development projects; more than 35 NGOs plan and implement training programs for extension workers, managers, and farmers; some 21 organizations work with the Bank to strengthen agricultural and livestock cooperatives; and eight NGOs assist with the construction and management of irrigation systems.

Many of the projects in the infrastructure and urban development sector involve the construction of homes or community facilities. NGOs prepare sites and services, organize credit schemes to enable individuals to borrow money for homes, build schools and health centers, and train community members in construction, maintenance, and community management. In 15 of the infrastructure projects, consultants from the World Organization for Rehabilitation through Training (ORT) worked with government to improve the construction and maintenance of transportation systems.

Several of the population and health projects, such as the Kenya Second Population Project, pioneered in introducing preventive health measures, family planning information, and education to the population via indigenous and grassroots NGOs.

In the industry and energy sector, local and international NGOs have helped small- and medium-scale entrepreneurs by making credit accessible and by training businesses in management and marketing techniques in 14 projects. In several power projects, the Washington-based National Rural Electrification Cooperative Association (NRECA) assisted in developing urban and rural power systems. In a very different type of NGO involvement, policy-advocacy NGOs over-

**Figure 4.1 World Bank projects involving NGOs, fiscal 1973-88**

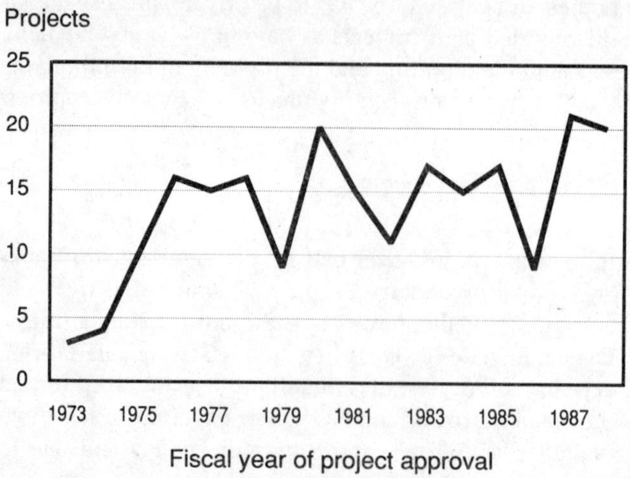

**Table 4.2 World Bank projects involving NGOs, by country and region, 1973-88**

| *Region/country* | *Number of projects* |
|---|---|
| *Africa* | |
| Benin | 1 |
| Burkina Faso | 3 |
| Burundi | 5 |
| Botswana | 6 |
| Cameroon | 8 |
| Central African Republic | 2 |
| Chad | 2 |
| Côte d'Ivoire | 1 |
| Equatorial Guinea | 1 |
| Gambia, The | 1 |
| Ghana | 2 |
| Guinea | 3 |
| Kenya | 9 |
| Lesotho | 5 |
| Liberia | 6 |
| Madagascar | 1 |
| Malawi | 3 |
| Mali | 3 |
| Niger | 7 |
| Nigeria | 5 |
| Rwanda | 4 |
| São Tomé and Principe | 1 |
| Senegal | 6 |
| Sierra Leone | 4 |
| Somalia | 1 |
| Swaziland | 3 |
| Tanzania | 1 |
| Togo | 1 |
| Uganda | 2 |
| Zaire | 10 |
| Zambia | 2 |
| Zimbabwe | 2 |
| Total | 111 |
| *Asia* | |
| Bangladesh | 3 |
| India | 23 |
| *Asia (cont.)* | |
| Indonesia | 14 |
| Korea, Republic of | 1 |
| Malaysia | 1 |
| Nepal | 2 |
| Philippines | 4 |
| Sri Lanka | 1 |
| Thailand | 2 |
| Total | 51 |
| *Europe, Middle East, and North Africa* | |
| Egypt | 5 |
| Jordan | 1 |
| Morocco | 2 |
| Pakistan | 1 |
| Tunisia | 1 |
| Turkey | 3 |
| Yemen Arab Republic | 3 |
| Total | 16 |
| *Latin America and the Caribbean* | |
| Bahamas | 1 |
| Bolivia | 4 |
| Brazil | 17 |
| Colombia | 4 |
| Dominican Republic | 2 |
| El Salvador | 2 |
| Guatemala | 1 |
| Haiti | 4 |
| Jamaica | 2 |
| Mexico | 2 |
| Paraguay | 1 |
| Total | 40 |

*Source:* World Bank data.

came substantial resistance from local authorities to bring about more equitable treatment of the poor in some of the larger projects, including the Itaparica Dam project in Brazil and the Narmada projects in India.

In one-third of the 20 education and training projects, NGOs have contributed to the planning and construction of schools and centers for adult education. In the other projects, NGOs worked with training components: developing teaching skills, improving curriculum, and organizing literacy and skills courses for adults.

Only six projects involve NGOs in the administration of relief and compensation and poverty alleviation programs. These are mounted to mitigate suffering during a period of structural adjustment intended to overcome national economic and financial crisis. NGOs have effectively reached the rural and urban poor, managing emergency nutrition programs, employment-generation programs, and village health projects, among others. Though compensation and poverty-relief programs of this type are only a small portion of Bank-NGO cooperation, the role of NGOs in this kind of activity is expanding. Both the Bank and NGOs have identified a need to collaborate on structural adjustment lending—not only to alleviate the impact on the poor, but to help design lending strategies that are more likely to better conditions for the low-income strata.

*Distribution by constituency and project phase*

The Bank has broken down NGOs in two ways—by constituency and by phase in the project cycle (Tables 4.3 and 4.4). Categorizing NGOs by constituency—international, indigenous/intermediary, or grass-roots—is a generally accepted approach:

- *International NGOs*—organizations typically originating in developed countries with widespread activities
- *Indigenous/intermediary NGOs*—groups organized at a national or subnational level, with almost all activities centered in the home country

**Table 4.3 World Bank projects involving NGOs, by type of NGO, 1973-88**

| *Region* | *International NGOs* | *Indigenous intermediary NGOs* | *Grass-roots NGOs* |
|---|---|---|---|
| Africa | 70 | 28 | 30 |
| Asia | 16 | 25 | 22 |
| Latin America and the Caribbean | 11 | 17 | 17 |
| Europe, Middle East, and North Africa | 7 | 5 | 6 |
| Total | 104 | 75 | 75 |

*Note:* Projects may involve more than one type of NGO.
*Source:* World Bank data.

**Table 4.4 Regional distribution of World Bank projects involving NGOs, by phase in project cycle, 1973-88**

| *Phase* | *Asia* | *Africa* | *Europe, Middle East, and North Africa* | *Latin America and the Caribbean* | *Total* | *Percentage* |
|---|---|---|---|---|---|---|
| Adviser | 18 | 37 | 8 | 12 | 75 | 26.7 |
| Designer | 1 | 19 | 0 | 13 | 33 | 11.7 |
| Implementor | 41 | 78 | 12 | 31 | 162 | 57.7 |
| Evaluator | 0 | 1 | 0 | 0 | 1 | 0.4 |
| Cofinancier | 0 | 8 | 2 | 0 | 10 | 3.6 |
| Total | 60 | 143 | 22 | 56 | 281 | 100.1 |

*Note:* In many cases, NGOs are instrumental in more than one phase of the project cycle. This explains why the total exceeds 218. Percentages do not add to 100 because of rounding.
*Source:* World Bank data.

- *Grass-roots NGOs*—community- or village-level, member-run groups working to develop themselves politically and/or economically.

In addition, activity is classified by phase in the project cycle. Though an overview yields a very general summary of activity, some interesting observations emerged from pairing participation by NGO constituency with participation by phase in the project cycle.

- Of those NGOs serving in advisory capacities, more than three-fourths are international NGOs. Advisers include NGOs contracted by the borrower as consultants, as when NRECA consultants work with power companies to improve rural electrification systems. The category also includes groups that advise farmers on cooperative development and market identification. Advocacy NGOs that provide the Bank information are advisers though they are not contracted by the borrower or the Bank.
- All large-scale cofinanciers are international NGOs. Cofinanciers are NGOs that commit by contract to fund a specific percentage of project costs or a particular project component (for example, training for community development workers, heavy machinery for road construction). On a smaller scale, some projects require relatively small financial or in-kind contributions from NGOs receiving grants.
- Grass-roots organizations are primarily active in the implementation stages. Implementation covers a wide range: training, organizing community health or women's groups, building schools, and administering small-scale loans. Grass-roots NGOs (for example, village cooperatives and herdsmen's associations) may be responsible for purchasing veterinary supplies, maintaining an irrigation system, or disseminating health information. In Asia, Latin America and the Caribbean, and Europe, the Middle East, and North Africa, implementation is more often carried out by indigenous and grass-roots organizations than by inter-

national NGOs. For example, in Asia, seven projects include one or more international NGOs in implementation and 27 projects involve indigenous and grass-roots NGOs. In the universe of 218 projects, only three grass-roots NGOs were found to be active in planning.

## The public-private continuum

The highly diverse group of development-oriented NGOs fills a void between the public and private sectors, enabling people to participate more fully in both. The public sector is often unable effectively to reach lower-income populations, and the formal private sector has little incentive to involve itself with those who have no resources. NGOs help bridge gaps, for example, by organizing coalitions of disenfranchised individuals to influence the political process, or by strengthening their ability to participate in the private and public sectors by providing services in health, education, and training.

A potentially more useful way to view NGOs than by constituency or project phase is according to the function they serve in development work. NGOs are often multisectoral. Their activities sometimes span more than one phase of the project cycle and may extend to influencing policy.

No taxonomy does complete justice to the wide diversity of institutions known as NGOs. We see two major means for categorization, one the degree to which the NGOs' activities serve public (common good) vs. private (market-oriented) purposes, and the other the degree to which the NGO is directed toward the interests of its own membership vs. oriented to a constituency beyond itself. Figure 4.2 places our five functional NGO types along two continua, public-private (left to right) and inner vs. other-directed (top to bottom). Literal interpretation of this figure will find fault, as many NGOs defy easy categorization. Cooperatives may be directed more toward public than private goals, or community associations devoted more to what would normally be considered private (vegetable gardening, water provision) than public ends (representing community interests with higher government bodies). However, the general placement of categories in this figure is illustrative of NGOs reviewed. It is offered as a suggestive guide for operational work involving NGOs.

**Figure 4.2 Public-private NGO spectrum**

Our five functional types of NGOs are described as follows:

1. *Community associations.* These member-run organizations provide information, assistance, and leadership for local communities and sometimes help public institutions connect effectively with local needs. They may also represent at the local level special interests such as farmers, small businesses, or water users. Community associations are typically formed by persons who recognize that pooling resources enables the community to work on its own development.

2. *Policy-advocacy groups.* At local, national, and international levels, these groups are advocates for those who are otherwise politically and economically ineffective. Many emphasize environmental, health, and public safety issues. Policy-advocacy groups often come into conflict with government officials and feed into larger political processes. These NGOs frequently serve as catalysts for collective action among the poor in societies unaccustomed to such behavior.

• *Community level.* Political action at the community level is akin to that of a political party. Driven by the desire to correct actual (and perceived) injustices, politically active community groups are often antigovernment and subject to frequent repression.

• *Indigenous/intermediary.* Members of these groups may not be members of the disenfranchised communities themselves. Unions and religious organizations are examples of indigenous NGOs that represent the powerless in fights for policy changes.

• *International.* International advocacy groups try to influence policy changes at national and international levels. Their activities usually center on specific issues such as the environment, minority rights, women, and child survival.

3. *Service-provider/intermediary.* These organizations, which can be international or indigenous, may help people to take advantage of government-sponsored programs or help donors and government to assess local needs. Through sharing values with both beneficiaries and government, the NGOs may educate to the benefit of both. They may assume service-provider roles, offering health care or education where government services do not reach. They also foster private sector development through credit administration and management and technical training for small-scale enterprises where these are not accessible to low-income people. While these NGOs may run income-generating enterprises to help support their activities, most are not-for-profit. Motivated not by the security and prestige of government work nor by the profits of private enterprise, staff and supporters tend to be drawn to the service-provider/intermediary NGO by an altruistic motivation to create an environment favorable to development.

4. *Contractors.* These NGOs become involved in Bank-sponsored projects as consultants to government agencies or financial institutions working to strengthen institutional capacity, or as contractors designated to construct roads, schools, and other public works. Though these NGOs often have activities other than contracting, many behave much like private contractors, often competing with private firms. Usually there are some differences: the NGO may be less tied to bottom-line profits, with income from sources other than contracting. This flexibility may manifest itself in a willingness to adapt operations to changing cir-

cumstances or to experiment with different approaches. NGO contractors often charge less because of lower overhead. They may be more effective than a private firm in using local labor and resources or in involving the community in planning. Most maintain a not-for-profit status, though consultants are paid market, or close to market, rates for their services.

5. *Cooperatives.* Defined as "voluntary organizations set up to protect and generate economic benefits for their members" (Cernea 1988, 13-14), cooperatives are formed when a task, such as obtaining credit, cannot be accomplished by an individual. Cooperatives distribute profit as dividends to members. They are often run on the principle of one vote per person. While many cooperatives are, in fact, full-fledged private enterprises, those with which development donors are concerned are generally dependent for an extended time on project-supplied concessional credit, inputs, and management training.

When the universe is viewed through the continuum, the type and the extent of NGO involvement are easier to understand and discuss (Tables 4.5 and 4.6). For example, we know that in 40 percent of the 218 projects, one or more service-provider/intermediary NGOs played significant roles as "brokers" between projects and beneficiaries. Looking at this group of 88 projects that involved service-provider/intermediary NGOs, we can observe patterns—in service-delivery capabilities, relationships with government and beneficiaries, and so on—more successfully than with "implementor" NGOs, which constitute an even more heterogeneous group of organizations and functions.

**Table 4.5 Frequency of NGO involvement in World Bank projects by type, as delineated by the "public-private" spectrum, and by region, 1973-88**

| | *Public-private continuum* | | | | |
|---|---|---|---|---|---|
| *Region* | *Community association* | *Policy-advocacy NGO* | *Service-provider/ intermediary NGO* | *Contractor* | *Cooperative* |
| Africa | 7 | 1 | 48 | 46 | 24 |
| Asia | 16 | 5 | 17 | 12 | 12 |
| Latin America and the Caribbean | 15 | 6 | 18 | 3 | 5 |
| Europe, Middle East, and North Africa | 4 | 0 | 5 | 7 | 4 |
| Total[a] | 42 | 12 | 88 | 68 | 45 |
| Percentage[b] | 19 (16) | 6 (5) | 40 (34) | 31 (27) | 21 (18) |

a. Since projects may involve more than one type of NGO, some may be double-counted across columns.
b. As a percentage of total projects in universe (218). Figures in parentheses are percentages of table total (255).
*Source:* World Bank data.

**Table 4.6 Frequency of NGO involvement in World Bank projects by type, as delineated by the "public-private" spectrum, and by sector, 1973-88**

| | *Public-private continuum* | | | | |
|---|---|---|---|---|---|
| *Sector* | *Community association* | *Policy-advocacy NGO* | *Service-provider/ intermediary NGO* | *Contractor* | *Cooperative* |
| Agriculture | 26 | 6 | 30 | 19 | 38 |
| Education and training | 2 | 0 | 8 | 10 | 0 |
| Population and health | 8 | 0 | 21 | 4 | 2 |
| Industry and energy | 0 | 3 | 5 | 13 | 2 |
| Infrastructure and urban development | 3 | 2 | 20 | 22 | 2 |
| Relief and compensation | 3 | 1 | 4 | 0 | 1 |
| Total[a] | 42 | 12 | 88 | 68 | 45 |
| Percentage[b] | 19 (16) | 6 (5) | 40 (34) | 31 (27) | 21 (18) |

a. Since projects may involve more than one type of NGO, some may be double-counted across columns.
b. As a percentage of total projects in universe (218). Figures in parentheses are percentages of table total (255).
*Source:* World Bank data.

Similarly, when we look at the involvement of cooperatives in projects, our focus immediately narrows from implementor to small, grass-roots organizations operating primarily in the agricultural sector in Africa. These numbers are more meaningful for framing issue discussions than for calibrating cross-regional comparisons: the predominance of African agricultural projects may be attributable to the generally greater number of such projects supported by the International Bank for Reconstruction and Development and the International Development Association. We have counted projects involving one or more cooperatives—the exact number involved (which ranges from more than 45 in the Bolivia Second Emergency Social Fund to some 5,000 in the India Dairy Development Project) was rarely available.

Of the 68 projects involving one or more contractor NGOs, over half are infrastructure or energy projects. This is probably because these types of projects are generally less in need of the brokering strengths of service-provider/intermediary NGOs and more in need of technical expertise. Though technical assistance from contractor NGOs is much the same as that from private sector contractors, experience shows that staff need to be aware of the differences (see section on sample findings).

While the public-private continuum categories do not contain homogeneous groups, they facilitate a sharper picture of NGO work with the Bank. The sample of 24 projects selected for in-depth analysis can be grouped along the spectrum, illustrating its utility (Figure 4.3).[5]

## Sample findings

Twenty-four projects were selected for intensive review roughly in numerical proportion to the universe—11 projects in Africa, six in Asia, five in Latin America and the Caribbean, and two in Europe, the Middle East, and North Africa. Many of these were selected because EXTIE and other Bank staff reported them as having particularly interesting outcomes. The sample is biased toward successful interactions, which should yield better insight. The sample also reflects the relative distribution by sector of projects with NGOs, with agricultural (10) and infrastructure and urban development (seven) projects predominating. The rest of the projects were selected to cover most types of Bank-NGO collaboration. Of the 24, four were chosen because of their controversiality—each having contributed to a change in either Bank or host-country policies on NGO, social, or environmental matters.

Projects were reviewed at the Bank. Four were also reviewed in the field through interviews with NGOs, beneficiaries, government officials, and knowledgeable Bank staff. Given the small size of the sample and the diversity of NGOs and development projects, lessons drawn from this review can only be inferential and suggestive of more general truths. Finally, as all 24 projects were either completed or well under way at the time of analysis, this is a retrospective review.

### *Community associations*

Of the 218 documented projects with NGO involvement, 42 (19 percent) involved one or more community associations. This small percentage may be a result of underreporting, as community associations were not at first included as NGOs by the former Bank-NGO liaison staff. Of the 42 projects, at least eight were designed to have community associations coordinated by intermediary NGOs. Over half the 42 are in the agricultural sector, including four community forestry projects and eight irrigation schemes involving water users' associations. Eight population and health projects depend on grass-roots NGOs to disseminate family planning and health care information and services. Of the 24 projects reviewed for this study, five incorporated community associations, often in conjunction with other types of NGOs, particularly service-provider/intermediary NGOs.

**Goals for community association involvement in projects.** A primary goal for grass-roots NGO involvement in a Bank project is sustainability. As an Operations Evaluation Department (1985) review of sustainability notes, aligning project objectives and activities with local needs and aspirations appears necessary for project success. This points to the need for community involve-

Figure 4.3 Public-private spectrum of NGOs involved in World Bank projects

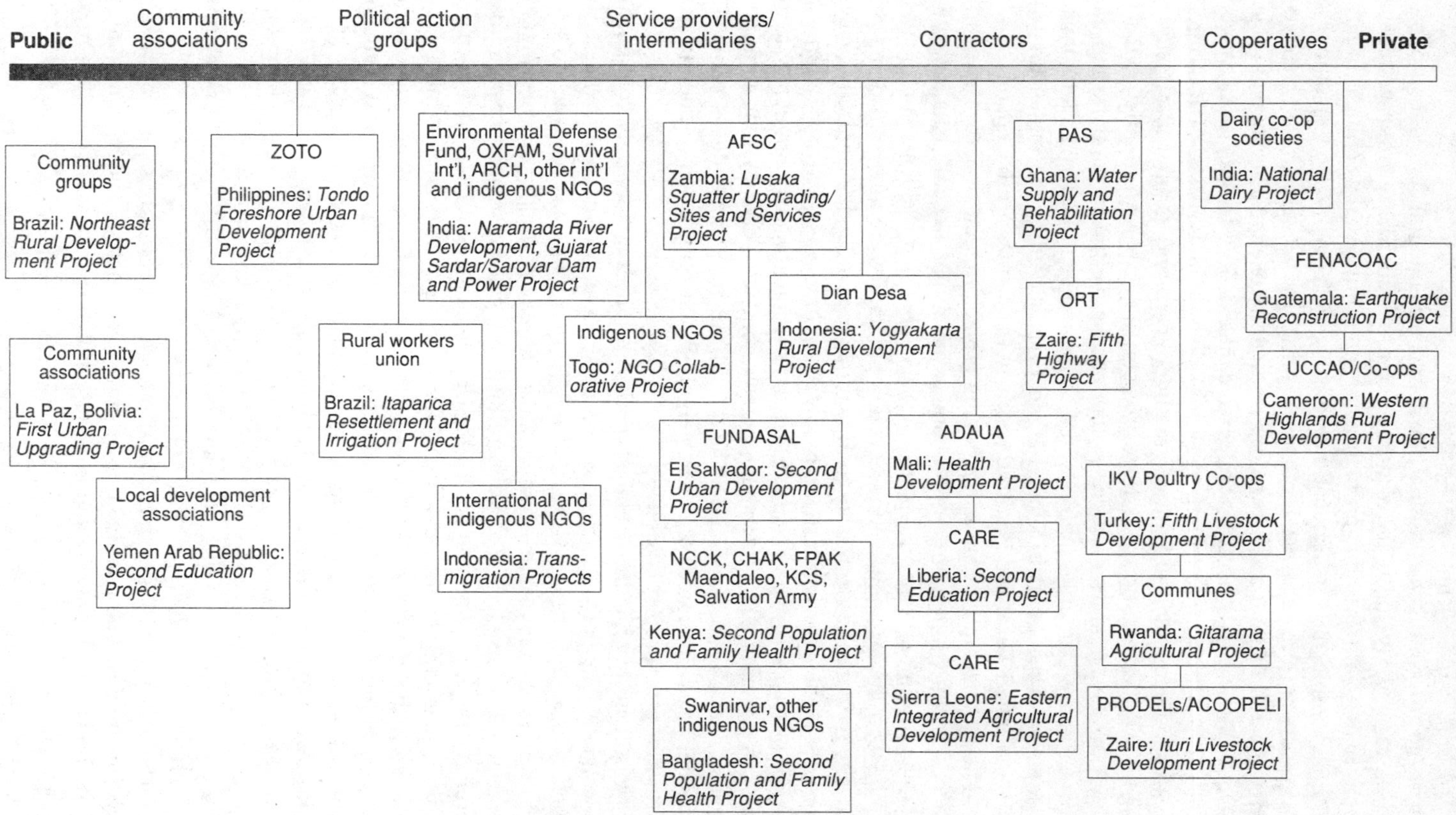

ment and grass-roots institutional development as integral components of project work, particularly during the planning phase, as beneficiary groups will be more inclined to organize around problems and opportunities they regard as important.

For example, the First Education Project in the Yemen Arab Republic showed practically no effect at the local level, primarily because it was planned and implemented without assessing rural community needs.[6] The Second Project is successful, primarily because it integrated the existing, country-wide network of Local Development Associations (LDAs),[7] community-based NGOs, into curriculum development for District Training Centers and introduced a Basic Training Fund for LDA-proposed village projects. Beneficiaries are satisfied that their needs are heard and met, there is continued government support, and the increased sense of mutual help inspired communities to undertake additional development projects. This Second Project has served as the model for similar LDA-oriented Third and Fourth Projects in the Yemen Arab Republic.

The La Paz, Bolivia, urban upgrading project yielded similar results through successful integration of neighborhood associations. Recent visits indicate that community improvements are still in place—but that residents continue to upgrade their homes and facilities. Their communities are now considered part of the city proper. The Zambia upgrading project, in which the Bank contracted the services of the American Friends Service Committee (AFSC) as an intermediary NGO, provides further evidence that the participation of community associations in planning and implementation contributes to reaching long-term project goals. Though the "mutual self-help" did not turn out quite as planned, the transition was a smooth one, and neighborhoods continued to undertake joint activities after project completion.

Sustainability means that development activities are not only continued, but become self-supporting. Thus cost recovery is a high-priority objective for community association involvement. If public authorities can recover most of the costs of a social investment, they are better able to extend the same program on a larger scale. As the La Paz project illustrates, when beneficiaries participate in project design and implementation through the community association, many are willing to contribute to costs. The resulting sense of ownership stimulates cooperation with the project. For example, as upgrading began, beneficiaries entered into a contract to pay their share of costs with nonindexed pesos. With the onset of inflation, which ranged from two to five digits during the project, HAM-BIRF (the project implementation unit) held meetings with beneficiaries and renegotiated their obligations to pay in U.S. dollar-equivalent terms. Beneficiaries agreed, even though they had no legal obligation to do so, primarily because they felt that the project was benefiting them and because HAM-BIRF tried to ensure their understanding of the repayment conditions.

Thus, community associations of intended beneficiaries have been seen as instrumental for the mobilization of opinion and action, and as communication links between community and government that can translate a project message from one to the other and help ensure that project commitments, such as cost recovery, are carried out.

**Analysis of interaction.** Successful integration of community associations rests on their involvement in project planning. The survey of the universe shows that very few grass-roots NGOs (both community associations and cooperatives) were active participants in the planning phase. An oft-mentioned reason is the fear that beneficiaries' expectations may be raised beyond the project's capability to deliver. It is also time-consuming to identify and consult local groups, who may be unaware of the options and unable to come quickly to a consensus. The La Paz and Zambia upgrading projects and the Yemen Arab Republic education projects indicate, however, that the benefits of involving grass-roots NGOs in planning outweigh its risks.

Though specific implementation procedures are best devised on a case-by-case basis, certain contractual and funding procedures have proven successful with community associations. The community-contract approach used by HAM-BIRF in La Paz, for example, is potentially replicable. A contract delineated the one of three upgrading options the community had selected, the amount each individual would owe, and the time each would commit to community projects. The community having the greatest number of residents signing up for the program and paying in advance for works earned priority on HAM-BIRF's list of communities to be upgraded. By requiring consensus and commitment before beginning, HAM-BIRF ensured the residents' understanding of and participation in the upgrading. This approach introduces peer pressure to induce residents to adhere to the terms of the contract. A community contract also helps to convince utility companies to extend services to target areas. When local political leaders promised free services (which never came), whole communities withdrew—at least temporarily. Since agreements had been made with communities and not individuals, the municipality was not bound to honor contracts with owners who did not choose to withdraw.

The proposal mechanism of the Yemen Arab Republic Education Projects has been particularly successful. The Local Development Associations of each village propose needed training courses and identify villagers who may serve as instructors or resource persons. Proposals are reviewed by District Councils, who advise on and monitor the District Training Centers that provide support services for courses. The LDAs are represented at all levels, including the National Board. Villagers are satisfied that their needs are being met through this process, and the government, both district and national, has expressed continued enthusiasm.

The Northeast Rural Development Projects in Brazil have taken an entirely different approach, in many ways similar to the Grass-roots Development Initiative in Togo. Both projects establish a grant-funding pool available to grass-roots NGOs, which have substantial flexibility as to the types of projects they will undertake. Though there have been a number of small shortcomings in both projects, two primary issues arose that are cross-regional and cross-sectoral:

- *Analysis of institutional capacity.* Problems with pilot projects in Togo indicated that local NGOs needed not only project funds but also funds and training for institutional strengthening. The revised policy is to analyze NGO institutional capacity and provide assistance where necessary before disbursing project grants. In Brazil, $200 million has been earmarked for the Support to Small Rural Communities Component, initially scheduled for disbursement within three years. Many of the implementing agencies, primarily rural workers unions and cooperatives, have not had the absorptive capacity to spend these funds effectively. Training and extra staffing have not solved the problem. Some intermediate NGOs have refused to collaborate in what they see as forcing funds on unprepared communities. Among other steps taken to alleviate this pressure, the project has been extended to eight years (Hennin and Parel 1989).

• *Identification of legitimate NGOs.* Creating selection criteria that both encourage legitimate community association initiative and discourage the formation of "ghost NGOs" (those formed to use the benefits of NGO status for commercial or political purposes, and which do little work at the grass-roots level) has proven difficult. For example, recent Bank observers in Northeast Brazil noted that in several cases, local government authorities had formed "NGOs" and used funds to cultivate patronage. Similar problems occurred in Togo. NGO representatives to the NGO-World Bank Committee have expressed fear that growing official interest in NGOs in general will stimulate a proliferation of these illegitimate NGOs.

**Context.** The identification of grass-roots NGOs includes analysis of the comparative strengths of existing community associations within their social, political, and economic contexts. The projects reviewed for this study illustrate the pitfalls of not doing so.

In the Zambia Upgrading Project of the American Friends Service Committee (AFSC), the field director helped with project design. The local government proposed implementation through ward development committees, which were delineated without respect to traditional clan units. The AFSC's project officers chose instead to work through local branches of UNIP, the national political party. This proved to be more workable because local UNIP units were composed of traditional village-type groups with village leaders, and UNIP had been active in social development projects when the government had shown little interest.

While this arrangement worked well for involving communities in implementation, its limitations became apparent when the time came to enforce repayment. UNIP leaders were unwilling to play such a role, and the ward councilors were too uninvolved for the project unit to motivate them as collectors. Many councilors campaigned against enforcement to gain political advantage. Cost recovery and maintenance were severely weakened because insufficient attention was given to the city council.

The La Paz community associations were thought to be representative of all residents and thus an effective vehicle for addressing the needs of the poor. However, while they were effective as intermediaries between the project and homeowners, an assessment of the beneficiaries revealed that many of the poorer residents, among whom renters outnumbered owners three to one, had been entirely overlooked. Although infrastructural improvements had not been made available to many renters, their rents had increased anyway because of the growing desirability of the area. Those renters who were not given access to water supplies or toilet facilities continued to use the river, undermining efforts to improve sanitation (Salmen 1987). Determining what the community associations' positions are vis-à-vis other area residents can enable the project to promote development with equity and to increase project effectiveness.

More than the usual amount of resources were devoted to assessing the existing community association network in the Yemen Arab Republic Education Project. Designers found that the Local Development Associations represented the interests of all members of a community, even though the leaders tended to be village elite. Designers also worked to ensure that institutional arrangements would facilitate the LDA-government relationship.

*Policy-advocacy groups*

Policy-advocacy groups are NGOs that bring to the attention of policymakers issues such as the environment or the rights of people politically and economically disenfranchised. Only 12 of the 218 projects record the involvement of these NGOs. However, since these projects have been particularly controversial for the Bank, the sample of 24 includes four of these. In all four cases, the NGOs have influenced changes in project implementation. As watchdogs of Bank and government planning and enforcement of environmental, resettlement, and upgrading policies, they have worked to focus international attention on actual and perceived injustices. Many work by lobbying Bank and government (donor and borrower) officials, the international press, and their own constituencies. Policy-advocacy NGOs have in some cases provided informal advice to the Bank on an ongoing basis. However, their primary stance, as regards both Bank and borrowing governments, may be better described as confrontational than collaborative.

**Advantages of involvement of policy-advocacy NGOs.** Interviews with Bank staff revealed three distinct types of contribution from policy-advocacy NGOs: their contributions to planning and design; the watchdog or monitoring roles they played during implementation; and their stimuli to corrective action. All three increased projects' responsiveness to the natural environment and to people unable to defend themselves (for example, impoverished groups threatened with resettlement as the result of a Bank-supported project).

Many agree on the importance of bringing advocacy NGOs into project design—rather than in the middle of implementation, when their input will likely consist of criticism of plans gone awry. In the Itaparica area of Northeast Brazil, the indigenous rural workers' union (Polo Sindical) was extremely effective in representing the interests of people to be resettled as the result of a dam project. Bank staff turned to the union, as well as to cooperatives, churches, and other representative organizations, to gain insight into the opinions of the affected population. As the union had developed technical expertise to supplement its political force, project staff found union contributions to a technical dialogue quite useful. Informal consultations continued throughout appraisal and implementation.

In the Tondo Foreshore Development Project in the Philippines, an indigenous advocacy organization forced its way into the planning process. Zone One Tondo Organization (ZOTO) was a people's movement consisting of 113 community organizations and supported by neighboring federations, Philippine church groups, and some international advocacy groups. The Philippine government had tried repeatedly since the 1960s to replace the squatter settlement with an industrial center, and ZOTO had repeatedly organized sufficient protest to delay these plans. ZOTO eventually also appealed to the World Bank, thereby helping to influence a change in project plans—from industrial development to squatter upgrading. The resulting project had a far more beneficial impact than the initially planned mass resettlement would have.

Advocacy NGOs intervening as watchdogs of implementation have uncovered problems that might otherwise have gone undetected during supervision missions. A good example comes from the Narmada River Development/ Sardar-Sarovar Dam and Power Project, where local NGOs reported to the Bank a "reinterpretation" of the land compensation agreement once it was put into action locally. Although the record clearly stated that two hectares of land should be given to each family, including the landless and encroachers, the government of Gujarat (or at least one local official) interpreted this to mean two hectares to each previous landholding. This would have given even extended families with three adult sons and families a total of two hectares, when they may have jointly worked fifteen hectares before. Faced with an NGO-organized uprising and tension with the Bank, the Chief Minister publicly accepted responsibility for the problem and reassured those who were resettled and the Bank that the government intended to cooperate in every way. While friction continues between those who were resettled and the government, the advocacy role that local NGOs played clearly helped prevent an inherently difficult situation from becoming even worse.

Similarly, Polo Sindical prodded Brazilian officials into action in the Itaparica Project. As the flooding date approached and resettlement plans had yet to be enacted, the union orchestrated a strike at the dam site, bringing the project to a standstill until demands were met. Though existing plans already fulfilled 95 percent of the union's demands, the union had not been informed and was thus reacting to plans from six months earlier. The CHESF (the Brazilian power utility subsidiary with implementation responsibility) had withheld the revised plans to prevent them from becoming an election year issue. The result of the strike was a contract between the unions and the CHESF, which created an atmosphere of constructive NGO-government cooperation that facilitated implementation (despite ongoing difficulties in providing irrigation to the resettled population).

A conclusion that came out of most interviews related to these projects is that advocacy NGOs have brought much useful information to the Bank, enabling project staff to design projects that are more responsive to social and environmental concerns. There is consensus on the need to involve these groups in project planning, implementation, and possibly evaluation. The indigenous advocacy groups in particular have shown themselves to be fairly reliable sources of information concerning beneficiaries' concerns, technical knowledge of local conditions, and the degree to which national governments' commitments to detailed resettlement and environmental protection plans are carried out by officials at state and local levels.

Thus, while policy-advocacy NGOs often bring uninvited criticism to a project, they also provide useful information and motivate borrower governments in ways that Bank staff cannot.

**Interaction.** While criticism from advocacy groups has contributed to constructive adaptations of project components, it has also generated negative impressions of NGO activity within the Bank. Though Bank staff answer letters from and meet regularly with NGO representatives, they are often put on the defensive by NGO materials that contain gross exaggerations of project problems, emphasize negative project effects without mentioning project benefits, or place what is perceived as undue responsibility for problems on the Bank. A good example of this is the huge letter campaign on the Itaparica Dam Project. Most letters expressed indignation that the Bank had helped build the Itaparica dam at all in light of the negative social and environmental impacts. In fact, the Bank was not directly involved in building the dam, but had supported a national energy loan that included Itaparica and, in large part due to NGO advocacy activities, sponsored a stand-alone resettlement and relief project.

Such tactics leave Bank staff considering proactive policies toward advocacy NGOs, instead of the defensive, reactive stance usually adopted. Some staff feel that the Bank must develop an offensive and preemptive public relations capacity. For example, some have suggested that the Bank should publicize its activities more through documentaries, which advocacy NGOs have often used successfully to depict the Bank in a negative light.

Bank staff are frustrated by the publication of dogmatic NGO materials written by people who have not visited a project and who have little idea of the Bank's role vis-à-vis government in its implementation. Indeed, as a survey of European NGOs' perceptions of the World Bank indicates, NGOs often have poor knowledge of Bank operations. From interviews with 30 of the larger European NGOs, Stephanie Baile (1986) concludes:

> *For most NGOs, the World Bank is a remote organization, far removed from their day-to-day activities. NGOs are very well informed about their national bilateral aid programs but largely ignorant of World Bank operations. Moreover, the information that they receive about the World Bank...is often controversial, partial, and biased.*
>
> *Interviews showed that some NGO leaders known for having negative attitudes toward the World Bank had come out with much more balanced views on the Bank when they had an opportunity to engage in discussion with World Bank officials on the occasion of World Bank seminars, symposia, or more informal social functions.* (5-6)

Increased emphasis on a two-way information flow that enables NGOs to view themselves as advisers to the Bank and the Bank to provide openings for NGO input might improve relations between the Bank and advocacy NGOs.

**Issues.** Understanding to what extent advocacy NGOs represent the interests of project beneficiaries is possibly the most difficult aspect of involving them in Bank projects. It may be particularly difficult to discern the degree to which international NGOs represent the views of local populations, especially concerning environmental and tribal rights issues. In the Indonesia Transmigration Projects, for example, the reactions of local NGOs to views expressed by international advocates reveal a difference of opinion. The views of both were published in 1986 and 1987 in the *Ecologist*. Survival International (SI) and other international NGOs presented an open letter to the Bank calling for it to suspend funding in light of the fact that the transmigration programs were designed to implement Indonesian government policies directly counter to those of the Bank.[8] Indonesian NGOs responded with a lengthy letter to the *Ecologist*, which stated that the transmigration program is "more of an ecological and natural resources mismanagement issue than a colonization issue" and "does not necessarily represent [a] grave threat to either the environment or indigenous peoples" ("Programme Slashed," *The Ecologist*, 1987, 41).

Developing country governments are often especially sensitive to the role of international advocacy NGOs. These NGOs use their influence with industrial country governments to put pressure on the Bank and on developing country governments. This behavior is sometimes perceived as an imposition on national sovereignty. Moreover, not all international advocacy NGOs are well informed about local circumstances.

The situation is sometimes further complicated by government-organized NGOs called GONGOs. In Madhya Pradesh, another Indian state in which massive resettlement will follow dam construction, the NGO network is extremely weak. One Bank staff member was invited to meet with a group of Madhya Pradesh NGOs that he assumed were representative of a budding community activist network. Instead, he found many of them to be "dummy" NGOs, sent by state officials to promote government opinions.

The Bank is limited in its ability to coordinate indigenous advocacy NGOs and borrower governments. Local advocacy groups are often perceived as threats to governmental authority. Government officials are not usually inclined to invite what may be seen as opposition groups into the planning of government programs. The Bank can play a role in improving this relationship by encouraging forums for discussion, for example, and by advocating NGO representation on various committees. State-level union members now sit on the national committee of Brazil's Northeast Development Project, and a local NGO leader sits on the government's Land Purchasing Committee in Gujarat.

Relationships between the Bank and advocacy NGOs are evolving. In the first stage, it was necessary for NGOs to generate sizable campaigns in order to capture enough international attention to force high-level policy decisions within the Bank and governments. Their activities were generally successful: a Bank

Environment Department has been established in the Policy, Planning, and External Affairs complex, and there are now environment divisions in all four regional technical departments. In addition, and partly due to this reorganization, greater attention is accorded to the effects of projects on the environment, indigenous tribes, and people who are resettled. In the second stage, when NGOs have established themselves as forces to be reckoned with, the relationship may be less confrontational. The Bank now seeks out the views of environmental NGOs on various policy and operational matters, and even the most critical of environmental groups have publicly supported some Bank work.

*Service providers/intermediaries*

Service-provider/intermediary NGOs have been involved in 88 Bank projects, 40 percent of the universe. These projects include those that deliver services to people or areas largely unreachable by the public and purely private sectors. The service-delivery function is perceived by many Bank staff to be the nongovernmental sector's greatest contribution. The important intermediary role assumed by many NGOs is that of acting as broker of values and information between donor/government and beneficiaries, using knowledge of both local circumstances and project objectives.

In the agricultural sector, NGOs implement training (managerial, agricultural, vocational) programs, organize and lend managerial assistance to cooperatives, provide financial assistance to grass-roots organizations, and coordinate community forestry activities.

Population and health is a sector to which NGOs seem particularly well-suited—primarily because of their relative strengths, compared with government and private health care, in extending information and services to less accessible populations. NGOs have been particularly good partners in urban development projects, where community involvement is often essential for success. NGOs have encouraged communities to voice their opinions to project managers and have generated self-help efforts to construct both individual dwellings and common facilities.

The interaction between the Bank or borrower and intermediary NGOs is noteworthy for pioneering approaches. Bank staff were taking chances on project models not previously tested in Bank-sponsored projects. While this study may draw attention to a number of problems, it also recognizes the benefit of such pilot projects as a basis for future projects.

**Goals for involving service-provider/intermediary NGOs in projects.** Many of the NGOs interviewed resent being perceived merely as service providers. Their goal is to serve as an institutional bridge linking project objectives and activities to the needs and environment of beneficiaries. Much of the discussion about NGOs' ties with large development institutions concerns a fear that NGOs will become too bureaucratic and will lose touch with local needs and eventually with original development goals. But there is also fear that by avoiding opportunities to influence development activities initiated by governments and large development institutions, NGOs will be unable to have much influence outside the immediate project environment. Reconciliation of project objectives with an NGO's goals and institutional capabilities, without distorting the NGO, is an overriding policy issue in Bank-intermediary NGO collaboration.

Goals that could be served by involving an intermediary NGO in a Bank-sponsored project include the following:

• *Translating beneficiary needs and knowledge of local conditions to the Bank or borrower.* This function can encompass advice given in informal discussions, formal representation of NGOs on project-planning or implementation teams, contractual agreements to perform beneficiary assessments, or other arrangements. When rural populations were not being effectively reached by the First Population Project in Kenya, indigenous NGOs (National Council of Churches of Kenya, Christian Health Association of Kenya, Kenya Catholic Secretariat) were informally consulted on ways to improve the effectiveness of the Second Project. The NGOs have since been formally incorporated into project dialogue and receive project funding to distribute family planning information and administer services.

• *Translating guidelines of project to communities.* As shown in the Zambia Upgrading Project example, intermediary NGOs may be able to translate the ideas of project managers on community self-help and repayment plans to beneficiaries. Another instance is the Guatemala Reconstruction Project, in which FENACOAC, a federation of 69 savings-and-loan cooperatives, took over the small-enterprise income-generation component. While BANVI, the national housing bank, was too far removed from small entrepreneurs to have interest in or the capacity for working with them, FENACOAC was able to notify its member cooperatives of available funding and assist them with preparing proposals to take advantage of it. The federation disbursed and collected 100 percent of project funds.

• *Organizing beneficiaries to take advantage of project benefits.* Beyond transferring information to beneficiaries, intermediary NGOs have catalyzed community association and cooperative formation. A good example of this is the work of the Development Foundation of Turkey (TKV) with poultry cooperatives. The TKV was contracted to replicate its successful cooperative model on a larger scale within the Fifth Livestock Development Project. The NGO promotes the project to farmers, encourages village consensus, trains professionals to provide technical assistance, provides administrative services, and sets up marketing and distribution centers. By organizing cooperatives of 20 farmers and providing support services, the TKV gives individuals access to project-funded credit.

• *Delivering services to less accessible populations.* Delivering services to people or areas unreached by government agencies or private firms is another valuable contribution of service-provider/intermediary NGOs. The issue for the Bank is how to take advantage of NGO expertise without compromising NGO goals and modes of operation. The Bangladesh and Kenya Population Projects have handled this with reasonable success. In both cases, the guidelines for NGO funding are fairly broad: as long as NGO programs contribute to national health and population objectives, they are free to choose their own methods of operation.

• *Serving as intermediaries to other NGOs.* This typically takes the form of financial intermediation, though other functions include geographical coordination, technical assistance, and training. Staff in some projects selected a particular NGO or NGO umbrella organization to review proposals and disseminate funds. FENACOAC, for example, served as a channel to smaller cooperatives. In the Togo Grass-roots Development Initiative, FONGTO, an umbrella organization, coordinates NGO activities and manages training programs for members that require institutional strengthening.

A common denominator among these predominantly successful examples of intermediary NGO-Bank collaboration is Bank/borrower recognition of the particular developmental objectives of each NGO. FENACOAC, the Kenyan NGOs, Swarnivar (Bangladesh NGO), and the TKV participate, for the most part, as organizations with individual goals and modes of operation—not as contractors concerned primarily with fulfilling, for a fee, terms of reference set by the Bank or a borrower.

The Bank staff's lack of recognition of an NGO's institutional agenda weakened the Zambia Upgrading Project. The AFSC joined the project with the objective of generating community participation in planning and construction; indeed, the Bank saw the AFSC's role as implementing the project's "community-development" component. Bank staff were skeptical of the efficacy of self-help construction, and the Lusaka City Council did not have the capacity to supervise large-scale community involvement in civic works. But pressure to build within the disbursement period led Bank staff to attach a rider to the final agreement: "should the procedure [of collective self-help] interfere with the progress of timely execution of the Project, the government shall, in consultation with the Bank, employ contractors to carry out the above-mentioned works" (letter for signature by authorized representatives of the World Bank and the Lusaka City Council). As a result, contractors had to incorporate community residents as workers, an arrangement that, for a number of reasons, was frustrating to all parties involved. Less time pressure and more flexibility for the AFSC might have increased the community's contribution to implementation.

Another Bank-NGO controversy arose in the El Salvador Second Urban Development Project, which FUNDASAL (Salvadorean Low-Income Housing Foundation) was asked to implement. While Bank staff were generally extremely responsive to the special needs of an NGO,[9] there was an ongoing controversy as to project objectives and how progress toward these should be addressed in evaluations. FUNDASAL saw housing as a means toward larger developmental goals, as "laying the foundations for a process of social change." But the Bank wondered, in the words of one staff member, "whether a low-cost construction project is the most appropriate vehicle to further these aims," and expressed concern over the lack of dependable hard data in the cost-benefit analysis of mutual help. The final compromise was to produce two separate evaluations of mutual help: one by FUNDASAL for "national consumption," considered "inappropriate to circulate within the Bank," and another for the Bank with less political content (according to Bank project file memoranda). This difference of opinion between Bank staff and FUNDASAL, however, had little if any effect on project performance inasmuch as FUNDASAL (unlike the AFSC in the Zambia project) had complete responsibility for implementation of the housing component (the only NGO to have had such extensive authority in a Bank-financed project).

**Interaction.** *Planning.* The Kenya Population Project illustrates the efficacy of inviting intermediary NGOs into the planning process before agreeing on an implementation strategy. Less tension and delay occur if goals and the resources to achieve them are agreed upon at the outset.

*Proposal preparation.* As a Bank consultant's report observes, donors are accustomed to an approach to funding that requires recipients to prepare detailed project proposals, often at their own expense, complete with cost estimates and a two-to-three year timetable. But perhaps NGOs that have had little interaction with international donors or little experience with a particular type of project should be assisted in obtaining the primary information necessary for preparing a budget and a proposal. For example, the Bank, with its experience and extensive access to research, can channel to NGOs state-of-the-art information on a particular type of project, advise NGO planners as to contingencies, and explain clearly the details of financing in Bank-sponsored projects.

*Institution building.* Projects involving a single intermediary NGO as implementor may require assistance in institution building before the loan or credit becomes effective. In Guatemala, for example, FENACOAC's role in financing small enterprises was delayed because the federation had insufficient staff to work with local cooperatives in developing and implementing activities. In Zambia, the Bank's disbursement procedure precluded the AFSC from training its community development team until the credit was effective. Thus, the training period itself cut into the already limited time allotted for community development.

*Reporting methods and mechanisms.* NGOs have been generally held to private contractor standards of strict accountability for expenditures and performance. They must submit periodic reports in each area and are sometimes subject to independent outside auditors. The need for accountability is not disputed. However, reporting procedures that emphasize quantitative achievements are seldom able to describe qualitative aspects of development that intermediary NGOs feel to be more essential—and for which they have often been brought into a project. The methods used in gathering this qualitative information are simple and informal. As the *Evaluation Source Book* of the American Council of Voluntary Agencies for Foreign Service (ACVAFS 1983) notes:

> *For the small-scale community programs that most PVOs operate, notes or tapes of carefully selected participant group discussions may be just as valid, and certainly more compatible, than a full-scale survey using a*

*closed-ended, computer-coded questionnaire. The choice of methods depends on what you want to know about a program as well as what produces the desired results.* (48)

Bank staff can assist in the development of a balanced reporting system by emphasizing to borrower governments the importance of incorporating qualitative assessment. For example, ongoing process evaluation using beneficiary assessment and focusing on NGOs' effects on the productivity of farmers and reelers has been built into a current community-based sericulture project in India. Bank staff can also encourage the funding of technical assistance to service-provider/intermediary NGOs to develop self-evaluation capabilities.

**Context.** As with other categories of NGOs, the context within which a service-provider/intermediary NGO operates is crucial to its successful involvement in project activity, as may be seen in the following two cases.

The Togo NGO Collaborative Project experienced delay because of insufficient attention to the relationship between the preexisting implementing umbrella NGO (CONGAT) and other NGOs. As implementation progressed, many NGOs felt that CONGAT did not act as a legitimate umbrella, primarily because it had developed a service branch that competed with member NGOs for donor funding. Many NGOs resented the dependence that resulted from CONGAT's control of funds. These formed a separate federation (SLONG) in opposition to CONGAT and its outspoken director. Though the two eventually joined to form FONGTO, which now channels project funds, the CONGAT director and his supporters, particularly donors from developed countries, may continue to harbor grievances.

Efforts to create umbrella groups for project purposes should be approached with caution. A sudden influx of assistance to a donor-created coordinating body can diminish NGO autonomy by making collaboration with other groups a precondition to donor support. If few NGOs are willing to submit their projects to the review of a coordinating committee, collaboration will be difficult. Such an attempt might also trample fledgling indigenous initiatives for coordination that, if given time, could eventually provide viable NGO representation to government and donors.

Unanticipated friction between NGOs and government agencies can also create tension and delay. A consultant's detailed analysis of a potential local intermediary NGO partner in the Indonesia Yogyakarta Rural Development Project provided a particularly vivid description of the NGO's political context. Her study helped the project avoid major coordination problems with the government. She found that the Bank, in discussing a community-development role for the NGO, had entirely overlooked Bang Des, the official body in charge of local development. The Bank had been working with BAPPEDAS, the provincial authority, whose director was engaged in a personality and power conflict with the Bang Des director. Both agencies were using Bank support of the NGO as a tool, thinking that, once the NGO and Bank resources were under their coordinating control, one agency would be strengthened against the other. The NGO itself was careful not to make a move without being requested to do so by national and local authorities. As it turned out, the NGO workers were allowed to participate only if they represented themselves to the villagers as Bang Des employees, thus negating any advantage they might have had as representatives of an outside agency or NGO.

*Contractor NGOs*

In 68 of the 218 projects (31 percent), NGOs participated as contractors; they agreed to implement project components, technical assistance, or public works strictly as delineated in requests for proposals. Contractor NGOs come to projects with special expertise, but generally not with independent development agendas. Of the 22 industry and energy sector projects, 13 included contractor NGOs, usually in a consultancy/technical assistance capacity: designing management and credit administration systems for banks, working with power companies to develop rural electrification systems, and similar activities. Within the infrastructure and urban development sector, 22 of the 41 projects involved NGOs as contractors. The World Organization for Rehabilitation and Training (ORT), which specializes in developing and managing transportation systems, worked in most of these.

In six of the 24 projects reviewed, NGOs could be categorized as contractors, as the roles they played are very close to those of private consulting or construction firms.

The Bank's Operational Directive states that "when NGOs act as consultants, they should be engaged following the Guidelines for the Use of Consultants by World Bank borrowers and by the World Bank as Executing Agency" (OMS 2.81 and OMS 2.50). Some consultant NGOs such as the ORT and the National Rural Electrification Cooperative Association (NRECA) are comfortable operating within these guidelines. They maintain a not-for-profit status and often initiate and manage independent development activities. For the Bank's purposes, these NGOs need no special policy adaptations. Nonetheless, these consulting entities are NGOs—further contributing to Bank staff confusion over definition. Other contractor NGOs, for lack of working capital or other reasons, cannot operate effectively within the procedures established for private firms.

A number of NGOs that agreed to work as contractors found that the terms inhibited them from incorporating methods of operation used in their own projects that might have contributed to project sustainability. As seen below, the benefits of involving this group of NGOs were not fully exploited; the NGOs might have been better incorporated if given more scope to use distinctive approaches in the project.

**Goals for involving contractor NGOs in projects.** A clear objective in incorporating a contractor NGO is to take advantage of its special knowledge or skills, perhaps regardless of the degree to which it is motivated by values. While differences in performance may be small, in some cases, a "value-driven" orientation may be a benefit. In the Ghana Water Supply and Rehabilitation Project, for example, Public Administration Services (PAS) was able to underbid private firms for the management consultancy. The PAS had some cost advantage because of its not-for-profit tax status and low overhead. The PAS's performance was also enhanced because its consultants were not preoccupied by profit considerations and were willing to lend assistance in areas beyond those delineated by the terms of reference.

Cost is often a factor in involving contractor NGOs. The low cost of NGO assistance is an advantage touted by many, although a conclusive comparison of NGO costs with those of government agencies and private firms has yet to be done. This small sample produced mixed results. In public works, CARE's road construction in Sierra Leone's Eastern Integrated Agricultural Project was relatively expensive, primarily because CARE refused to compromise on quality. However, in the Liberia Second Education Project, CARE was able to construct primary schools at a cost estimated to be 30 percent less than that of for-profit contractors. In technical assistance components, the PAS was relatively less expensive to hire, while ORT consultants are paid market or near-market rates.

The Bank's experience with CARE as a contractor in Liberia supports the contention that, because the NGO was hired primarily for its low-cost construction capability, it did not contribute as fully as it might have. CARE was initially assumed by the Bank to be working as a service-provider/intermediary, since CARE considers one of its strengths to be the motivating of communities in self-help efforts. In both Liberia and Sierra Leone, however, CARE implemented only its primary tasks as delineated in contracts. In Liberia, CARE was selected to build 100 schools (85 of which were completed). CARE's proven track record of cost-efficient construction, made cheaper with voluntary community labor, made it a much more attractive candidate than local contractors (well-known to be too expensive, ill-equipped, and only moderately skilled) or the Ministry of Public Works (which judged itself incapable of such a large undertaking).

CARE did not work with Liberian communities to create a role for the village schools, and some buildings went unused. The project completion report and a later government review of the education sector noted that many schools had deteriorated because villages had not been involved in planning for maintenance. The CARE project manager said that because Liberia was his first CARE country assignment, he was not forceful enough in dealing with the Bank on participation issues; if he were to deal with the Bank now, he would assure CARE of a role in community organization as well as in construction.

**Contracting procedures.** Agreements with contractor NGOs are usually similar to those with private firms. The project delays and implementation obstacles caused by lack of attention to the special needs of some contractor NGOs indicate a need for flexibility in contracting procedures.

Whereas private contractors typically work on an expense-reimbursement cycle, a not-for-profit NGO is unlikely to have the capital reserves necessary to fund construction while awaiting reimbursement. This became clear to project staff working on the Mali Health Development Project, in which l'Association pour le Developpement d'une Architecture Naturel et d'un Urbanisme Africans (ADAUA), an NGO from Burkina Faso, was contracted to build health centers. ADAUA was selected because of its expertise in stabilized-soil construction technology. Problems arose when the NGO tried to undertake work on three sites simultaneously, thereby overextending its supervisory and financial capacity. Funds were disbursed through the Ministry of Health, contingent on verification and certification of work completed. Such certification was the responsibility of the Ministry of Public Works, which was often slow to inspect and certify work completed. The ministry sought to block further advances to ADAUA, which was treated as a private contractor. The Ministry of Health, in turn, occasionally authorized further advances. In the final analysis, the system of control and verification broke down, important sums could not be fully accounted for, and the government imposed force account procedures.

The Bank might alleviate such financial difficulties by setting up a special revolving fund to cover expenses while awaiting reimbursement; in that way the highly successful El Salvador Second Urban Development Project made allowances for FUNDASAL's financial position.

In the Yogyakarta Rural Development Project, Dian Desa, an appropriate-technology NGO, was also subject to government rigidity on contractors. It had agreed with the Bank and Public Health Department to construct ferrous cement water cisterns that could collect water during the dry season. When the NGO found itself covering expenses and persistently requesting reimbursement, it was told that it was not a "bona-fide" contractor and would have to go through government for all procurement. Since tanks were constructed simultaneously in many areas, the use of a single supplier for all of them caused delays. Additionally, the government did not permit forward purchase of cement needed to begin construction when a water shortage eased.

Because these agreements are often dependent on borrower government policies, the Bank can be instrumental in influencing flexible terms. It will help when Bank staff recognize types of special contracting arrangements that might be necessary when involving an NGO.

**Identification and selection of contractor NGOs versus public agencies or private for-profit firms.** Questions have been raised about the temporary nature of building local NGO capacity, compared to the benefit of increasing government or private capacity. While an NGO may appear to be the only viable option in a country with an underdeveloped private sector, allowing the NGO to meet project-created demand may delay the growth of private (for-profit) firms.

This may point to a need for NGOs to help "work themselves out of business." This could be done, for example, by emphasizing the training of government or private workers. A contract might also stipulate NGO support of the private sector in the form of subcontracting to local firms, or require training local people during the project. The training component of the Mali Health Project has been considered a moderately successful ADAUA achievement, though it is still too early to gauge the multiplier effect in generating new entrepreneurial ventures. In Sierra Leone, where CARE was contracted for road construction, it handed its heavy machinery on to the Ministry of Public Works after implementation. Similarly, NGOs might be encouraged to sell their machinery at concessional prices or with soft financing.

Contracting with NGOs—with the possible exception of consultant NGOs, such as the ORT—often involves issues beyond those inherent in hiring private firms. If an NGO is deemed the best alternative, it is important to analyze the NGO's institutional capacity and the special contracting arrangement necessary and to consider whether the NGO's strengths are being put to full use under the contracting arrangement.

### *Cooperatives*

Forty-five of the 218 projects involved creation of or coordination with cooperatives. While some cooperatives are comprised of artisans, most are organizations of low-income farmers. Of these, 25 are in agricultural projects in Africa. Many are oriented toward crop production and marketing, livestock development, or dairy production. Several key issues arose from an institutionally oriented review of the six projects in the sample 24 with cooperative involvement.

**Goals for involving cooperatives in projects.** The Bank has categorized "production-related" people's organizations as a type of NGO (OMS 5.30). Cooperatives work for the benefit of members and their principal objective is to increase incomes; they do not, therefore, always fit the conventional image of NGOs as altruistic and service-oriented. The Bank's goal in supporting cooperatives is to enable their eventual self-sustaining, autonomous activity as private firms. Cooperatives can be considered NGOs only if one recognizes that they have ends beyond the strictly economic—for example, social equity. Then they may be included with other organizations working to enable primarily low-income persons to participate more fully in the private and public sectors.

Three of the cooperative projects in our sample are widely considered successful by Bank staff interviewed. The Ituri Livestock Project in Zaire illustrates how cooperatives can achieve both increased income and greater political leverage. The project-implementation unit catalyzed the formation of 117 livestock producers' associations (PRODELs) and a federation (ACOOPELI) that pools PRODEL resources for purchasing veterinary medicines and represents herders' interests to the project unit, government, and donors. The enthusiastic response of farmers to cooperative ideas was unexpected: far beyond the planned cattle-dipping program, the PRODELs sell veterinary supplies, manage communal pastures, curb rustling, and defend herdsmen's interests at the local level.

In the Turkey Livestock Project, more than 800 farmers in 12 regions benefit from cooperatives started by the Development Foundation of Turkey. In the much-acclaimed India Dairy Project, the Bank's switch from support of state-run dairy operations to support of Operation Flood[10] has enabled the project to cover all but one of India's states and territories, with more than 30,000 Dairy Cooperative Societies. A staff appraisal report noted that Operation Flood activities have "demonstrated profound social and economic consequences, as cooperative profits are used to finance communal resources of education, water supplies, health services, and access roads."

**Issues arising from the involvement of cooperatives in project activity.** From the review of these three cooperative NGOs and one not considered a success, UCCAO in Cameroon, we raise three issues:

1. The sustainability of cooperatives is still a question in the Zaire and Turkey Livestock Projects. Enabling grass-roots economic organizations to operate free of project support (donor funding, intermediary NGO support services) is possibly the most difficult aspect of implementation. The Development Foundation of Turkey (TKV) continues to supply managerial and technical services for which member farmers do not pay. It is not clear how the cooperatives would remain competitive if they were bereft of TKV services or had to pay for them out of profits. In Zaire, the PRODELs and ACOOPELI continue to receive support in subsequent projects. ACOOPELI still relies on donated veterinary supplies from Canada.

2. Proper institutional analysis is as important in dealing with cooperatives and other NGOs as it is in working with public or purely private entities. Sustainability is not just a financial issue but also an institutional one. UCCAO, a union of six Western Province cooperatives in the Cameroon Western Highlands Project, was active only in the processing and marketing of arabica coffee. In the absence of strong government services in the West, however, UCCAO's functions were expanded to fill the needs of the entire agricultural development project. This included coffee production—and small animal husbandry, tree planting, bottomland development, water supply, food production, and extension services. The burden proved too large for UCCAO; the nature of the organization was changed by the influx of funding and responsibilities, some of which later had to be transferred to government agricultural services.

3. A final issue is that of examining the cooperative network within context. The Cameroon Project tried to support cooperatives without consideration of UCCAO's position vis-à-vis its member cooperatives or their members. During project preparation, it appeared that UCCAO was a functionally representative organ of the cooperatives—but, in fact, the cooperatives saw UCCAO as purely a service organization and had closely limited its power. By gaining control over project resources and developing an implementation network parallel to the cooperative network, UCCAO increased its influence. The cooperative managers think their interests have not been met through this arrangement. To farmer-members, whose interests often differ from those of managers, UCCAO is a far-removed, almost governmental body. An Operations Evaluation Department review (1988) further substantiated the "need for a more detailed understanding of the power realities in the institutional and political environment in which rural development projects operate" (60).

### The Bank's role in facilitating relations between governments and NGOs

Borrower government cooperation determines whether the integration of NGOs into Bank-sponsored projects is successful. The stipulation that the Bank's funds must, according to its Articles of Agreement, go through government often discourages NGOs that might otherwise see great potential in participating in a Bank-sponsored project. Depending on the country, NGOs can often receive funding from private and bilateral donors more directly; bureaucratic obstacles inherent in working through government agencies put the Bank at a comparative disadvantage. The Bank is well positioned, however, to foster effective relationships between governments and NGOs.

Michael Bratton's summary (1989) of NGO-government relations in Africa applies to a number of the projects reviewed in all regions:

> *Whether NGOs are international or community-based, all operate within the boundaries of a nation-state and at the pleasure of a sovereign government. Because governments resist any reduction of their leadership role in development, they are likely to seek to control NGOs by enacting legal and administrative regulations to govern the voluntary sector. For their part, NGOs are among the only formal organizations to enjoy a degree of autonomy from government and to have a direct presence among mobilized communities at the grass-roots level....Governments and NGOs therefore find themselves in a new and challenging juxtaposition that requires leaders on both sides to ponder the potential for conflict or complementarity between their institutions.* (570)

Many of the bureaucratic obstacles that delayed implementation in Bank-sponsored projects were manifestations of government hesitancy to allow autonomous NGO activity. The issue for the Bank is how best to design a government-NGO partnership in which the government is aware of, yet does not control, NGO activities. Turning otherwise autonomous institutions into de facto branches of government could squelch those aspects of NGOs that make them particularly valuable to development.

In some projects, the conflict was at the national level, where officials were hesitant to relinquish responsibilities to an outside agency—afraid that channeling control or funding to NGOs would reduce their own leadership role. This helps to explain the Guatemalan government's hesitance to transfer administration of the Reconstruction Project's small-enterprise-development component from BANVI (the national housing bank) to FENACOAC, a federation viewed as unsympathetic to the government.

This fear can be combined with the desire of central government agencies not to look incompetent. In Turkey, the Ministry of Agriculture (MAFRA) displayed such sentiments in its lack of cooperation with the TKV in the Livestock Project. Though government priorities lay elsewhere, the Bank pushed hard to add the poultry component, specifying the TKV as implementor because of the NGO's proven successes. Using the premise that some TKV enterprises operate with commercial methods and generate income, MAFRA balked at reimbursing expenses. Project officers note, however, MAFRA's own lack of success with poultry projects.

In other cases, national officials were fully supportive of NGO participation, but state or local officials viewed NGO involvement as threatening. The project performance audit report for the India Dairy Project states that "without [state government's] negative influences, the outcome of Operation Flood and the Bank-assisted projects doubtless would have been greater than that actually attained." Though national officials expressed willingness to support Operation Flood, state officials had little incentive to support the cooperative movement and much to gain in propagating state-run dairies. These, though unsanitary and inefficient, maintain thousands of jobs. Politicians cultivate urban votes by holding down producer prices and protecting the interests of private dairies and middlemen.

Sometimes authorities find it easier to work with NGOs at the local level. In the Kenya Population Project, NGO-government coordination generally happens more often and with better results at the district and local levels than at the national level. While supportive of NGO involvement, national officials are concerned with macro-policy issues and delineation of responsibilities along ministry lines. Coordination at the micro-level is informal, stimulated by the need to share resources.

The reactions of government to NGO participation in Bank-financed projects have an economic basis insofar as the government sees NGOs as diluting scarce development resources. In most developing countries, legitimate demands on government far outstrip financial resources. In addition, procedural difficulties arise because official agreements with NGOs are often awkwardly new to governments, NGOs, and the Bank. Finally, there may be political problems. The political perspective is the most complex; Bank staff may find it hard to understand the political environment within which NGOs operate and to help a confrontational government-NGO relationship evolve into a cooperative one.

As Michael Bratton (1989) has observed, governments that derive legitimacy from their capacity to make good on promises of economic and social advancement will not want to admit they have performed poorly, because this has implications for their right to power. As in the Sierra Leone project, in which the government was frustrated at CARE's receiving credit from beneficiaries for government-financed road construction, governments may be unwilling to allow others to get credit for development activities. The challenge for Bank staff is to convince government that NGO-supported projects can extend government capabilities, without competing with the public sector for local power bases.

The antigovernment stance of many advocacy NGOs sometimes makes them almost off-limits to Bank staff, who must be careful not to offend a host government. In the early days of both the Tondo Foreshore and Narmada Dam projects, Bank staff were severely reprimanded by government and Bank management for speaking with indigenous NGOs. The Philippine and Indian governments felt threatened by the actual or potential organized opposition these groups represented. In both cases, the NGOs proved to be invaluable sources of local information to the Bank, thus moving from a confrontational to an informal advisory stance. While ZOTO continued to be repressed by the Philippine government, the Indian NGO's local knowledge and political base eventually won it respect from the government. In the Brazil projects (Itaparica and Northeast Development), the rural workers unions began as outside agitators but eventually negotiated a contract with the power utility subsidiary. Labor unions are also represented at the national level in the Northeast Development Project, and they receive a percentage of project funds to implement training programs for local NGOs.

The acceptance of policy-advocacy groups by government seems to depend on official attitudes toward dissent, the NGOs' abilities to organize local power bases, and their willingness to move beyond confrontation to negotiation. While the Bank's primary relationships are with its member governments, its willingness to listen to the views of advocacy groups can influence governments to take such views seriously.

There have been relatively few examples of fully collaborative trilateral arrangements among governments, NGOs, and the Bank. The Yemen Arab Republic Education Projects have met with success because officials are convinced that the projects both fulfill beneficiary needs and reflect well on government. Government representation at every level is more a symbol of support than a controlling influence. The Kenya Population projects are also building what is expected to become a replicable model. The National Council for Population and Development (NCPD) is responsible for coordinating all family planning-related NGO activity. NGOs see the advantages to such centralized functions and are generally positive about the NCPD's future capabilities.

Some more recent projects are indicative of changing government attitudes toward NGOs. Many of the most promising NGO-government linkages have been in Asian countries, where governments are relatively strong and thus less threatened by NGOs. In the Philippines, for example, NGO leaders are working with President Aquino's government on a health development project, as well as on such policy issues as land reform and rural employment generation. In Latin America, projects such as Bolivia's Emergency Social Fund show encouraging changes: NGOs work with government to plan, design, and implement projects that will address the needs of those hardest hit by recession and structural adjustment. NGO partners are becoming more acceptable—especially for service delivery. Latin American governments tend to be vocally supportive of community participation, but their motives in involving NGOs may sometimes center more on the cultivation of political support and cost recovery than on empowerment of the poor (Annis 1987). Because many Latin American NGOs see their basic role as helping poor people become more assertive and better organized, many NGO-government relationships will continue to have antagonistic overtones.

NGO involvement in Bank-financed projects is more prevalent in Africa than anywhere else, in part because governmental institutions are relatively weak there. But the weakness of African governments may also make NGO-government tensions more difficult to reconcile in this region. Many of the problems mentioned in this chapter tend to be more severe in Africa than elsewhere, though recent experiences, such as the promising Grass-roots Development Initiatives Project in Togo, illustrate the increasing willingness of governments, even in Africa, to entrust project responsibilities to NGOs.

## Conclusions and recommendations

This chapter has reviewed the nature and scope of NGO involvement in 24 Bank projects. For the period 1973-88, 218 projects were identified that have involved NGOs, representing less than 6 percent of Bank projects. Our sample represents approximately 11 percent of these Bank projects. The review shows that, in general, NGOs have contributed positively to Bank projects by facilitating beneficiaries' participation, by highlighting environmental issues, and by assisting in the delivery of services to low-income groups. Questions have arisen and will continue to arise on the proper role of NGOs in Bank projects. Bank-NGO collaboration must be informed by a balanced assessment of the strengths and weaknesses of NGOs.

The potential benefits of NGO's participation in Bank projects are several:

• They have demonstrated skills and experience in identifying community needs, promoting community participation, and building grass-roots institutions.

• They have been articulate and forceful contributors to policy reform, particularly on issues concerning the environment.

• They have provided innovative models for action that have been scaled up or replicated by governments nationwide.

• They sometimes have a comparative advantage in the low-cost delivery of services to relatively vulnerable and inaccessible groups of beneficiaries, and augment the potential for cost recovery.

• They have a long-term commitment to development efforts and play a strong advocacy role on behalf of disadvantaged groups. This is a potentially valuable asset in the context of poverty reduction. Development of autonomous, self-reliant grass-roots organizations has been shown to be correlated with project sustainability (OED 1985). Additionally, as noted at Bank-NGO meetings, the priority placed on mitigating the negative effects of structural and sectoral adjustment loans on the poor (or changing the design of program loans to enhance their positive effects on the poor) points to the growing need to solicit NGO input from the preparation stage.

The Bank should also be aware of the limitations of NGOs and the pitfalls in working with them.

• The advocacy role of NGOs often injects a sense of antagonism into their relations with governments.

• The strong interest of many NGOs in local problems and their commitment to grass-roots action tend to make them less sensitive to macroeconomic problems and to the need for an enabling macroeconomic environment.

• NGOs may be hostile not only to governments but to one another. Parochial interests could cause them to behave defensively. This tendency merits attention in development projects with inter-NGO collaboration.

• NGOs are generally poor in financial and managerial resources. This is particularly true of indigenous NGOs, which have often been unable to scale up their activities.

The scope and quality of Bank-NGO collaboration can be improved in several ways. First, the Bank should increase its understanding of NGOs' operational functions and purposes; second, NGOs should contribute more to project design; and third, Bank collaboration with borrower governments should help create an enabling environment in which NGOs may operate to their fullest potential.

*Increased Bank staff awareness of NGOs*

It is clear from the many interviews conducted with Bank staff for this review that most have an incomplete understanding of NGOs and their potential contribution to development. A good understanding of the nature, scope, and diversity of NGOs—and the contributions different types of NGOs can make to Bank projects—would be most useful to operational staff working on projects with potential for Bank-NGO collaboration. Contributing toward increasing Bank awareness have been EXTIE's advisory service, Operational Directive No. 14.70 (1989), staff and consultant reports,[11] and staff training seminars.

Bank staff were able to identify with reasonable accuracy only the NGOs at the center of our spectrum (see Figure 4.2). Some staff thought that community associations were quasi-governmental bodies (though these groups were not part of the formal government apparatus) and that political action groups, particularly those close to the communities of beneficiaries, were para-political bodies (though they had no formal political affiliation). Contractor NGOs were often thought to be in the for-profit private sector while cooperatives were treated as a class by themselves, yet much closer to private enterprises than organizations commonly perceived as NGOs. It is likely that the increased exposure of Bank staff to NGOs through operational work will improve their understanding and appreciation of these important development agents.

*Recommendations*

1. *Foster understanding of the strengths and weaknesses of the Bank and NGOs.* This review underscores the need for the Bank to devote greater resources to increasing the understanding of potential NGO partners from several perspectives: the compatibility of their goals with those of the Bank; their technical expertise and experience; their institutional soundness; and the quality of their relationships with government, other donors, other NGOs, and beneficiaries. Considerable work has already been done to compile directories and to analyze country-level NGO activities. The Bank's NGO liaison office (EXTIE), many regional offices, resident representatives, and others are collecting infor-

mation and facilitating Bank-NGO contacts. The Bank has also begun to furnish more information about its activities to NGOs to improve their understanding of Bank capabilities and limitations and to encourage NGO involvement early in the project cycle. Clearly, further extending these activities will call for an increased allocation of Bank resources.

2. *Increase Bank staff training*. Bank staff working on sectors with potential for collaboration with NGOs should be properly equipped to work with them. For example, short-term training may be organized to teach staff more about NGOs and their potential role in Bank projects. Opportunities may be created for Bank staff to meet NGO leaders and key government officials who have experience in working with NGOs. Staff may also learn from NGO leaders and experts invited to join Bank missions.

3. *Initiate sector work on NGOs*. The Bank's knowledge of NGOs can be enhanced through systematic sector work on their operations in countries and sectors where the potential for Bank-NGO collaboration seems reasonably bright. In many cases, the related fieldwork and analysis of data can be entrusted to local consultants. Expanded sector work is a cost-effective means for Bank staff to assess the level of development and the strengths and weaknesses of NGOs.

*The role of NGOs in project work*

The NGOs' most valuable contributions to development—their vision and grassroots-level experience—have been overlooked in many of the Bank-NGO interactions. The effective development NGO, especially the intermediary NGO, can understand and articulate people's needs and initiate action to meet them better than many other agencies. Most of these NGOs act as a bridge between beneficiaries and the outside world, imparting new knowledge and motivating people in ways compatible with their cultural beliefs and traditions. The communication of project objectives and procedures to beneficiaries and of beneficiaries' values and behavior to project managers, the provision of services to beneficiaries, and the sustainability of project achievements through their incorporation in the culture are dimensions to which both the Bank and NGOs attach the greatest importance. NGOs' strengths can be fully used only when they are able to play a more active role in Bank projects.

In the past, NGOs were used in Bank projects primarily (in 58 percent of the cases) as implementors. Those involved in project design and planning accounted for only 12 percent of the cases. Some types of NGOs, such as community associations, have had very limited involvement in Bank projects. An unintended consequence of this approach is the tendency to limit NGOs to the role of service providers, though their strength lies in long-term community development. This has led to a mismatch in several Bank projects between the comparative advantage of NGOs and the roles prescribed for them by the Bank. But when NGOs were identified with great care and their potential capabilities in given project contexts systematically evaluated, a better fit emerged between the NGOs and Bank projects. The role of local development associations in the Yemen

Arab Republic Education Projects and that of FUNDASAL in the El Salvador Second Urban Development Project illustrate this point.

*Recommendations*

1. *Involve NGOs further upstream.* As noted, NGOs generally become involved in Bank projects during implementation. But it is in the planning and design stages that NGOs' distinct experience and vision can best be brought into the decisionmaking process. This is particularly true of community associations and policy-advocacy NGOs. The NGO can be more effective during project implementation if it has had a role in the design stage.

2. *Develop creative financing mechanisms.* Experience with NGOs has shown that the funding arrangements typically used for private, for-profit entities often hinder NGO participation in projects. The typically undercapitalized financial structures and nonprofit orientation of NGOs point to the need for more flexible funding mechanisms. A revolving fund, for example, can make advances available so as to facilitate disbursements to local beneficiary groups in time. Balancing accountability with autonomy requires carefully negotiated agreements among the borrower, the Bank, and the NGO on expenditure approval and disbursement processes for payments through special accounts and funds, government-NGO contracts, or other appropriate mechanisms.

3. *Learn from NGO involvement in projects.* NGOs impart intangible yet important inputs of motivation, education, and organization. How an NGO interacts with and influences beneficiary response deserves to be noted and transferred. Participant observation, in particular, can assist development managers in gaining an appreciation of the diverse attributes of the NGO, many of which contribute to sustainable development.

*The NGO-government-Bank triad*

The Bank lends primarily to governments. Whether NGOs are involved in Bank operations, except policy dialogue and informal consultations, depends on the approval of borrowing governments. The relationship between NGOs and governments in many of the projects reviewed (TKV/Turkey, PRODELs/Zaire, CARE/Sierra Leone, Dairy Coops/India, Dian Desa/Indonesia) adversely affected project success. The problems were diverse: rivalry and jealousy among NGOs, NGO dissatisfaction with the contractor role, corruption, and so on. In most cases the Bank's influence on the situation was limited. In this study, for example, only one of the 24 projects reviewed, the Yemen Arab Republic Second Education Project, demonstrated a harmonious, mutually supportive relationship among the NGO, the government, and the Bank. Too often NGOs, governments, and donors have not had a shared understanding of their relationships in a project. The links between NGOs, governments, and the Bank need to be strengthened in the interests of project effectiveness and sustainability.

*Recommendations*

1. *Provide institutional assistance to both NGOs and governments to better enable each to deal with the other for development ends.* Many NGOs in all five categories have institutional needs—financial, administrative, managerial—that could be addressed through technical assistance in accounting, record keeping, monitoring, and evaluation. Well-managed NGOs will be better able to collaborate with governments. Similarly, governments may need assistance in improving their capacity to work effectively with NGOs, for example, in setting up public information or NGO-liaison offices and recruiting persons with NGO experience for public agencies.

2. *Strengthen Bank-NGO dialogue.* Effective involvement of NGOs in relevant Bank projects will require seeing the NGO as a development institution in its own right. With the recent emphasis given by Bank senior management to the incorporation of NGOs in Bank work, many managers and staff have started to make the operational and policy adaptations necessary for effective collaboration with NGOs. The Bank is making a concerted effort to draw on NGO expertise in crucial policy areas such as environmental impact, community initiatives, developing country debt, microenterprises, and structural adjustment, among others. Increasing communication with NGOs—through the NGO-World Bank Committee, NGO consortia, and regional or national meetings—further opens channels between the Bank and NGOs worldwide. In this climate of growing mutual interest in collaboration, the Bank should give serious consideration to a proactive brokering role; it should sponsor occasional conferences and workshops for the dissemination of innovative NGO experiences and development perspectives. As governments, NGOs, and the Bank come to appreciate their common goals and distinct characteristics, the foundation is being laid for sound partnerships and lasting development.

## Notes

1. Delivered September 27, 1988.
2. Given April 22, 1988.
3. Established in 1982, the NGO-World Bank Committee is composed of development NGOs and NGO consortia from throughout the world and senior Bank managers and staff from the four regional offices and Policy, Research, and External Affairs. At its annual meetings, the Committee seeks to encourage dialogue between the Bank and NGOs on broad issues of development policy, to facilitate operational collaboration, and to promote cooperation in development education (from a paper presented to the World Bank's Board of Directors).
4. EXTIE is developing a data base on Bank projects involving NGOs and on the NGOs with which the Bank has had dealings that is expected to help in systematizing and monitoring NGO involvement in Bank projects.
5. Projects that involved more than one type of NGO are listed under the type that played the more important role.

6. It was virtually impossible to reach rural communities at all in the immediate aftermath of a civil war.
7. LDAs grew up during the civil war as communities sought to develop mutual use facilities and infrastructure. They are parallel to a local government structure but can in no way be considered agents of the national government. They are led by elected village elders and financed from taxes on produce sales (later augmented by government contributions of customs revenues).
8. SI quotes the Bank as being committed to preserving the cultural identity and individual and collective rights of project-affected tribals (World Bank Operational Manual Statement 2.34), while the government is quoted as advocating active assimilation of Irian Jayans into the Indonesian culture (*Pelita*, May 1985; *Indonesia: News and Views* VI, 1986, in SI letter to President Conable, January 1988).
9. A special revolving credit fund was set up to allow continued operation while waiting for expense reimbursements. The repayment period for the loan was extended to enable FUNDASAL to complete projects and recoup losses caused by rising political and economic instability.
10. Operation Flood is based on the Anand model, which has several key institutional features: member-elected boards, democratic and accountable operations, employment of professional managers, cooperative ownership and management of processing, marketing, and production assets, and autonomy of decisionmaking related to pricing. Each Dairy Cooperative Society is a member of a regional producer's union, which in turn is a member of a state federation. Federation representatives participate in the policymaking of the National Cooperative Dairy Federation of India.
11. See particularly Cernea (1988).

# 5

# Recent Experience and Emerging Trends

*David Beckmann*

At the start of 1988, the World Bank began an institution-wide effort to expand its work with NGOs. The turning point was an instruction from the Bank's senior management to all operational staff, which has been followed up by periodic Bank-wide reviews of progress. This final chapter discusses what the Bank's recent outreach to NGOs has achieved, draws lessons from emerging experience, and projects how the Bank's work with NGOs is likely to evolve to the end of the century.[1]

## Recent experience

The previous chapter, by Salmen and Eaves, is a retrospective review of the Bank's work with NGOs from 1973 to 1988. The Bank accumulated experience with NGOs gradually during that period, often through the initiative of individual Bank staff. Salmen and Eaves started their study just as the Bank-wide NGO initiative began, and the recommendations with which their study concludes have helped to shape policy. To increase staff understanding of NGOs, the Bank issued operational guidelines, set up an advisory office, data bases, and training seminars, and carried out general and country-level studies of NGOs. The Bank's management has repeatedly urged staff to bring NGOs into project work at the planning stage, some projects have created new institutions to help fund NGOs, and the Bank has monitored its experience with NGOs. The Bank has encouraged governments and NGOs to work together, and NGO-Bank discussions have become more prevalent and influential.

The Bank's NGO initiative turned out to be part of an international wave of interest in NGOs. The dramatic spread of democracy in the 1980s, which climaxed in 1989 with the sudden emergence of democracies throughout Eastern Europe, has led to more favorable government attitudes toward citizens' groups in many countries. More generally, ineffective public sector programs and tight fiscal constraints have made many governments more aware of their limitations and more interested in what NGOs can contribute. Bilateral development agencies provide substantial funding to NGOs, and most multilateral development agencies have at least begun to develop links with NGOs. These broader trends have pushed the Bank's work with NGOs forward.

The Bank has used an inclusive and pragmatic definition of "nongovernmental organization." Preceding chapters highlight the differences among NGOs, but all NGOs pose some of the same problems and opportunities for the Bank. By its Articles of Agreement, the Bank's shareholders and borrowers are its member governments, so Bank collaboration with any NGO (whether a farmers' association, Oxfam, or the Boy Scouts) calls for similar institutional and legal arrangements. The Bank has long experience with the public and commercial private sectors in most developing countries, but has in the past had relatively little knowledge about the continuum of nongovernmental organizations.

*Patterns among projects*

Table 5.1 and the figures on the following pages compare the NGO-related projects that the Bank approved in its 1989 and 1990 fiscal years with some of the patterns Salmen and Eaves noted for 1973-88. Figure 5.1 highlights the sharp increase of NGO involvement in Bank-financed projects. Of the projects the Bank approved in fiscal 1989 and 1990, 96 involved NGOs—up from an average of 14 projects a year for fiscal 1973-88. The review of NGO involvement in fiscal 1991 projects is not yet complete, but NGOs feature in at least 80 of the 229 projects approved in fiscal 1991.

Figure 5.2 highlights the other main change from the pattern of the past. During fiscal 1973-87, 60 percent of the NGOs involved in Bank-financed projects were grass-roots or other indigenous NGOs. That figure increased to 80 percent for fiscal 1988-90, and the preliminary figure for fiscal 1991 is 86 percent. When local NGOs are well-developed, they tend to be more effective than international NGOs, and the latter are increasingly shifting from direct operations to support for local NGOs. When it comes to NGO involvement in government programs or policy discussions, most governments are more inclined to support, or take criticism from, local NGOs.

Figure 5.1 also shows that the regional distribution of Bank-financed projects in which NGOs have been involved has stayed remarkably constant. The preceding chapter outlined reasons why about half the NGO-related projects have been in Africa, with another quarter in Asia. The United Nations Development Program (UNDP), which has also been expanding work with NGOs, has noted a similar regional pattern among its NGO-related projects.

**Table 5.1 Patterns in Bank-NGO collaboration, fiscal 1973-88 and 1989-90**

| | *Fiscal 1973-88* | | *Fiscal 1989-90* | |
|---|---|---|---|---|
| *Region* | *Projects* | *Percent* | *Projects* | *Percent* |
| Africa | 111 | 51 | 49 | 51 |
| Asia | 51 | 24 | 22 | 23 |
| Europe, Middle East, and North Africa | 16 | 7 | 7 | 7 |
| Latin America and the Caribbean | 40 | 18 | 18 | 19 |
| Total | 218 | 100 | 96 | 100 |
| *Sector* | *Projects* | *Percent* | *Projects* | *Percent* |
| Agriculture/rural development | 102 | 47 | 33 | 34 |
| Environment | 2 | 1 | 6 | 6 |
| Education/training | 20 | 9 | 9 | 9 |
| Population/health | 26 | 12 | 15 | 16 |
| Industry/energy | 22 | 10 | 5 | 5 |
| Infrastructure/urban development | 41 | 19 | 13 | 14 |
| Relief | 3 | 1 | 2 | 2 |
| Adjustment-related | 2 | 1 | 12 | 13 |
| Women in development | .. | .. | 1 | 1 |
| Total | 218 | 100 | 96 | 100 |
| *Type of NGO* | *NGOs* | *Percent* | *NGOs* | *Percent* |
| Grass-roots[a] | 75 | 30 | 59 | 42 |
| Indigenous intermediary | 75 | 30 | 54 | 38 |
| International | 104 | 40 | 29 | 20 |
| Total[b] | 254 | 100 | 142 | 100 |
| *Function* | *Projects with function* | *Percent* | *Projects with function* | *Percent* |
| Advice | 75 | 27 | 14 | 9 |
| Design | 33 | 12 | 30 | 19 |
| Implementation | 162 | 57 | 88 | 57 |
| Monitoring and evaluation | 1 | 0 | 11 | 7 |
| Cofinancing | 10 | 4 | 13 | 8 |
| Total[b] | 281 | 100 | 156 | 100 |

a. Grass-roots groups are organizations of poor people. Indigenous intermediary groups are other indigenous groups.
b. Exceeds number of cases because NGO involvement in one project sometimes falls into more than one category.
*Source*: World Bank data.

**Figure 5.1 Operational collaboration between NGOs and the World Bank, by region, fiscal 1973-90**

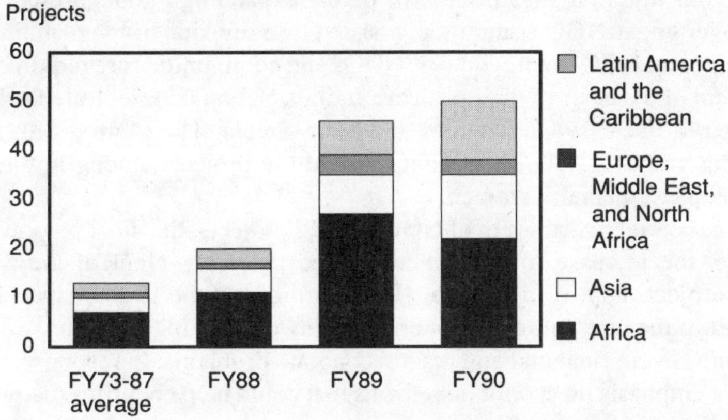


The Bank's management has urged staff to involve NGOs in the design of Bank-financed projects. There have been some notable examples of this. The Agriculture Services Project in Burundi provides for consultancies by local NGOs to adapt extension to women farmers. A Filipino NGO that had pioneered a collaborative health program with governmental agencies in Mindanao later played a key role in planning for the program's replication in other provinces as a part of a Bank-financed health project. Many instances of NGO advice during fiscal 1973-88 were relatively insignificant, and the apparent decrease in this type of Bank-NGO interaction is probably due mainly to changed reporting. But in view of the management's urging, it is striking that the growth of NGO involvement at the design stage has been modest.

Some Bank-financed projects now include funding for NGOs. The Bank's first free-standing NGO project, the Togo Grass-roots Initiative Project, was approved in fiscal 1989. It provides grants of $3 million to community-based

**Figure 5.2 Operational collaboration between NGOs and the World Bank, by type of NGO, fiscal 1973-87 and 1988-90**

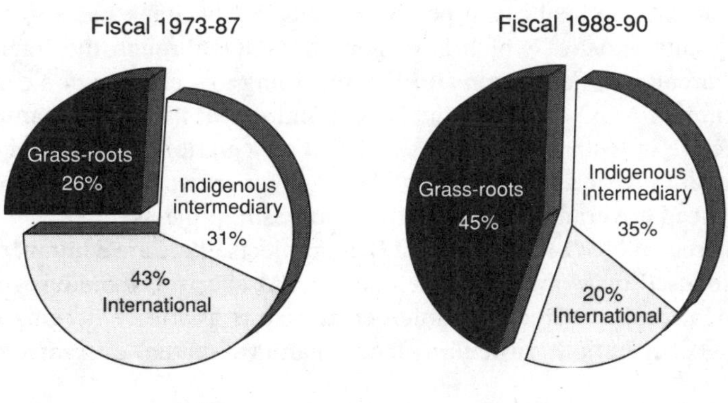

development projects designed and carried out by NGOs and project beneficiaries. The Bank used advances from its Special Project Preparation Facility to develop this initiative on a pilot basis before expanding it to its present scale. A joint government-NGO committee, assisted by a division of the planning ministry, decides on NGO grant requests. NGOs and communities are required to meet 30 percent of the costs of their projects. India's National Sericulture Project, also approved in fiscal 1989, provides another example. The Central Silk Board is providing grants in support of NGO sericulture projects among low-caste and tribal people, especially women.

In the sectoral distribution of NGO-related projects, the most obvious change has been the increase in adjustment-related projects—eight of the 50 NGO-related projects approved in fiscal 1990. Throughout the 1980s, especially after the onset of the international debt crisis, many developing countries were struggling with severe financial and macroeconomic problems. In response, the Bank put more emphasis on economic reforms that could help countries recover financial stability and growth. Structural adjustment loans, which provide balance of payments assistance in support of policy reform, grew to a quarter of the Bank's lending. Increasingly, the Bank also focused on the poverty impact of economic crisis and the additional costs that needed economic reforms sometimes entail for the poor. One way to address the social problems associated with adjustment has been to help governments set up special funds, through which international donors can support NGO- and community-initiated social programs. Bolivia's Emergency Social Fund was an early, successful example. It channeled some $170 million to poverty-focused community projects, $43 million of it through NGOs. Similar funds are being set up in other countries, mostly in Africa and Latin America.

The Bank is funding a growing number of environmental protection projects, and all of them involve NGOs. In Madagascar, for example, the Bank helped organize a joint government-NGO process to develop a national environment plan. Local groups and international environmental groups took part in the task forces, and the Bank is now financing implementation of the plan.

NGO involvement in Bank-financed population and health projects continues at a high level. Virtually all Bank-financed population and health projects feature a major role for the local family planning association or community-based health groups. For African health and population NGOs, the Bank has a special program of grants, most of which have gone to NGOs through the International Planned Parenthood Federation (IPPF). According to a consultant's evaluation, the government-NGO meetings and NGO training that the IPPF organized have been effective in fostering government-NGO cooperation in the sector in much of Sub-Saharan Africa. They have set the stage for greater NGO involvement in Bank-financed governmental population and health projects.

Among recent NGO-related World Bank projects, there are a number of components focused on women in development and one free-standing women-in-development project. Credit for microenterprise is another emerging focus of Bank-NGO cooperation, particularly the formation of mutual-guarantee schemes, often among women. For example, Ghana's Private Small and Medium Enterprise Development Project supports a pilot mutual-guarantee scheme to bridge the gap between formal banking institutions and microentrepreneurs, with assistance from Women's World Banking-Ghana.

Agriculture is still the sector in which NGOs are most frequently involved. These are normally producer or user groups (irrigation associations, herders' organizations, or cooperatives). Compared to the 1970s, much more of the Bank's agricultural lending now is in support of institutional and policy reforms at the national level (higher prices for farmers, for example), and farmers' groups are less likely to be directly involved in such projects. In a few cases, however, the Bank is supporting changes in government policies toward farmers' groups. In Cameroon, for example, a Bank study showed that cooperatives were more vigorous in the region where they had received less assistance and control from the government. A project under preparation will support steps to make cooperatives throughout the country more independent from government.

Similarly, the Bank's lending for urban development has shifted from neighborhood-specific projects in the 1970s toward programs designed to strengthen municipal government and housing finance institutions. This shift has meant less direct involvement with neighborhood organizations, but in some instances the Bank is helping to put into place systems of official cooperation with those organizations and other NGOs. In Indonesia, the Bank financed a successful program of neighborhood (kampung) improvement in the 1970s. It was a top-down program but improved water supply, roads, and drainage in many poorly serviced neighborhoods. When Indonesia's oil revenues dropped, the government was compelled to stop kampung improvement. But two pilot UNDP-financed projects demonstrated an alternative, more participatory approach that costs the government less and fills gaps left by the kampung improvement of the past. The new approach stresses aspects of neighborhood improvement, such as sanitation and public health, in which local people need to play an active role. The Bank is now financing the application of this approach on a large scale in Jakarta and other cities. NGOs are working with neighborhood associations to help them function more democratically and strengthen their capacity to take on these new responsibilities.

### *Dialogue between NGOs and the World Bank*

The rapid expansion of NGO involvement in Bank-financed operations has taken place against a backdrop of intensified policy discussion between NGOs and the Bank. The NGO-World Bank Committee, a panel composed of senior Bank managers and 26 NGO leaders from around the world, is one forum for the exchange of views.[2] Formed in 1982, it has become much more active in the last few years. Advice from the Committee has influenced the Bank's operational outreach to NGOs. The Committee has also focused on two other themes. A debate about the poverty impact of adjustment has evolved into a discussion of NGO ideas about an alternative vision of development. This vision puts less emphasis on growth in production and exports and more emphasis on justice, sustainability, and democracy. A debate about the Bank's policies regarding public access to internal documents broadened into a discussion of how the Bank can be more supportive of popular participation in development decisions.

An international network of environmental NGOs has played an important role in getting the Bank to devote more attention to environmental issues. Poorly implemented Bank-financed projects on the edge of the Brazilian Amazon provoked Washington environmental groups to start lobbying the Bank in the early 1980s. They brought pressure to bear through their testimony before committees of the U.S. Congress. They also banded together with environmental groups in Europe and, later, in a growing number of developing countries. Environmental groups in the industrial countries became more convincing as they increasingly drew on eyewitness reports from grass-roots NGOs in developing countries. Partly in response to NGO criticism, the Bank has dramatically expanded its work on environmental issues. The Bank has adopted more rigorous environmental policies and project review practices; it is factoring environmental considerations into its advice on economic policy issues.

Some NGOs that do advocacy work on poverty issues have also been working to influence the Bank. Washington-based advocacy groups concerned with poverty have been best placed, most active, and most influential, but international NGO networks working on poverty issues are also emerging, and poverty and environmental NGOs are increasingly working together in efforts to influence the Bank. Advocacy groups have stressed the impact of Bank-supported adjustment on poor people, and they have strongly encouraged the Bank's outreach to developing country NGOs. Washington and London groups teamed up to lobby their governments and the Bank about the allocation of funds from the International Development Association (IDA), the Bank's concessional affiliate. IDA allocations now depend more than before on how much effort recipient governments are making to reduce poverty. The Bank used its *World Development Report 1990* to urge bilateral aid agencies to make a parallel shift and allocate more of their resources to developing country governments making serious efforts to reduce poverty.

There have also been a number of regional and country-level meetings between NGOs and Bank staff, some of them organized by the Bank and others by NGOs. In India and Zimbabwe, national NGO-World Bank consultation committees have been established. SOLIDARIOS, the largest secular coalition of NGOs in Latin America, organized a meeting between the Bank and NGOs in the Southern Cone of Latin America. The meeting focused on adjustment issues and on the opportunities and problems of Bank-supported government programs of funding for NGOs (PACT 1990).

More than in the past, Bank staff are seeking out NGO perspectives on project design and, in some instances, policy issues. In the early stages of planning a tropical forest protection project in Cameroon, for example, Bank staff sought the advice of both local and international NGOs. The Bank mailed draft guidance for Bank staff on community involvement in environmental assessments to hundreds of NGOs, including anyone who requested it, to seek suggestions. When the Bank decided to revise its forestry policy, it invited a group of some 50 environmental NGOs from around the world to Washington to discuss a new policy paper in draft.

## Emerging lessons

This section draws lessons from the Bank's recent experience, particularly lessons that add to the analysis presented in the previous chapters.

*Success in cooperation between NGOs and the World Bank*

When the Bank's management asked operational staff to identify countries, sectors, and projects in which to pursue an expansion of the Bank's work with NGOs, the staff response was much more extensive than any of the managers involved had expected. The relatively strong and continuing response from operational staff on this issue suggests that working with NGOs indeed makes sense in some country and project contexts.

There is great scope for further expansion of Bank-NGO cooperation over time. But since the Bank's work with NGOs has been growing rapidly, there are risks of superficiality or clumsiness, and insensitive World Bank attention to NGOs could, in some situations, do more harm than good. Thus, the Bank is not now especially urging staff to involve NGOs in more Bank-related activities. The stress is rather on the quality of NGO involvement—the involvement of beneficiary groups and other NGOs in project planning, attention to NGOs in the Bank's analysis of development issues and dialogue with governments, and adequate Bank attention to NGO components during project implementation.

The Bank has monitored progress through frequent reports to its board and senior management. Emerging experience conforms with the generally positive impression that Salmen and Eaves gleaned from past experience. Changes inside the Bank and in the pattern of recent projects indicate that the Bank is improving its work with NGOs along the lines that Salmen and Eaves suggested. The Bank's knowledge about NGO involvement in its projects depends mainly on reports by the Bank staff involved, mostly appraisal reports (which are based on project plans). But the Bank is also getting critical feedback on some projects from NGOs, and the Bank's NGO office is now commissioning independent monitoring studies and concentrating more on projects under implementation. The Bank commissioned NGO reviews of planning for the Guatemala Social Investment Fund and of a proposed project to improve water supply and address other high-priority issues for women in four states of Mexico. The Bank also commissioned an Indonesian NGO to review the Bank's overall interaction with NGOs in Indonesia.

### *Bank influence on government policies toward NGOs*

The fact that the Bank and other international agencies are interested in NGOs has made many governments more aware of NGOs and, in some cases, encouraged efforts to strengthen government-NGO cooperation. In some situations, the Bank's government counterparts have long been working with NGOs. In more situations, the Bank's interest in NGOs is fostering new connections between officials and NGOs. Guatemala has been a good example. The government of Guatemala was eager to work with community groups and NGOs, but politically driven haste and lack of coordination among ministries weakened its initial efforts. When the government asked the Bank to help plan a Social Investment Fund, modeled in part on Bolivia's Emergency Social Fund, the Bank made sure that NGOs were involved in the planning. The dialogue between government and NGOs broke down in the run-up to national elections, but the groundwork has been laid for a nonpartisan and effective mechanism of government funding for NGOs.

Increasingly, the Bank is studying NGOs in the course of its analysis of country and sector issues. This should make the Bank's work with NGOs more knowledgeable and sensitive, and it also brings NGO issues into the Bank's policy dialogue with member governments. The Bank has done a major study of NGO microenterprise development programs in Colombia. In Nepal, a Bank review of poverty issues discussed the contribution of NGOs and broached recommendations to government, NGOs, and donors to enhance what NGOs are doing for the country's development.

The government of Indonesia has long kept tight control over organizations at the village level, and local officials have often restricted NGOs that work with the poor. These official attitudes have been changing gradually, however. A Bank study documented the remarkable progress that Indonesia has made against poverty, but urged more encouragement for community initiative and NGOs. Government policy has become markedly more favorable toward NGOs, and the Bank's growing awareness of NGOs may have contributed to this process.

The government of Bangladesh has overregulated NGOs. An NGO needs official approval to get started, for every new project, and for every year's plan. This has typically required the approval of a lengthy application by numerous government agencies. The Bank's studies demonstrated the important work that NGOs are doing to reduce poverty, notably through credit schemes such as Grameen Bank. The World Bank and other official development agencies and donors urged the government to reduce its regulation of NGOs. The World Bank pressed this issue at the highest levels and at one point offered to support deregulation of NGOs with a fast-disbursing "poverty adjustment loan," but the government declined. When NGOs and the Bank asked that officials at least clarify the regulations, NGOs were dismayed to find that regulations were even more complicated than they had realized. Bangladeshi NGOs were later able to negotiate simplified regulations, and the Bank's work on the issue may have helped set the stage. But the Bangladesh experience indicates that the Bank is limited in what it can achieve by pressing for change in government policies toward NGOs.

In another case, Zaire, the Bank's staff decided that a frontal effort to improve the government's overall relationship with NGOs would end up tightening government control over them. So instead, the Bank simply funded NGOs through various projects.

*Difficulties for governments and the Bank*

The main concern that developing country governments have expressed about World Bank cooperation with NGOs is nationalistic. They do not want the Bank's assistance to be unduly influenced by political ideologies, business interests, or NGO pressures in the industrial countries. Some developing country NGOs are almost entirely dependent on funding from industrial country NGOs. When they also use NGO networks to bring World Bank pressure to bear on their own governments, some officials become concerned about "NGO colonialism."

Some governments are also concerned that NGOs represent a domestic political threat. Unpopular authoritarian governments tend to be most nervous—not without reason, given examples such as the role of NGOs in toppling the Marcos government in the Philippines, for example, or the prevalence of former NGO leaders in Chile's post-Pinochet government. In some countries, such as Mexico, church-state issues complicate government's relationship with religiously motivated NGOs. More generally, civil servants may resent competition from NGOs, especially when NGOs are administering an increasing share of foreign assistance or, as is sometimes the case, are better paid and equipped than government offices. Some governments (such as Sudan) argue that it would be imprudent for them to pass on borrowed money to NGOs, particularly as grants. It is always an issue how far NGOs that get government money should be subject to the government's financial control practices (which are cumbersome but can help to restrain corruption).

The World Bank needs to be sensitive to such concerns among its government counterparts. NGO involvement in Bank-financed projects is least in the countries and regions where governments are least inclined to work with NGOs.

In addition, the Bank's own operating procedures make work with NGOs difficult in several ways. First, the Bank commits money at the beginning of a project on the basis of agreements that specify what the project will entail. Bank staff time is concentrated on a project at the planning stage and is much more limited during implementation. This pattern is most obviously appropriate for the types of projects the Bank funded in its early years: if a major highway was well-planned, implementation was relatively routine. But beneficiary groups and other NGOs are not likely to evolve according to any planner's blueprint.

Of the projects for which completion or evaluation reports were done in fiscal 1988-89, 23 featured NGO involvement. The bulk of these completed NGO-related investments were in agriculture and rural development, and the NGOs involved were normally farmers' organizations. The most striking finding from a review of these projects was that official planners had seldom predicted correctly how the NGOs would perform. In the Mali Sud Agricultural Project, for example, a network of village associations emerged to take on local responsibility for distribution of project inputs and for marketing of cotton. The network has today assumed a broader role at the village level by investing in community health and social services. These developments were not anticipated. More often, project planners expected beneficiary groups to be more effective than they turned out to be. The cooperative improvement component of the Indonesia Second Transmigration Project was not as successful as expected, in part because the transmigrants came from different communities and were not quick to develop mutual trust. More adequate study of beneficiary groups and consultation with them at the planning stage would reduce uncertainty about how they will behave. But beneficiary groups are bound to be somewhat unpredictable, and (as Brown and Korten argue in Chapter 3) flexibility is a hallmark of voluntary organizations. The Bank's legal agreements and its reduced involvement in projects during implementation sometimes discourage flexibility.

Another difficulty for the Bank in working with NGOs is limited staff time. The Bank has about 3,000 higher-level staff, compared, for example, to at least 12,000 active voluntary organizations in India alone. A typical Bank task manager could be responsible for overseeing preparation of a $150 million project and, at the same time, supervising the implementation of two similar-sized projects in the same or neighboring countries. The Bank has been given increasing responsibilities for country-level economic analysis, policy dialogue, and aid coordination. Bank staff have also been asked to pay more attention to social and environmental issues (and to NGOs), but to maintain traditional excellence on economic and technical issues. Meanwhile, the Bank's lending has been expanding faster than its administrative budget. Under these circumstances, it is remarkable that Bank staff have done as much as they have to reach out to NGOs.

Finally, the Bank's pace is often different from that of NGOs with which it is working. While it often takes a year or two between the identification of a Bank-financed project and the beginning of implementation, NGOs tend to have a shorter planning horizon. In some cases, an NGO's component has been delayed because of problems in other components of a large project or broader issues between the Bank and the government. In other instances, the Bank has pushed forward with a loan when some of the NGOs involved felt that they needed more time to prepare. In Bangladesh, for example, the Bank and the government were in discussion for at least six years about the possibility of a semigovernmental foundation that would channel loans and grants to NGOs. Leading NGOs in Bangladesh were involved in these discussions for at least three years. But when the government was finally ready to proceed, a few respected NGO leaders protested that the foundation was starting with too much money. The new foundation decided to begin operations on a small scale, without financing or other assistance from the Bank.

*Difficulties for NGOs*

Recent experience also reveals some problems that involvement with the World Bank poses for NGOs. Most important, NGOs are used to working with official development institutions that give them grants, and engagement with the Bank is much more complex and difficult. Brown and Korten end their chapter in this book with advice for "donors," a term they mean to include the World Bank. But the Bank is not a donor. It lends money to governments (on highly concessional terms in the poorest countries) and invites NGOs to help make official projects more effective. Many NGOs welcome opportunities to work, often as independent partners, within larger development processes. But this requires a shift in orientation and usually some independent funding.

For example, a U.S. private voluntary organization, OEF International, took an active role in the preliminary stages of a Mexican project designed to meet the priority needs of women in several states. OEF's representative went to Mexico repeatedly, sometimes as a consultant to the Bank, but sometimes at OEF expense. Her proposal that Mexican NGOs should play a major role in the project was rejected by government and Bank planners, but OEF then helped train staff in government agencies to work with groups of women in ways that would encourage decisionmaking and initiative by the women themselves. The government and the Bank agreed that OEF should continue to provide training during project implementation, but Mexican officials later questioned whether a Mexican institution would not be more appropriate. OEF has spent significant resources on this project, and its staff have found the progress frustrating. They are pleased with their contribution to an important large-scale project, but disappointed that their investment has not led to the continuing role and income for OEF that they expected (Terrell 1990).

Within the Bank, there has been extended debate about the possibility of allocating a relatively small sum to a fund that the Bank's operational staff could use to help developing country NGOs engage in Bank-financed projects. The Bank's special program for African population NGOs has shown that grant funding for NGOs can be a fruitful adjunct to the Bank's normal operations, and two less operational, specialized lines of NGO grants have emerged (a program to help developing country institutions contribute to the development debate, and ad hoc grants to women-in-development NGOs). The Bank's management decided against the proposal for grants to help developing country NGOs work with the Bank, however. The main arguments against it have been the tightness of the Bank's own budget, concerns about the staff-time cost of administering grants, and the risk of raising false expectations among NGOs that the Bank is about to become a major new channel of direct funding.

A second problem NGOs have encountered in trying to work with the Bank is the difficulty of cooperation among NGOs. Each NGO has its own history and constituency, and NGOs often compete against each other for funding. The pilot stages of the Togo Grass-roots Initiative Project were marred by controversy, partly because the Bank moved too quickly, but partly because of preexisting tensions among the NGOs. Tensions regarding the national association of NGOs exploded when the government asked NGOs to elect representatives to a government-NGO committee. At the global level, the NGO-World Bank Committee is a unique opportunity for NGOs to debate official development policy. The Committee NGOs have had long and torturous debates among themselves about elections, procedures, and what they together want to say to the World Bank.

Third, engagement with the Bank has highlighted weaknesses among NGOs on issues of public policy. Many NGOs want to contribute on policy issues, and they often give valuable feedback or general advice. But NGOs are seldom staffed adequately to make detailed, practical suggestions for policy change. For example, international NGOs have urged that the Bank and governments seek advice from local NGOs about adjustment policies. Some governments would be reluctant to do so, but, in practice, the binding constraint has been on the NGO side (Clark 1991). NGOs have not been able to take much advantage of a standing invitation from the Bank (expressed repeatedly to the NGOs on the NGO-World Bank Committee) to support NGO-organized consultations on adjustment issues in particular countries.

NGOs have not generally been strong on self-evaluation. Much of what NGOs write about themselves is oriented toward fund raising. The people who work in NGOs tend to be action-oriented and individualistic, traits that discourage institutionalized programs of self-evaluation. Much of the NGO evaluation that has been done has been sponsored by bilateral aid agencies as their funding for NGOs has increased. As NGO interaction with developing country governments grows, NGOs are contributing helpful critiques of the effectiveness of official programs, but the process also casts new light on the strengths and weaknesses of NGOs.

The main disappointment of the Bank's work with NGOs to date is that it has not done much to involve poor people themselves in the planning of Bank-financed projects. Few beneficiary groups have been engaged in such planning, and when other NGOs have been involved they have seldom insisted on or helped engage beneficiary groups. While some NGO leaders stress what voluntary organizations do to empower the poor, the Bank's experience suggests that many voluntary organizations are, in practice, still primarily involved in service delivery.

Many Bank-financed projects in which NGOs have made a major contribution involve different types of NGOs working together—indigenous intermediary NGOs together with international NGOs or with organizations of poor people.[3] In Zaire, a project agency was not implementing its agreements with the Bank about resettlement for a dam. Local community organizations that had been receiving funds from Oxfam provided information that Oxfam brought to the Bank's attention. The Bank communicated its concern to the project agency and sent a consultant to help improve the situation.

*New intermediaries*

When NGOs are involved in Bank-financed projects, they often serve as intermediaries between official agencies and poor people. NGOs help channel resources to the poor, act as advocates for the poor, or sometimes help the poor get organized to act and speak for themselves. In the Kwale Water Project, a local NGO, Kenya Women for Health Organization (KWAHO), served as an "ombudsman" for communities with project authorities. KWAHO also helped organize local water committees to deal with the authorities and manage the operation of pumps.

In a number of countries, new intermediaries, such as Bolivia's Emergency Social Fund, are emerging to channel official funds to grass-roots organizations and other NGOs. As opportunities to work with governments and intergovernmental institutions grow, NGO associations are also growing in number and strength. Although the Guatemala Social Investment Fund has not yet started, it has already had a beneficial impact among NGOs in Guatemala; the opportunity to take part in the planning has given them incentive to work together. Under the leadership of their association (ASINDES) and with assistance from an international NGO consortium (PACT), NGOs have been meeting by sector to share experience, recommend criteria for government funding, and coordinate planning among themselves.

A new breed of intermediaries between NGOs and the Bank is also emerging. Washington-based environmental groups set up the Bank Information Center to channel information from the Bank and from Washington NGOs to developing country NGOs. Advocacy groups in Washington that are concerned with poverty formed the Development Banks Assessment Network to coordinate their work on Bank issues. The social and environmental activists who have been assembling at annual meetings of the World Bank and the International Monetary Fund have constituted themselves as the International NGO Forum on World Bank and IMF Lending. The Bank itself has established an NGO liaison office, helped develop the NGO-World Bank Committee into a serious policy forum, and supports Bank-NGO consultation committees in India and Zimbabwe.

## Toward the future

NGO-World Bank interaction seems almost sure to expand further and to become more important. This section outlines four trends that seem likely to persist to the end of the century and that will frame the Bank's work with NGOs.

*Continued growth of NGOs*

NGOs are likely to continue growing in number, diversity, and technical capacity. Several factors that have contributed to rapid NGO growth in recent decades will endure. NGO growth in the developing countries has been due partly to rising levels of income and education, and some developing countries are likely to achieve further economic and social progress in the 1990s. As people escape abject poverty and ignorance, they are more likely and better able to join together in associations to address social issues.

Improvement in communications and transportation has been a second factor underlying the growth of NGOs. More economical jet travel and international telephone connections have made it easier for NGO networks to work together across borders. The number of international NGOs (including trade and professional associations) grew more than tenfold between 1970 and 1989—from an estimated 2,300 to 24,000 (Paul Ghils, Union of International Association, private correspondence). Many NGOs have been quick to begin using fax machines and electronic mail, and the pace of change in communication technologies is accelerating. The information revolution is also reaching low-income communities. Poor people in remote areas hear on their radios what is happening worldwide. The cases in which small communities threatened by resettlement have been able to recruit international political support suggest that low-income people may, over time, increasingly use improved communications to speak out as well as to listen.

Finally, NGOs in the developing countries have also been strengthened by a growing flow of finance from bilateral aid agencies, and official agencies (now including multilateral agencies such as the World Bank) are more supportive of NGOs than ever. The current level of official enthusiasm is likely to subside as working with NGOs becomes more routine and NGO limitations are more visible. But processes already in motion among the official aid agencies will provide NGOs with substantial additional resources and opportunities.

### *NGOs and governments*

A second trend that will shape the Bank's future work with NGOs is the intensification of relationships between NGOs and governments. This is a trend that recent developments and world events have accelerated and likely will propel into the future. Most important, democracy has spread to virtually all of Latin America and Eastern Europe, and there are democratic stirrings and scattered successes throughout Asia and Africa. Democratic governments tend to be much more supportive of NGOs than authoritarian governments.

In addition, there has been an even more widespread shift in thinking about what governments can and should do for their people. Global recession at the start of the 1980s spurred new concern about economic efficiency and a widespread shift away from reliance on the public sector. As the 1990s begin, environmental and poverty concerns are higher priorities again in many countries, but skepticism remains about what public bureaucracies alone can accomplish in dealing with these problems. Policymakers in many countries are stressing what the voluntary sector can do to help. In the United States, for example, President George Bush coined the phrase "a thousand points of light" to emphasize the importance of the voluntary sector. In the Soviet Union, President Mikhail Gorbachev's reforms have included an expanded role for citizens' groups of many kinds.

While many governments have become more interested in NGOs, NGOs' attitudes toward governments are also changing. In the past, most NGOs were content to work at the community level. The debt and development crisis in the 1980s and mounting environmental problems prompted some NGOs to look up from traditional projects and focus on larger developments at the national and international levels. A growing number began to foster in-house capacity to analyze and contribute to official policies and programs. For example, Oxfam (U.K.) now has a department devoted to work on international debt, official aid, and other policy issues.

The relation between developing and industrial country NGOs is a hotly debated issue among NGOs (Drabek 1987). Some developing country NGOs want the industrial country NGOs that fund them to reduce their direct involvement and control. As developing country NGOs try to reduce their heavy dependence on funding from industrial country NGOs, local contributions and funding from their own governments are the main options. Government funding risks increasing government control, of course. Yet in some situations, government funding can be a helpful supplement to funding from local and foreign private sources. A developing country NGO with funding from various sources, including its own government, will have more room to maneuver according to its own priorities.

Helping governments develop sensitive and effective programs of funding for NGOs is a role the Bank is likely to play. Most of the Bank-financed programs of funding for NGOs are too new to draw firm conclusions, but the Bank has done a first review of grass-roots development funds. The Bank has also reviewed India's experience with government schemes to support NGO family planning and health programs. These schemes have not been very effective for two reasons: (1) they do not provide enough money to command much attention from either officials or NGOs, and (2) the government's population program does not have any NGO liaison staff at the state or district levels. A survey of NGOs working in health and family planning in six states found that three-quarters of them had never heard of the government's grant schemes. A follow-up meeting that brought NGOs, government officials, and Bank staff together resulted in several other suggestions, notably that government introduce more flexibility and responsiveness into its programs of NGO funding. The findings from the study and workshop are influencing the administration of ongoing Bank-financed population projects and have become a subject of discussion between the Bank and sectoral officials. The Bank is now engaged in a cross-sectoral review of Indian governmental programs of grants to NGOs.

More generally, the Bank may play a growing role in encouraging government policies that contribute to an effective voluntary sector. The Bank has already done work along these lines in some countries and has begun cross-country research. An example from the Philippines offers a promising illustration of specific policy reforms to encourage the work of NGOs. An NGO umbrella association, Asian NGO Coalition, arranged a series of NGO meetings with the Philippine planning department to develop recommendations regarding public policies toward NGOs. These meetings clarified the channels through which NGOs receive funding from government agencies and foreign sources, and also suggested clear and decentralized procedures for government approvals. Participants proposed that every government department establish an NGO liaison office and identified a need for publicity among NGOs about import tax advantages that were already on the books. The conclusions became official policy through a cabinet resolution. The United Nations Development Programme (UNDP) and the Food and Agriculture Organization (FAO) (in this case, not the World Bank) supported this policy development process.

Other agencies can do as well or better than the Bank in providing the four other types of support for NGOs that Brown and Korten outline: direct financial support; support for intermediary organizations; links for voluntary organizations' feedback to donors; and the promotion of intersectoral partnerships. But the World Bank might be uniquely effective in helping to create "political space" for NGOs, because of its substantial policy influence with government and other international agencies in many developing countries. The Bank's Articles of Agreement forbid it from making decisions on political grounds or taking part in a country's politics, so the Bank is limited in what it can say about a country's basic political ground rules (about freedom of speech, for example). But governments can encourage the voluntary sector through deregulation and tax advantages, and Bank analysis on such issues would closely parallel what the Bank has often done on the same issues as they relate to the commercial sector. The Bank can also legitimately insist on measures to encourage popular participation where they are important to the effectiveness of the development activities the Bank supports.

### *Greater popular participation in development decisions*

Many governments and intergovernmental agencies are again stressing the importance of having the people participate in development decisions. Popular participation makes government programs more responsive to real needs and stimulates community initiative. This theme has been sounded often in the past, with little practical result. But the recent spread of democracy in the developing countries makes the political context more favorable than it has been for many years. And the end of the Cold War has made industrial country governments less willing to support a Marcos or Mobutu with foreign assistance.

Many NGOs have long emphasized popular participation. During the past 20 years, NGO thinking and practice have been evolving from traditional charity activities (food distribution) to developmental approaches (credit for microenterprise) and to community organization (helping poor neighborhoods organize to demand minimal public services). NGO rhetoric on popular participation is often ahead of practice. But many NGOs today self-consciously invite communities to help shape NGO projects, and some NGOs see their main purpose as helping communities organize to exercise a wider influence. Sophisticated community organization techniques (such as those pioneered by Saul Allinsky in Chicago or Paulo Friere in Brazil) are now practiced by some NGOs throughout the world. NGOs with experience in promoting community participation stress the complexity and difficulty of the process, even on a small scale, and the literature on popular participation in developing countries returns again and again to the same 20 to 25 examples that have demonstrated the possibility of participatory approaches in government-sponsored, large-scale projects.

A series of Bank studies in the late 1980s helped make the case that strong beneficiary organizations are important to the success and sustainability of many types of official projects (Cernea 1985; Paul 1987; Salmen 1987 and 1990; EDI 1988; Strategic Planning and Review Department 1989; and Nagle and Ghose 1990). These studies show that beneficiary participation is especially critical when a project is designed to help a specific group of people, especially if the beneficiaries must themselves do something to make the project work (adopt new practices or pay part of the cost). More recently, the Bank has become convinced that public participation in decisionmaking is needed to reduce the environmental and social side-effects that large infrastructure projects often entail. The main recommendation to emerge from the Bank's reviews of adjustment lending is that the Bank should do more to make sure that governments really "own" adjustment programs, partly by checking whether government officials discuss them with the public.

The Bank's experience with projects that involve beneficiaries in planning is limited but growing, especially in urban development, rural water supply, population and social services, and irrigation and other subsectors of agriculture. The Bank's current environmental assessment policy calls on borrowing member governments to consult with affected communities and local NGOs in the planning and implementation of all environmentally sensitive projects, including many large infrastructure projects.

Stimulated by the NGO-World Bank Committee and guided by a review of the Bank's own experience to date, the Bank embarked in 1991 on a modest program of action and learning on the issue of popular participation. The Bank's top management committed the Bank to a four-point program: (1) effective implementation of the community involvement provisions of the Bank's environmental assessment policy; (2) continued efforts to involve NGOs in Bank-supported operations, especially in planning; (3) a review of what the Bank's operational directives say about participation and the extent to which they are being implemented; and (4) a Bank-wide process to learn better how the Bank can support popular participation more widely. The learning process will draw lessons from 20 exceptionally participatory Bank-supported operational activities. A learning group of staff from various parts of the Bank has been commissioned to accelerate the Bank's process of learning about participation and to recommend ways the Bank's own operational practices may need to change in order to widen its support of popular participation.

Meanwhile, a debate has emerged about the Bank's role in supporting good governance more generally. This debate has been joined on the Bank's board, which brings together representatives of the Bank's 152 member governments. The Bank's Articles of Agreement preclude the Bank's involvement in member governments' internal politics, and developing country governments are concerned that the Bank and other foreign agencies may be moving toward more intrusive conditionality. Yet predictability, openness, and accountability in governance are demonstrably important to economic and social development. The problems of Africa, in particular, have dramatized the futility of external support for development under corrupt and oppressive regimes. Thus, the debate is not about whether the Bank should concern itself about governance more than in the past. The debate is about how far the Bank should go in this direction.

*Greater public understanding*

Increasingly, NGOs are influencing public opinion and public policy on pressing global issues such as the environment. The World Bank is an important instrument of international cooperation on several of the issues that are most urgent from a planetary perspective—reducing poverty, stemming environmental destruction, and helping the former Communist countries succeed economically. Yet, NGOs typically criticize the Bank for not saying and doing more, and the Bank has so far done little to help NGOs build political support.

The political impact of NGOs is growing. Many NGOs are aligned with social movements, and social movements seem generally to have gained strength and power in recent decades. Again, the mass media have been a factor. The United States' civil rights movement of the 1950s and 1960s, for example, was fueled by press coverage of local officials repressing protests. The recent spread of democracy and the more widespread reassessment of what governments can do have added to the freedom and influence of social movements.

Issues that pose threats to all of human civilization are eliciting international social movements. For example, grass-roots movements for disarmament sprung up simultaneously in North America and Western Europe in the early 1980s, when few governments were inclined to pursue disarmament. Religious groups, environmental groups, labor unions, and other NGOs now all maintain constant communication across national borders, and NGOs are gaining experience in lobbying various governments and international organizations in a coordinated way. And because industrial countries loom large in the global economy and in international politics, many developing country NGOs are urging industrial country NGOs to help them, not only by sending money and expertise, but also by influencing public policies back home.

The evolution of the Christian churches' response to international development illustrates the trend toward NGO policy advocacy. At the end of the Second World War, many churches set up international relief and development agencies (for example, Catholic Relief Services). These agencies continue to grow, but their programs in the developing countries have become subordinate to the developing country church leaders they assist. In the 1960s, the Vatican, the World Council of Churches, and others began to stress the need for church involvement in public policy issues such as international trade and aid. In the 1970s, a new generation of church-related agencies (for example, the United States' Bread for the World) were organized to lobby industrial country governments about global development issues.

Many NGOs are weak in economic and technical analysis. For example, nearly all NGOs active in international development feel that banks and governments in the industrial countries should assume more of the cost of overcoming problems of developing country debt. Yet relatively few NGOs know the ins and outs of the debt issue, or are actively involved in lobbying for more forthcoming debt policy. And few of the NGOs that are active in debt issues turn to the World Bank to draw from its analysis, despite its central role in the day-to-day work of helping developing countries cope with their debt problems. This is partly because NGOs often distrust the World Bank. And although World Bank reports are mines of information and analysis on such questions and typically suggest practical steps that would favor the developing countries, they are usually couched in technical, diplomatic prose.

Operational interaction in the developing countries is gradually deepening NGO and World Bank understanding of each other's perspectives, and policy discussions between NGOs and the World Bank have resulted in learning on both sides. Over the last several years, the Bank has become much more openly self-critical, and its publications have become a bit more inviting. At the same time, leading NGO analysts increasingly use the Bank, not only as a foil, but also as a source of information and perspective.

The survival of civilization, and perhaps of humanity itself, depends on more vigorous action to protect the planet, reduce mass poverty, and minimize the risk of war. The thaw in East-West relations makes international cooperation on these issues more likely. These overarching realities are pushing the World Bank and NGOs to work together in building public understanding of global development issues. The Bank is rightly urging NGOs to support and draw from its rich operational experience, and NGOs are rightly urging the Bank to speak out more clearly and forcefully about what more ought to be done.

## Notes

1. This chapter draws on the ongoing work of the International Economic Relations Division of the Bank's External Affairs Department, which has overall responsibility for the Bank's relations with NGOs. Kris Martin, Aubrey Williams, and Maxine Stough contributed to this chapter.
2. The NGO members of the Committee come from various types of NGOs and different parts of the world. Three-fifths come from developing country NGOs. Some represent large coalitions of NGOs, such as InterAction (the association of U.S. private voluntary organizations) or the World Council of Churches. The Committee NGOs themselves elect new members as old members' terms expire. No group of 26 people could "represent"

the tens of thousands of NGOs active in developing countries, but the NGOs on the Committee are diverse and tied into a broad range of NGO networks.

3. Paul Nelson at the University of Wisconsin, who is writing a dissertation on the Bank and NGOs, identified some 50 projects approved during 1973-89 in which NGOs were involved in especially important ways. Although his analysis is not yet complete, this pattern stands out clearly.

# References


Ackoff, Russell. 1974. *Redesigning the Future*. New York: Wiley.

Adam, Hussein, and L. David Brown. 1987. "Forum of African Voluntary Development Organizations: Observations of the Dakar Conference, May/June 1987." *World Development* 15 (Supplement, Autumn): 251-53.

American Council of Voluntary Agencies for Foreign Service (ACVAFS). 1983. *Evaluation Source Book*. Washington, D.C.

Annis, Sheldon. 1987. "Can Small-scale Development be a Large-scale Policy? The Case of Latin America." *World Development* 15 (Supplement, Autumn): 129-34.

———. 1988. "Small-Scale Development, Large-Scale Policy?" In Sheldon Annis and Peter Hakim, editors, *Direct to the Poor: Grassroots Development in Latin America*. Boulder: Lynne Rienner Publishers.

———. 1989. "What is Not the Same about the Urban Poor: The Case of Mexico City." In John Lewis, editor, *Strengthening the Poor: What Have We Learned?* Washington, D.C.: Overseas Development Council.

Asian NGO Coalition (ANGOC). 1988a. "Democratizing Asian Development: A Commitment to Leadership." ANGOC Monograph Series No. 7, Asian NGO Coalition, Manila, Philippines.

———. 1988b. *NGO Strategic Management in Asia: Focus on Bangladesh, Indonesia, and the Philippines*. Manila: ANGOC.

Association of Development Agencies in Bangladesh (ADAB). 1989. *Future Strategies and Vision of NGOs in Bangladesh*. Dhaka: ADAB.

Bagadion, Benjamin U. 1989. "The Evolution of the Policy Context: A Historical Overview." In Frances F. Korten and Robert Y. Siy, Jr., editors, *Transforming a Bureaucracy: The Experience of the Philippine National Irrigation Administration*. West Hartford, CT: Kumarian Press.

Baile, Stephanie. 1986. "Survey of European Nongovernmental Aid Organizations: A Guide to NGOs and their Perception of the World Bank." World Bank, European Office, Paris.

Ben-Ner, A. 1986. "Nonprofit Organizations: Why do They Exist in Market Economies?" In Susan Rose-Ackerman, editor, *The Economics of Nonprofit Institutions*. New York: Oxford University Press.

Berg, Robert J. 1987. *Nongovernmental Organizations: New Force in Third World Development and Politics*. East Lansing: Center for Advanced Study of International Development, Michigan State University.

Bratton, Michael. 1988. "Poverty, Organization and Policy: Towards a Voice for Africa's Rural Poor." Paper prepared for a colloquium on the Changing Nature of Third World Poverty: A Policy Perspective, sponsored by the Center for the Advanced Study of International Development, Michigan State University, Lansing, March 13-15.

———. 1989. "The Politics of Government-N.G.O. Relations in Africa." *World Development* 17(4): 569-87.

Brodhead, Tim. 1987. "NGOs: In One Year, Out the Other?" *World Development* 15 (Supplement, Autumn): 1-6.

Brodhead, Tim, Brent Herbert-Copley, and Anne-Marie Lambert. 1988. *Bridges of Hope? Canada Voluntary Agencies in the Third World*. Ottawa, Canada: The North-South Institute.

Brown, L. David. Forthcoming. "Private Voluntary Organizations and Development Partnerships." In P. Khandwalla, *Organizational Behavior and Social Development*. New Delhi: Sage Publications.

Brown, L. David, and J.C. Brown. 1983. "Environmental Microcosms and Ideological Negotiations." In M. Bazerman and R. Lewicki, editors, *Negotiating Inside Organizations*. Beverly Hills, CA: Sage.

Brown, L. David, and J.G. Covey. 1987a. "Development Organizations and Organization Development: Toward an Expanded Paradigm for Organization Development." In R.W. Woodman and W.E. Pasmore, editors, *Research in Organizational Change and Development,* Vol I. Greenwich, CT: JAI Press.

———. 1987b. "Organizing and Managing Private Development Agencies." Working Paper 128, Program on NonProfit Organizations, Yale Institution for Social and Policy Sciences, New Haven, CT.

Brown, L. David, and David C. Korten. 1989. *The Role of Voluntary Organizations in Development*. Boston, MA: Institute for Development Research.

Brown, L. David, and R. Tandon. 1983. "Ideology and Political Economy in Research: Action Research and Participatory Research." *Journal of Applied Behavioral Science* 10(3).

Canadian Council for International Cooperation (CCIC). 1988. *"Mind if I Cut in?"* Report of the CCIC Task Force on CIDA-NGO Funding Relationships. Ottawa.

Cernea, Michael. 1988. *Nongovernmental Organizations and Local Development*. World Bank Discussion Paper 40. Washington, D.C.

———, editor. 1985. *Putting People First: Sociological Variables in Rural Development*. New York: Oxford University Press.

Chambers, Robert. 1986. "Normal Professionalism, New Paradigms and Development." Discussion Paper 227. Brighton, U.K.: Institute of Development Studies.

Clark, John. 1991. *Democratizing Development: The Role of Voluntary Organizations.* West Hartford, CT: Kumarian Press.

Commission of the European Communities (CEE). 1981. *Evaluation Study of 26 Co-financed NGO Projects in Five Countries.* SEC (81)105.

Conger, Jay, Rabindra Kanungo, and Associates. 1988. *Charismatic Leadership: The Elusive Factor in Organizational Effectiveness.* San Francisco: Jossey-Bass.

de Soto, Hernando. 1987. In *The Challenge of Democracy,* A Conference on Efforts Underway to Advance the Cause of Democracy throughout the World, sponsored by the National Endowment for Democracy, May 18-19, Washington, D.C.

Diamond, Larry. Forthcoming. "Beyond Authoritarianism and Totalitarianism: Strategies for Democratization." *The Washington Quarterly.*

Diamond, Larry, Juan J. Linz, and Seymour Martin Lipset. 1988. "Democracy in Developing Countries: Facilitating and Obstructing Factors." In Raymond D. Gatil, editor, *Freedom in the World: Political Rights and Civil Liberties, 1987-88.* New York: Freedom House.

Douglas, James. 1987. "Political Theories of Nonprofit Organization." In Powell (1987).

Drabek, Anne Gordon. 1987. "Development Alternatives: The Challenge for NGOs—An Overview of the Issues." *World Development* 15 (Supplement, Autumn): x-xiii.

Drucker, Peter E. 1989. "What Business Can Learn from Nonprofits." *Harvard Business Review* 67(4): 88-93.

———. 1990. *Managing the Nonprofit Organization.* New York: Harper Collins.

Durning, Alan B. 1989. "Action at the Grassroots: Fighting Poverty and Environmental Decline." World Watch Paper 88. World Watch Institute, Washington, D.C.

Economic Development Institute (EDI). 1988. "Readings in Community Participation." World Bank, Washington, D.C.

Elliot, Charles. 1987a. *Comfortable Compassion? Poverty, Power and the Church.* London: Hodder and Stoughton.

———. 1987b. "Some Aspects of Relations between the North and the South in the NGO Sector." *World Development* 15 (Supplement, Autumn): 57-68.

Ellis, Gene. 1984. "Making PVOs Count More: A Proposal." In Robert F. Gorman, editor, *Private Voluntary Organizations as Agents of Development.* Boulder, CO: Westview Press.

Esman, Milton J., and Norman T. Uphoff. 1984. *Local Organizations: Intermediaries in Rural Development.* Ithaca: Cornell University Press.

Etzioni, Amitai. 1961. *A Comparative Analysis of Complex Organizations.* New York: Free Press.

Foley, Dolores. 1989. "Nongovernmental Organizations as Catalysts of Policy

Reform and Social Change: A Case Study of the International Planned Parenthood Federation." Ph.D. dissertation, University of Southern California.

Fowler, Alan. 1989. "Why is Managing Social Development Different?" *NGO Management* 12(January-March).

Frantz, Telmo Rudi. 1987. "The Role of NGOs in the Strengthening of Civil Society." *World Development* 15 (Supplement, Autumn): 121-27.

Gronbjerg, Kirsten A. 1989. "Developing A Universe of Nonprofit Organizations: Methodological Considerations." *Nonprofit and Voluntary Sector Quarterly* 18(1): 63-80.

Hall, Peter Dobkin. 1987. "A Historical Overview of the Private Nonprofit Sector." In Powell (1987).

Hansmann, Henry. 1980. "The Role of Nonprofit Enterprise." *The Yale Law Journal* 89 (5): 835-901.

———. 1987. "Economic Theories of Nonprofit Organization." In Powell (1987).

Hellinger, Stephen, Douglas Hellinger, and Fred M. O'Regan. 1988. *Aid for Just Development: Report on the Future of Foreign Assistance*. Boulder: Lynne Rienner Publishers.

Hennin, Christopher J., and Miriam Parel. 1989. "Report on NGOs in Northeast Brazil." World Bank, Latin America and the Caribbean Regional Office, Washington, D.C.

Hursh-Cesar, Gerald, and Associates. 1986. *Development Effectiveness of Private Voluntary Organizations*. Washington, D.C.: USAID.

Hyden, Goran. 1983. *No Shortcuts to Progress: African Development Management in Perspective*. Berkeley: University of California Press.

Iffrig, Andree, and David C. Korten. 1988. "Banjarnegara and the YPPSE: A Case of Local Government/NGO Collaboration." A case study. Institute for Development Studies (LSP), Jakarta, Indonesia.

Independent Sector. 1986. *Dimensions of the Independent Sector: A Statistical Profile*. Washington, D.C.: Independent Sector.

Independent Sector. 1988. *Dimensions of the Independent Sector: A Statistical Profile*. Interim Update, Fall. Washington, D.C.: Independent Sector.

InterAction. 1985. *Diversity in Development: U.S. Voluntary Assistance to Africa*. New York: InterAction.

———. 1989. *Monday Developments* (June 26).

James, Estelle. 1982. "The Nonprofit Sector in International Perspective: The Case of Sri Lanka." *Journal of Comparative Economics* 6 (June): 99-129.

———. 1987. "The Nonprofit Sector in Comparative Perspective." In Powell (1987).

Japanese NGO Center for International Cooperation (JANIC). 1988. *Directory of Nongovernmental Organizations in Japan: NGOs Active in Development Cooperation*. Tokyo: JANIC.

Jenkins, J. Craig. 1987. "Nonprofit Organizations and Policy Advocacy." In Powell (1987).

Jorgensen, Jan, Taieb Hafsi, and Moses Kiggundu. 1986. "Toward a Market Imperfections Theory of Organizational Structure in Developing Countries."

*Journal of Management Studies* 23 (4): 417-42.

Kanter, Rosabeth Moss. 1983. *The Change Masters: Innovation for Productivity in the American Corporation.* New York: Simon and Schuster.

Kanter, Rosabeth Moss, and David V. Summers. 1987. "Doing Well While Doing Good: Dilemmas of Performance Measurement in Nonprofit Organizations and the Need for a Multiple-Constituency Approach." In Powell (1987).

Knoke, David. 1988. "Incentives in Collective Action Organizations." *American Sociological Review* 53:311-29.

Korten, David C. 1980. "Community Organization and Rural Development: A Learning Process Approach." *Public Administration Review* 40(5): 480-511.

———. 1984. "Strategic Organization for People-Centered Development." *Public Administration Review* 44:341-52.

———. 1987. "Third Generation NGO Strategies: A Key to People-Centered Development." *World Development* 15 (Supplement, Autumn):145-59.

———. 1988. "New Roles and Challenges for Asian NGOs." In *Proceedings of the ANGOC Regional Seminar on NGO Strategic Management in Asia.* Manila: ANGOC.

———. 1990. *Getting to the 21st Century: Voluntary Development Action and the Global Agenda.* West Hartford, CT: Kumarian Press.

———, editor. 1986. *Community Management: Asian Experience and Perspectives.* West Hartford, CT: Kumarian Press.

Korten, David C., and Rudi Klauss, editors. 1984. *People-Centered Development: Contributions toward Theory and Planning Frameworks.* West Hartford, CT: Kumarian Press.

Kothari, R. 1984. "Party and State in Our Times: The Rise of Nonparty Political Formation." *Alternatives* IX (Spring): 541-64.

Kramer, Ralph. 1981. *Voluntary Agencies in the Welfare State.* Berkeley: University of California Press.

Landim, Leilah. 1987. "Non-Governmental Organizations in Latin America." *World Development* 15 (Supplement, Autumn): 29-38.

Macy, Joanna. 1983. *Dharma and Development: Religion as Resource in the Sarvodaya Self-Help Movement.* West Hartford, CT: Kumarian Press.

Mirvis, Philip, and Edward Hackett. 1983. "Work and Work Force Characteristics in the Nonprofit Sector." *Monthly Labor Review* (April): 10-11.

Montgomery, John D. 1988. *Bureaucrats and People: Grassroots Participation in Third World Development.* Baltimore: Johns Hopkins University Press.

Morss, Elliott. 1984. "Institutional Destruction Resulting from Donor and Project Proliferation in Sub-Saharan African Countries." *World Development* 12 (4): 465-70.

Morss, Elliott, and Victoria Morss. 1982. *U.S. Foreign Aid.* Boulder, CO: Westview Press.

Nagle, William, J., and Sanjoy Ghose. 1990. "Beneficiary Participation in World Bank-Supported Projects." Strategic Planning and Review Department Working Paper. World Bank, Washington, D.C.

Nerfin, Marc. 1986. "Neither Prince Nor Merchant: Citizen—An Introduction to the Third System." *International Foundation for Development Alternatives Dossier 56* (November/December).

Olson, Mancur. 1971. *The Logic of Collective Action*. Cambridge, MA: Harvard University Press.

Operations Evaluation Department (OED). 1985. *Sustainability of Projects: First Review of Experience*. Washington, D.C.: World Bank.

———. 1988. *Rural Development: World Bank Experience 1965-86*. Washington, D.C.: World Bank.

Organization for Economic Cooperation and Development (OECD). 1988. *Voluntary Aid for Development: The Role of Nongovernmental Organizations*. Paris.

———. 1989. "Summary Record of the 560th Meeting held on 22nd-23rd November 1988 at the Chateau de la Muette, Paris on Cooperation with Non-Governmental Organizations." DAC OECD, Paris. Draft prepared January 13.

OECD, Development Assistance Committee. 1986. *Development Cooperation: 1986 Report*. Paris: OECD.

Osborne, K.O.H., and G.A. Armstrong. 1982. *An Evaluation of the Joint Funding Scheme*. London: Ministry of Overseas Development.

Ostrander, Susan A. 1989. "The Problem of Poverty and Why Philanthropy Neglects It." In Virginia A. Hodgkinson, Richard W. Lyman, and Associates, editors, *The Future of the Nonprofit Sector*. San Francisco: Jossey-Bass Publishers.

Ouchi, William. 1979. "A Conceptual Framework for the Design of Organizational Control Mechanisms." *Management Science* 25 (9): 833-48.

———. 1980. "Markets, Hierarchies and Clans." *Administrative Science Quarterly*.

Padron, Mario. 1988. "Structural Adjustment Policies: Some Consequences for the Poor, NGOs and Solidarity Agencies." Paper presented at the 1988 InterAction Annual Forum, Philadelphia, PA, May 1-4.

Paul, Samuel. 1982. *Managing Development Programs: The Lessons of Success*. Boulder, CO: Westview Press.

———. 1987. *Community Participation in Development Projects: The World Bank Experience*. World Bank Discussion Paper 6. Washington, D.C.

———. 1988. "Governments and Grass-roots Organizations: From Coexistence to Collaboration." In John P. Lewis, editor, *Strengthening the Poor*. Washington, D.C.: Overseas Development Council.

Peters, Tom, and Robert H. Waterman. 1982. *In Search of Excellence: Lessons from Americas's Best Run Companies*. New York: Harper and Row.

Powell, Walter W. 1987. *The Nonprofit Sector: A Research Handbook*. New Haven: Yale University Press.

Private Agencies Collaborating Together (PACT). 1984. "Voluntary Resource Organizations in South Asia: Investigative Summary." Communications Development Service, PACT, New York.

———. 1990. *Steps Toward a Social Investment Fund*. New York: PACT.

"Programme Slashed in Response to Transmigration Campaign." 1987. *The Ecologist* 17 (1): 41.

Pyle, David F. 1981. "From Project to Program: The Study of the Scaling-up/Implementation Process of a Community-Level, Integrated Health, Nutrition, Population Intervention in Maharashtra (India)." Ph.D. dissertation. Massachusetts Institute of Technology, Cambridge, MA.

Ramanathan, K.V. 1982. *Management Control in Nonprofit Organizations.* New York: Wiley.

Robert R. Nathan Associates, Inc. 1982. *An Evaluation of Private Agencies Collaborating Together.* Prepared for PACT and USAID Office of Private and Voluntary Cooperation.

Rose-Ackerman, Susan, editor. 1980. *The Economics of Nonprofit Institutions: Studies in Structure and Policy.* Yale Studies on Nonprofit Organization. New York: Oxford University Press.

Salamon, L.M. 1987. "Partners in Public Service: The Scope and Theory of Government-NGO Relations." In Powell (1987).

Salmen, Lawrence F. 1987. *Listen to the People: Participant-Observer Evaluation of Development Projects.* New York: Oxford University Press.

———. 1990. "Institutional Dimensions of Poverty Reduction." World Bank, Africa Technical Department, Washington, D.C.

Sasono, Adi. 1989. "NGOs' Roles and Social Movement in Developing Democracy: The South-East Asian Experiences." *New Asian Visions* 6 (1): 14-26.

Satawan, N., M. Swara, N. Sutjipta, W. Suteja, and W. Winda. 1984. *Studi Perbandingan Subak Dalam Sistem Irigasi Non-PU dan Subak Dalam Sistem Irigasi PU: Kasus Subak Timul Baru dan Subak Ceulak Kabupaten Gianyar.* Denpasar: Universitas Udayana.

Schneider, Bertrand. 1988. *The Barefoot Revolution: A Report to the Club of Rome.* London: Intermediate Technology Publications.

Siy, Robert Y., Jr. 1986. "Averting the Bureaucratization of Community-Managed Resource—the Case of the Zanjeras." In Korten (1986).

Smillie, Ian. 1988. "Strengthening Collaboration with NGOs: The Strangulation Technique." Available from Ian Smillie, 618 Melbourne Ave., Ottawa, Ontario, Canada K2A 1X1.

Smith, Brian H. 1984. "U.S. and Canadian PVOs as Transnational Development Institutions." In Robert F. Gorman, editor, *Private Voluntary Organizations as Agents of Development.* Boulder, CO: Westview Press.

———. 1987. "An Agenda of Future Tasks for International and Indigenous NGOs: Views from the North." *World Development* 15 (Supplement, Autumn): 87-93.

Sommer, John G. 1977. *Beyond Charity: U.S. Voluntary Aid for a Changing Third World.* Washington, D.C.: Overseas Development Council.

Strategic Planning and Review Department. 1989. "Strengthening Popular Participation in World Bank-Supported Activities." Prepared for NGO-World Bank Committee. World Bank, Washington, D.C.

Tandon, Rajesh. 1987. "The Relationship between Non-Governmental Organizations and Government." Society for Participatory Research in Asia, New Delhi, August.

———. 1989. "The State and Voluntary Agencies in India." In Richard Holloway, editor, *Doing Development: Government, NGOs and the Rural Poor in Asia*. London: Earthscan Publications.

Tandon, Rajesh, and L. David Brown. 1981. "Organization-Building for Rural Development: An Experiment in India." *Journal of Applied Behavioral Science* 17 (2): 172-89.

Tendler, Judith. 1982. *Turning Voluntary Agencies into Development Agencies*. A.I.D. Program Evaluation Discussion Paper 12. Washington, D.C.: U.S. Agency for International Development.

———. 1987. *What Ever Happened to Poverty Alleviation?* New York: Ford Foundation.

Terrell, Nena. 1990. "Women, Water, and Development in Mexico: A Case Study of NGO Collaboration in a World Bank Project." Prepared for the World Bank. OEF International, Washington, D.C.

Unger, Roberto Mangabeira. 1987. *Plasticity into Power: Comparative-Historical Studies on the Institutional Conditions of Economic and Military Success*. Cambridge: Cambridge University Press.

Uphoff, Norman. 1987. "Drawing on Social Energy in Project Implementation: A Learning Process Experience in Sri Lanka." Paper presented at the American Society for Public Administration meetings, Boston, March.

U.S. Agency for International Development (USAID). 1988. *The Effectiveness of Private Voluntary Organizations*. Advisory Committee on Voluntary Foreign Aid, 1988 Report. Washington, D.C.: USAID.

Van Til, Jon. 1988. *Mapping the Third Sector: Voluntarism in a Changing Social Economy*. New York: The Foundation Center.

Weisbrod, B.A. 1988. *The Nonprofit Economy*. Cambridge, MA: Harvard University Press.

Williams, Aubrey. 1990. "A Growing Role for NGOs in Development." *Finance and Development* (December): 31-33.

Williamson, Oliver. 1975. *Markets and Hierarchies: Analysis and Antitrust Policy*. New York: Free Press.

Williamson, Oliver, and William Ouchi. 1981. "The Markets and Hierarchies and Visible Hand Perspective." In A.H. van de Ven and W.F. Joyce, editors, *Perspectives on Organization and Behavior*. New York: Wiley.

Witjes, Ben. 1987. "The Indonesian Law on Social Organizations: A Study of the Sociopolitical Context and the Consequences for Indonesian and Foreign NGOs." NOVIB, The Hague.

World Bank. 1988. *World Development Report 1988*. Washington, D.C.

———. 1990. *World Development Report 1990*. Washington, D.C.

Ziswa, Valentine. 1988. "Recipient/South Perspectives: A Commentary." In *Justice in the Aid Relationship? A Dialogue on Partnership*. Vienna: International Council on Social Welfare.

# About the Editors and Contributors

**Samuel Paul** is advisor in the Public Sector Management and Private Sector Development Division of the World Bank. A former director of the Indian Institute of Management at Ahmedabad, he is the author of *Managing Development Programs: The Lessons of Success* (Boulder, CO: Westview Press, 1984).

**Arturo Israel** is senior advisor in the Infrastructure and Urban Development Department of the World Bank. He is the author of *Institutional Development: Incentives to Performance* (Baltimore, MD: Johns Hopkins University Press, 1987).

**David C. Korten** is president and founder of the People-Centered Development Forum in Manila, Philippines, and a senior associate of the Institute for Development Research in Boston, Massachusetts. He is the author of *Getting to the 21st Century* (Hartford, CT: Kumarian Press, 1990).

**L. David Brown** is president of the Institute of Development Research and professor of organizational behavior at Boston University, Boston, Massachusetts. He is currently working on a book entitled *Bridging Organizations in Social Development.*

**Lawrence F. Salmen** is a senior social scientist in the Africa Technical Department of the World Bank. He is the author of *Listen to the People* (New York: Oxford University Press, 1987).

**A. Paige Eaves** is a volunteer with Habitat for Humanity International. She is a former consultant and researcher in the Public Sector Management and Private Sector Development Division of the World Bank.

**David Beckmann** is president of Bread for the World, a U.S. nongovernmental organization concerned with hunger and poverty issues. A former principal international relations officer of the World Bank responsible for NGO-Bank relations, he is the author of *Friday Morning Reflections at the World Bank: Essays on Values and Development* (Washington, D.C.: Seven Locks Press, 1991).